AF324857

Deinstitutionalization
Program and Policy Development

SYRACUSE SPECIAL EDUCATION AND REHABILITATION
MONOGRAPH SERIES, 12

Deinstitutionalization

Program and Policy Development

JAMES L. PAUL,

DONALD J. STEDMAN,

and G. RONALD NEUFELD, *Editors*

SYRACUSE UNIVERSITY PRESS   1977

Copyright © 1977 by Syracuse University Press

Syracuse, New York 13210

All Rights Reserved

First Edition

An earlier version of Chapter 8, "The Law," appeared in Turnbull, H.R., and Turnbull, A. P., "Deinstitutionalization and the Law," *Mental Retardation* 13(2)(1975):14–20.

Library of Congress Cataloging in Publication Data

Main entry under title:

Deinstitutionalization.

    (Syracuse special education and rehabilitation
monograph series; 12)
    Includes bibliographies and index.
    1. Handicapped—United States. 2. Mentally
handicapped—United States. I. Paul, James L.
II. Stedman, Donald J. III. Neufeld, G. Ronald.
IV. Series: Syracuse Special
education and rehabilitation monograph series; 12.
HV1553.D44   362.3'0973   76-58557
ISBN O-8156-0132-8

Manufactured in the United States of America

Contents

Foreword

N O SOCIAL MOVEMENT has been initiated with such abruptness or with so little planning as has been deinstitutionalization—a movement which is being pursued in the United States and elsewhere as an approach to better meet the needs of the handicapped. Administrators of state programs, legislators of both state and national governments, university professors, and community planners—all of whom pride themselves on their ability to plan—often moved with little more than an administrative decision to reduce the size of institutional populations under the guise of deinstitutionalization and normalization. Logic, careful total planning, and thoughtful leadership often have been conspicuous by their absence. This book provides an orientation to an issue which should have had much thought and deliberation before the first resident of a state or federally supported institution was returned to the community as a part of this program.

The lack of preplanning has resulted in a number of serious problems, among which are community readiness for and citizen attitudes toward institutional patients; archaic building and housing codes; inaccessible transportation systems, community services, and public buildings and street curbs; appropriate employment or training; social, and medical services. Often the establishment of new community-based mini-institutions, which provide little not previously experienced by the resident but which contribute to a dollar profit by those who are enterprising and have organized these facilities, are seen as substitutes for previous institutional placements. Each of these negative issues is an outgrowth of the lack of both program and policy at all levels of local, state, and national governments. A myriad of second-order problems likewise await solution.

The ramifications of the concept of deinstitutionalization are many. They cut across almost every aspect of community life and accentuate some elements which are not always the concerns of the family. This book provides a focus for the valid consideration of these complex issues. Its authors deal with a broad spectrum of problems which are vital to the successful implementation of a program of deinstitutionalization within any organization. Unless the problems emphasized in this book are considered, fully understood, and completely and appropriately addressed, deinstitutionalization becomes a hollow shibboleth which adds no luster either to the agency which spawned it or to the human dignity of those who bear the brunt of faulty planning. This book is a positive statement in an otherwise problematic social movement.

William M. Cruickshank, Editor
Syracuse Special Education and
Rehabilitation Monograph Series

Contributing Authors

Barbara J. Anderson is Developmental Research Psychologist, Social and Behavioral Sciences Branch, National Institute of Child Health and Human Development, National Institutes of Health, Bethesda, Maryland.

William M. Cruickshank is Director of the Institute for Mental Retardation and Related Disabilities, University of Michigan, Ann Arbor, Michigan.

Dan W. Davis is Assistant Professor of Pediatrics and Education, University of North Carolina School of Medicine, Chapel Hill, North Carolina.

Paul R. Dokecki is Professor of Psychology and Special Education and Director of Programs for Human Development Specialists, George Peabody College, Nashville, Tennessee.

Jacqueline Farah is Coordinator of Community Education, Epilepsy Center of Oregon, Portland, Oregon.

Paula Breen Hammer is Associate Director of Developmental Disabilities Technical Assistance System, University of North Carolina, Chapel Hill, North Carolina.

Elsie D. Helsel is Associate Professor of Education, Coordinator of Special Education, and Director of the Ohio University Affiliated Center for Human Development, Ohio University, Athens, Ohio.

Jennifer Howse is Executive Director of the Willowbrook Review Panel, New York State Department of Mental Hygiene, New York, New York.

Edward Humberger is Assistant Professor of Political Science, Northeastern University, Boston, Massachusetts.

G. Ronald Neufeld is Co-Director of Developmental Disabilities Technical Assistance System, University of North Carolina, Chapel Hill, North Carolina.

James L. Paul is Associate Professor and Director of Graduate Studies, Division *x*

of Special Education, School of Education, and Director of Training, Developmental Disabilities Technical Assistance System, University of North Carolina, Chapel Hill, North Carolina.

Rebecca Posante-Loro is a doctoral student in the Division of Special Education, University of North Carolina, Chapel Hill, North Carolina.

William C. Rhodes is Professor of Psychology, University of Michigan, Ann Arbor, Michigan.

R. C. Scheerenberger is Superintendent of the Central Wisconsin Colony and Training School, State of Wisconsin Department of Health and Social Services, Madison, Wisconsin.

Philip S. Strain is Supervisor of Research for Children and Youth, Middle Tennessee Psychiatric Institute, Nashville, Tennessee.

Donald J. Stedman is Professor of Education and Chairman of the Division of Special Education, School of Education, and Associate Director of the Frank Porter Graham Child Development Center, University of North Carolina, Chapel Hill, North Carolina.

Richard C. Surles is Director of the Model Area Program/Management Information System, State of North Carolina Department of Human Resources, Raleigh, North Carolina.

Donald E. Taylor is Assistant Secretary, Department of Human Resources, and Executive Director of the North Carolina Office for Children, Raleigh, North Carolina.

Ronald L. Thiele is Dean of the School of Allied Health and Social Professions, East Carolina University, Greenville, North Carolina.

Pascal L. Trohanis is Assistant Professor of Education, School of Education, and Associate Director of Public Awareness and Media, Developmental Disabilities Technical Assistance System, University of North Carolina, Chapel Hill, North Carolina.

Ann Turnbull is Assistant Professor of Education, Division of Special Education, School of Education, University of North Carolina, Chapel Hill, North Carolina.

H. Rutherford Turnbull III is Assistant Director, Institute of Government, University of North Carolina, Chapel Hill, North Carolina.

Ronald Wiegerink is Associate Professor of Education, Division of Special Education, and Director of Developmental Disabilities Technical Assistance System, University of North Carolina, Chapel Hill, North Carolina.

Introduction

DONALD J. STEDMAN

INSTITUTIONS ARE SOCIETY'S GLUE. When they are eroded or diluted, the sizing of society's fabric tends to disintegrate.

In this book the term "institution" is used in a fairly broad sense. It does not refer simply to the sociological phenomenon; nor does it always refer to those great walled asylums in the rural sections of our states where we have isolated large numbers of our fellow citizens for what we perceive as their deviancy. Both concepts are used. Institutions are organizations as well as places.

This book is an attempt to draw together discussions on the institutions and institutionalization and their undoing among the handicapped citizens of our society.

Over the past fifty years the history of services for the handicapped has been a checkered one. It has been largely a search for residential care. The initial plaintive cries of parents and other advocates were the main source of public conscience. Persuasion was the main tool for change. More and better institutions were our goals.

In the 1950s, it became evident that a substantial political constituency was present to act on behalf of handicapped citizens which could bring new change through one of the nation's greatest institutions, the United States Congress. Federal legislation on behalf of the mentally retarded and other handicapped persons developed rapidly and substantially, leading to significant pieces of state legislation throughout the country.

Subsequent changes in the political administrations in the early 1960s saw advocates for handicapped persons flood toward the executive branch of the federal government, finding congenial support in the Kennedy administration.

By the late 1960s the legislative and executive branches had been largely abandoned in favor of the effective utilization of the judicial branch and the newly found routes of legal advocacy, not now for institutionalization but for *de*institutionalization.

In the 1970s there is some disenchantment with the capacity to follow through on judicial decisions and consent decrees, and the concept of widespread advocacy for the successful deinstitutionalization of the handicapped is the major organized thrust.

Deinstitutionalization means to most people in the developmental disabilities fields the physical removal of a handicapped person from a state institution and the placing of that person in a community at home or a replacement home. Those who have attempted this relocation find that it is more than physical removal. It is often a state of mind and requires the re-socialization and preparation for re-entry of a human being into a socialized community setting.

The head winds against deinstitutionalization are predictable. The community at large has never been well informed and has always been significantly threatened by people who are different. Sophisticated resistance such as zoning laws—and unsophisticated resistance such as resentment against the presence of handicapped citizens in the community—forms a spectrum of difficulty which must be rationally approached and understood on a grand scale if deinstitutionalization is to be successful as a movement toward the reintegration of handicapped persons into our society.

The best routes for successful deinstitutionalization and the development of effective community alternatives are not clear. However, a variety of demonstration activities and points of view lend support to the notions that deinstitutionalization can be successfully accomplished.

The broad viewpoint presented in this book, together with the stimulating responses which readers are bound to accumulate, will serve to carry deinstitutionalization even further forward.

It should become clear in the reading that there are three major factors to consider in order to complete the bonding process between person, family, and community which is required to assure deinstitutionalization:

1. *Personal transition.* There are difficulties in the transition between institutional life and the community. Often a person has been completely socialized to one environment and finds it extremely difficult to succeed when introduced to a new environment. This culture shock encountered by many retarded and physically handicapped persons returning from long periods of residential care results in immediate and sometimes difficult reactions which often lead to immediate reinstitutionalization rather

than continued community placement. The personal transition period must be very carefully planned and requires a great deal of assistance in the early weeks and months of a person's return to the community.

2. *Overcoming community resistance.* There often is attitudinal and physical resistance on the part of total communities and substantial parts of them through both subtle and more direct means. The resistance may be economic rather than attitudinal. The priorities of communities which are not set in the direction of support for developmentally disabled persons amount to a denial of rights and access as well as re-entry to the community itself. A good deinstitutionalization project requires a clear and sequenced plan for overcoming community resistance in both the active and passive forms.

3. *Family undoing.* It must be remembered that for every person institutionalized in the past and now in a residential program, there is at least one family that has arrived at the decision to institutionalize the person in the first place. Undoing that decision requires a great deal of care in order to provide for effective long-term deinstitutionalization and community placement.

Elsewhere in this book space will be devoted to two of the three major factors affecting deinstitutionalization—the overcoming of community resistance and the personal transition problems of the deinstitutionalized person. The third, and most important factor in my view, is the factor of "family undoing."

Family undoing refers to the fact that deinstitutionalization in most cases requires a painful reversal and revisitation of earlier decisions to separate the child from the family. Most families sought residential care for months or even years before relief was provided. Many conceded *only* because of strong professional recommendation to institutionalize their son or daughter. Now the wound is reopened and resistance to the re-entry process should be understandable and expected.

One cannot understand the difficulty of deinstitutionalization for many families without revisiting the period during which the decision was made to institutionalize the child.

It is an interesting phenomenon in our culture, and indeed among our species, that the strongest of personal attachments is between mother and child. There is a psychological cord tying the two together in a protective/dependent bond that can be severed only with great trauma and difficulty. Mothers have followed their children, where fathers have faltered. The maternal drive is obvious and ever present. It provides a strong influence upon our society.

Yet, there are circumstances under which mothers and fathers rationally participate in a planned separation from their child—where, because the child is different, the bond is cut and the mother delivers the child into the care of others, perhaps for a lifetime. It happens daily around the country when families institutionalize their handicapped children.

The separation is not always authentic maternal permission. It is often couched in "what is best" for her family or for her child. It is often a sorrowful experience and constitutes a major psychological event for all involved.

Unlike the reverse phenomenon of adopting a child, institutionalization seeks to overcome, rather than encourage, a biological and emotional investment in the child.

Yet, the practice persists and it is incumbent upon the professional to recognize the psychological mechanisms that operate in the antecedent and consequent conditions as well as in the separation process itself. Whether one is a physician, social worker, educator, clergyman, psychologist, lawyer, spouse, brother, or sister, it is extremely important to try to understand the decision to separate the mother and child. The consequences to them may be dependent upon the actions and words of others.

In no condition is the decision to institutionalize more frequent than in cases of severe and profound mental retardation accompanying birth defect or physical handicap. Those working in the field of mental retardation encounter the process often and realize its complexities and idiosyncrasies. For them, placement for the child and restoration of the family, whatever the decision, is a major task involving precise judgment, some preventive mental health, and, often, remedial counseling.

The advent of the child with a birth defect or the discovery of an exceptional child can lead many families to disorganization, ambivalence, grief, hostility, and doubt. This would hardly seem the atmosphere in which to make any decision on the long-term management of a child. However, this is often precisely the psychological atmosphere within which the decision to institutionalize is attempted.

A variety or combination of psychological conditions may exist. The mother is often gripped in an over-reaction to the child's condition. Her grief is for the child and for herself, and depression, guilt, loneliness, and maternal doubt and blame may ensue. In her search for understanding of the "why" and the "how" of the child's condition, she is often incapable of entertaining some ambivalent feelings about her need to reject the child.

The father, often forgotten by those who would attempt to support the mother in a time of tension and grief, may be equally angry, apprehensive, and stricken with feelings of inadequacy in the situation. His attempts at reshaping the world are usually intellectualization, rationalization, and brave attempts to play his role as the "steady force" in the family at the risk of his own stability.

The other children in the family may be equally affected. The boys may be puzzled and, depending on their age and level of identification, may take on some of the psychological symptoms of the mother or father. Teenage sisters can become apprehensive and, in their identification with mother, examine their own futures and attempt to divide their attentions between themselves and their mother's feelings concerning the event.

Grandparents are often sympathetic and readily identify with their children and their children's fears.

The truth of the matter is that nobody reacts very sanely during the initial impact phases of the advent of a handicapped child into a family. In most cases the family is totally unprepared for the child's exceptionality and is more or less traumatized, depending upon a number of pre-existing factors, knowledge of which are of the utmost importance to the clinician or counselor.

No two families are alike, either in their makeup or in their activity pattern. Neither are they alike in terms of their strength, cohesiveness, and resiliency. It is often difficult to predict the reaction of a family to a handicapped child.

On the other hand, there are some observable categories of family patterns that are worth consideration in a discussion of the impact of handicapped children on family integrity.

THE OLDER PARENTS

There are cases in which the advent of a visibly handicapped and mentally retarded child is a function of maternal age. This appears to be the case with Downs Syndrome (mongolism), and since this clinical syndrome includes the largest homogeneous group of mentally retarded children in the population, it constitutes a fairly large group of families which have in common advanced parental age. In general, the child may represent a "surprise," may be unplanned, and perhaps unwanted, even if normal. On the other hand, it may represent a serious attempt to begin a "second" family, since the other children have moved into high school or even college-age groups. The older parents may be ill prepared to face the problem of a handicapped infant and less flexible in their consideration of the topic of child care, with or without residential placement. While the older parents are likely to be more secure economically and materially than the younger family, they are no less vulnerable to the emotional challenge of a handicapped child and the possible question of institutionalization. In some cases, the advent of the handicapped child is coupled with premenopausal or midmenopausal psychological change in the mother and pre- and midclimacteric change in the father. This can compound the difficulty of counseling and may warrant close psychiatric attention and more extensive therapeutic intervention. In no case should the older couple be seen as a higher risk for a heavy impact; rather, the conditions under which decisions are made about the child differ significantly from those conditions usually surrounding the younger couple with or without other children.

THE ISOLATED COUPLE

The young couple who are geographically isolated from family and friends because of a recent move for a new job or for advanced education are often a very vulnerable family when attempting to deal with the problem of institutionalization and a handicapped child. Maternal isolation in time of need for emotional support is risky business in any case, but when it is tied to the birth of a handicapped child, it can be extremely deteriorating and potentially destructive to the marriage and family integrity. In such cases, it would seem important to mobilize family or fraternal ties in order to bring immediate supportive counseling and assistance to the mother in the young family before entertaining the notion of institutionalization or long-term care for the child.

THE PROFESSIONAL FAMILY

While we often credit the higher trained or highly educated parent with the ability to understand and deal with events that are emotionally charged, the kinds of defenses often mobilized by the professional parent are not always conducive to the acceptance and intelligent handling of the problem of the advent of an exceptional child and the issue of institutionalization. Frequently, the professional parent attempts to deal with the issue in such a mechanical and emotionless fashion that little opportunity is available to discharge the emotion-laden impact of the child who is different. This, in a way, can be more difficult to deal with than the parent who falls apart emotionally in attempting to deal with the problem. Great care should be taken by people attempting to deal with this kind of family to provide a constructive channel of emotional discharge, while guarding against depression and anger in reaction to an inability to deal with the problem at an emotional level.

THE LOW-INCOME FAMILY

The family with little means is no less susceptible to the advent of a child who is visibly different, but also may have less access to systems and programs for care of the child than does the middle-income family. The area of interaction of mental health and social class is still not clear, but it would seem that there is less appreciation for the long-term implications of mental retardation in the lower-class family. This may constitute a problem in bringing the child into a residential care program when, in fact, it is highly desirable and necessary.

In addition, there is substantial support for judgements that lower-class parents are more authoritarian and lower in verbal intelligence than middle-class parents. This makes counseling difficult, especially since there is often a low degree of psychological mindedness and consequent difficulty in expressing and evaluating feelings about the problem.

THE DISTURBED FAMILY

Some families are already on shaky ground when a handicapped infant arrives. Because any addition to the family can serve to cause imbalance in the family, the arrival of a handicapped infant can be a particularly difficult situation to handle. The child may trigger an existing underlying problem already present in family relationships or may serve to exaggerate a situation that had been under control or of only minimal disruption to the family. All families are constantly undergoing change and having to adapt to different degrees and kinds of problems generated by children or other factors such as finances, health, occupational adjustments, and aging. The disturbed family may displace its difficulties onto the exceptional child, and that displacement may severely cloud issues such as the decision to institutionalize the child. It is extremely important to try to define situtations in which the advent of an exceptional baby has generated or simply triggered emotional instability in intra- or interfamily activities.

THE LARGE FAMILY

The median family size in this country is 3.5 persons, but there are many instances in which the handicapped infant is the fifth, sixth, seventh, or eighth child in the ordinal position of the children in the family. Large families usually indicate greater stresses on the parents, and the sheer logistics of large family management and the geometric increases in the number of possible interactions between family members is a factor to consider in working with the large family on the issue of institutionalization. The fact that the family is large should not automatically indicate that residential care is the best decision. Decision for residential care should be based on logistics, space, and management time on the mother's part. Indeed, the large family may offer more support to the mother in facing and accepting the issue of a handicapped child than that received by the mother with no other children.

THE BROKEN HOME

There are instances when divorced parents, newly bereaved parents, or separated couples find themselves having to deal with the problem of an exceptional infant, born in or out of wedlock, and, perhaps, the issue of institutionalization as a solution. Maternal love may be no less strong, even if the mother is not interested in re-establishing or maintaining the family unit. Of prime concern here is the lack of immediate emotional support of one parent for the other as a way of dissipating the impact of the advent of the handicapped child. Often, the family of the parents are less than happy with the fact that the family is a broken one and may not be mobilized or used as shock absorbers prior to or at the time of discussing the decision to institutionalize the child.

THE "RELIGIOUS" FAMILY

It is not uncommon for families to see the handicapped infant as the "Will of God" and to accept it on those terms. This may be a sincere effort to cope with the situation or a rationalization to avoid direct responsibility for decision-making about the child's future care. In general, religious affiliation is a positive factor for preventing the disintegration of the family unit, but both parents must be made aware of the need for their instrumentality in deciding about institutionalization. In these situations, the family priest, minister, or rabbi can be of great value in indirect or direct supportive counseling around the impact of the handicapped child on the family.

THE "AVERAGE" FAMILY

I have already indicated that no two families are alike and that there is no such thing as the "average" family. However, in the sense that the age of the prents, their proximity to their family, their income level, and other factors are like the majority of families in the country, there is a unit which might be construed as the average family. In cases such as this, and because they may have a benign history, we may overlook the fact that the impact of the handicapped child can be, even so, very traumatic and potentially disorganizing. No matter how calm the surface of the water may appear to be, there may well be, lurking beneath the surface, extreme struggles of conscience, feelings of guilt and apprehension, anger, and hostility that will not serve the best purposes of the continued stability of the family unit. One should not be suspicious of the family that fails to fall apart in the face of the impact of the handicapped child, but one should not be misguided by apparent family tranquility. Great effort should be made to discreetly probe the level of understanding and acceptance in the family and the strength of the family's defenses in the situation.

There is no automatic indicator for institutionalization or for deinstitutionalization. While some professionals hold that certain kinds of defects, certain kinds of families, and certain kinds of circumstances automatically dictate the institutionalization of the child, this is clearly not the case, and neither is it the case for deinstitutionalization. The nature of families is complexity, flexibility, varying degrees and quantities of strength, and, above all, people who themselves are capable of decision-making. Because of these facts, it is strongly felt that the basic decision to institutionalize or to deinstitutionalize should be made in concert with parents and that this responsibility cannot be taken over by anyone outside the family. There is some protest that it is easier for the parents, particularly the mother, if someone else in fact makes the decision for the family. It is difficult to determine for whom this is more helpful. It is difficult to observe a family struggling with the difficulties of the decision, and it is, perhaps, natural for outsiders to attempt to rescue the family in the situation. While there is no guarantee that when the family does make the decision it will be any easier, there is less guarantee that a decision made from the outside will be of value to the family in the long run.

It would seem that at least three major factors are involved in attempting to assist the family in coping with the decision to institutionalize and also to deinstitutionalize their child.

The first is the degree of isolation of the family, both geographically and emotionally, from sources of emotional and material support in the immediate situation in which the decision is being attempted.

The second is the extent to which the family has experience in utilizing emotional supports. This may well be through religious, fraternal, or strong social affiliation. It may be through family and social ties. It may be in the form of a more systemized professional counseling experience or, perhaps, contact with systems that offer support.

The third is the extent to which the family has access to and makes use of a supportive person who can be objective in the situation. In most cases, this will be the minister, family physician, or, in some cases, the family lawyer. In other cases, it may be an educator or some other person who has been close to the family and is seen as a person in whom the parents may confide. In no event is it a simple situation in which simple rules or criteria may be applied in order to automatically develop an answer to the question, "Should this child be institutionalized?" People are involved in decision-making and in dealing with decision-making situations. Where people are involved, decision-making is never a simple matter. Beyond that, it can be an emotionally charged, physically and psychologically exhausting, situation with implications for the long-term stability of the family and its members; it can also have the potential for further development of the child in question.

So, to revisit this process, perhaps twenty years after the smoothing and accommodating have made the decision a comfortable one, is a perhaps dangerous and volatile undertaking.

Certainly, the person to be deinstitutionalized has that right. There is no basis made here for violating the right of least restrictive alternative to education and care. There is, however, a good way and a poor way to go about securing these rights. One good way is to take into account the need for careful family undoing—else we may deinstitutionalize one and institutionalize another as a result.

REVIEW AND PREVIEW

Deinstitutionalization may be considered in two major dimensions. One is that having to do with large social organizations and remote physical facilities. The other has to do with the personal experience of those affected by institutional structures and processes. This book has been introduced by focusing on the philosophical domain—the impact of institutionalization and desinstitutionalization on families. The book continues this theme in discussing the process of institutionalization. By starting here we hope to convey the importance of examining deinstitutionalization from this perspective and to provide a balance to the more extensive presentation of the less personal dimension of deinstitutionalization. Most of the book deals with theoretical, organizational, political, legislative, economic, and programmatic aspects of deinstitutionalization.

The first section provides an orienting framework for defining and understanding deinstitutionalization. The second section presents major aspects of the theory and issues involved in deinstitutionalization, including labeling and stigma, policy and politics, productive roles of consumers, and the transformation of organized caregiving. The third section presents basic topics involved in the structure of institutional change and deinstitutionalization. These topics include accountability and the legal, organizational, and programmatic aspects of deinstitutionalization involved in making services more accountable to clients. These aspects include program planning, monitoring, and evaluation at local, regional, and state levels.

This is not a how-to-do-it book on deinstitutionalization. It is, rather, an examination of the major topics and issues involved in an effort to provide a more comprehensive base of concepts and information for deinstitutionalization. The book will be a useful resource for training in deinstitutionalization. It will also be a helpful professional overview of deinstitutionalization for those involved in developing, administering, or influencing policies relevant to deinstitutionalization.

I. Definition

1

Deinstitutionalization in Pespective

R. C. SCHEERENBERGER

DEINSTITUTIONALIZATION is one of the most significant concepts affecting contemporary programs for mentally retarded persons. As with most innovative concepts, it has been variously interpreted and applied with results that have been both positive and negative. In some instances, the retarded have definitely gained from deinstitutionalization; in others, they have not. Regrettably, deinstitutionalization occasionally fosters undesirable attitudes toward the needs of retarded persons in residential facilities.

We shall attempt to place deinstitutionalization in some perspective. In order to accomplish this task, it is necessary to posit a definition of deinstitutionalization and to examine its relationship to several variables.

Deinstitutionalization has been defined by the National Association of Superintendents of Public Residential Facilities for the Mentally Retarded (1974):

> Deinstitutionalization encompasses three interrelated processes: (1) prevention of admission by finding and developing alternative community methods of care and training; (2) return to the community of all residents who have been prepared through programs of habilitation and training to function adequately in appropriate local settings; and (3) establishment and maintenance of a responsive residential environment which protects human and civil rights and which contributes to the expeditious return of the individual to normal community living, whenever possible [pp. 3, 4].

This definition addresses itself not only to the discharge of retarded persons from residential to local settings, but also to preventing residential care. This dual connotation is most important and places a primary responsibility on communities to develop appropriate services. Without quality local programs, deinstitutionalization is impossible.

It is difficult to place deinstitutionalization in perspective since it potentially involves the entire gamut of human services ranging over a persons's total life span. For the sake of discussion, however, let us consider deinstitutionalization as it relates to the retarded person, society, parents, and finally, the residential facility. To some degree, this represents an artificial division since the four aspects usually act in unison.

THE RETARDED PERSON

One of the factors which has had great impact on the retarded as indiduals as well as their programming in general has been the increased recognition of their rights as citizens. Since 1971, a series of Federal court decisions has confirmed the rights of the retarded to receive appropriate treatment and services in the least restrictive setting. The landmark case involved *Wyat* vs. *Stickney* (1972). This suit was brought against the Alabama Department of Mental Hygiene, alleging the failure of the state to provide proper treatment for the mentally retarded in a public residential school. The ultimate decision was significant and precedent setting, not only because it declared the constitutional rights of the retarded to habilitation were being violated, but the final document inlcuded a twenty-page appendix which defined minimum treatment standards for the state school to meet. Several of these standards are pertinent to the present discussion:

No borderline or mildly retarded person shall be a resident of the institution.

No person shall be admitted to the institution unless a prior determination shall have been made that residence in the institution is the least restrictive habilitation setting.

Residents shall have a right to the least restrictive conditions necessary to achieve the purposes of habilitation. To this end, the institution shall make every attempt to move residents from: (a) more to less structured living; (b) larger to smaller facilities; (c) larger to smaller living units; (d) group to individual residence; (e) segregated from the community to integrated living in the community; (f) dependent to independent living [p. 3].

A subsequent court case in the state of Wisconsin (*Lessard* vs. *Schmidt* 1973) resulted in further restricting admissions. According to this decision, a retarded person can be admitted involuntarily to a residential facility only if he is "dangerous to himself or to others."

These basic decision have been reconfirmed in a number of subsequent court actions. In essence, the courts have declared that a residential facility shall be used only as a last resort and only if the child's needs can be met.

Correspondingly, several court actions have stipulated that at least education and training must be offered to the retarded person in the community. The two landmark cases in this area involved Pennsylvania and Washington, D.C. In 1971, a three-judge federal district court panel upheld a consent agreement between the Pennsylvania Association for Retarded Children and the Commonwealth of Pennsylvania guaranteeing every retarded child in the state the right of a free public education. This position was upheld and expanded by *Mills* vs. *the Board of Education* in 1972 (*Basic Rights . . .* , 1973). The latter judgment held that no child in Washington, D.C., could be denied a public education because of mental, behavioral, physical, or emotional handicaps or deficiencies.

While many of these decisions are being challenged at a higher level, most states are responding to their intents by formulating and developing new programs for the retarded. A number of states, for example, are actively pursuing right-to-education laws and are redesigning admission criteria and procedures to guarantee individual rights.

It is important to recognize that courts do not function in isolation. Their decisions usually reflect the prevailing attitudes and level of receptivity of the population in general. As stated by Friedman (1973) in his text on the history of American law, "as long as the country endures, so will its system of law, co-extensive with society, reflecting its wishes and needs. . . . The law is a mirror held up against life" (p. 595). He also pointed out that the two most active legal interests of the twentieth century have been the idea of equality before the law and the demand for equality of opportunity, which follows when formal equality fails in its purpose (from the standpoint of an oppressed or subordinate group). Both observations are certainly true in the case of the mentally retarded and other developmentally disabled persons.

Furthermore, while there is a current emphasis on deinstitutionalization, it should be remembered that only 3 percent of the retarded has ever been in a residential facility. The trend toward serving the mildly and moderately retarded in the community and its effect on residential populations and admissions was well documented by Goldstein as early as

1959. Finally, we are beginning to realize the goals outlined by President Kennedy in 1963:

> To stimulate improvements in a level of care given the mentally disabled in our state and private institutions and to reorient those programs to a community-centered approach.
>
> To reduce, over a number of years, by hundreds of thousands, the persons confined to these institutions.
>
> To retain in and return to the community the mentally ill and retarded, and to restore and revitalize their lives through better health programs and strengthened educational rehabilitation programs.
>
> To reinforce the will and capacity of our communities to meet these problems, in order that the communities, in turn, can reinforce the will and capacity of individuals and individual families [pp. 13-14].

To summarize, the retarded are coming into their own. Their rights as citizens are being recognized and local communities are making a genuine effort to meet their needs.

SOCIETY

The retarded are few and usually identifiable. Society, on the other hand, is a rather amorphous phenomenon, subject to individual definition. Rather than pursue an extensive dialogue on society in its broadest context, let us refer briefly to three aspects: the general citizenry, generic services, and sociopolitical institutions.

The General Citizenry

Perhaps one of the most misused and maligned group of citizens are those classified as "average." Frequently, one hears such comments as "the people don't want the retarded in their community," or "the community isn't ready." Experiences by many persons, however, tend to belie these observations. Both Michigan and Wisconsin, for example, which have been very active in developing foster and group homes, have encountered no major community resistance. Former residents have been received extremely well by the community.

Occasionally, however, there is some objection to the group homes for the retarded. One would hope that the 1974 decision by the New York State Court of Appeals (the highest state court in New York) will prevail throughout the country. In this instance (*City of White Plains* vs. *Ferraioli),* the court was dealing specifically with the question of zoning and single-family dwellings as they relate to group homes for the developmentally disabled. The decision rendered stated:

> the group home set up a theory, size, appearance, and structure to resemble a family unit fit within the definition of family, for purposes of a zoning ordinance. So long as the group home bears the generic character of a family unit as a relatively permanent household and is not a framework for transience or transient living, it conforms to the purpose of the ordinance. Moreover, in no sense is a group home an institutional arrangement, which would be another matter. Indeed, the purpose of the group home is to be quite the contrary of an institution and to be a home like other homes [Lauber 1974].

If this decision is upheld by other states, there seems to be little question that group homes will become an increasingly visible alternative to the natural home or residential facility. This again demonstrates the degree to which courts at all levels are responding to the rights and needs of retarded persons.

The general citizenry has definite responsibilities for the retarded. It must:

1. Respect the rights of the retarded, including the right to fail.
2. Respond to retarded persons as individuals rather than as a member of a subgroup.
3. Provide for their specialized needs.

The citizenry, in turn, realistically expects:

1. The retarded will respect the rights of others.
2. The retarded will be reasonably self-controlled in terms of behavior and social conduct.
3. The retarded will contribute to the benefit of society through gainful employment, whenever possible.

Above all, the public should feel entirely confident that the retarded will not be neglected. The citizenry has every right to be outraged when deinstitutionalization results in the dehumanization reported by *Time* magazine on December 17, 1973.

> Since _______ state started emptying its mental hospitals of thousands of inmates six years ago, many of them have been jammed into tiny rooms, basements, and garages, and fed a semi-starvation diet of rice and chicken necks. . . . They are taken from the steps of mental institutions by operators who jam them into what can only be described as a private jail and confiscate their monthly welfare checks.

Deinstitutionalization assumes well-monitored, quality community programs and reasonable living circumstances. Specifically, there should exist: (1) a local or regional body with statutory authority and accountability to plan, implement, and coordinate programs for the retarded; (2) an independent standard-setting and monitoring agency; (3) highly sophisticated back-up services, including technical consultancy; (4) strong, effective advocacy programs; and (5) substantial financial support (Scheerenberger 1974).

Taken collectively, these comments indicate that experiences to date support the notion that communities are ready and willing to accept the retarded into the mainstream of life consistent with local standards. They also imply that the local citizenry expects persons and agencies directly involved with deinstitutionalization to provide adequate programs and to insure that the rights of the retarded are respected at all times.

Generic Services

It is imperative that, as more retarded individuals are served in the community, generic as well as specialized services become increasingly available. Generic services refer to any health, education, welfare, rehabilitation, or employment agency in the community which serves a broad spectrum of persons, including the developmentally disabled (Jaslow 1967). Excluded are special progrms intended solely or primarily for the developmentally disabled.

In a study conducted by Scheerenberger (1970), the majority of generic agencies surveyed were not serving the mentally retarded, nor did they appear particularly sensitive to their needs. While this situation is changing, the problem of generic services, especially for the more severely and profoundly multiply handicapped child, remains acute. The philosophies and attitudes of many agencies are not compatible with serving a child with such problems.

It is also rather common to place unrealistic expectancies upon general practitioners, regardless of their professional field. For example, several years ago, a rather prominent organization declared that the physician should assume responsibility for the life planning and coordination of services for the retarded. This presents several problems. First, mental retardation is not a major aspect of a physician's training; nor is the physician or any other professional in a position to act as a life planner without recourse to adequate information and technical consultancy for himself and programming for his client and family. Easily accessible fixed points of referral are important. In many areas of the country, the residential facility serves as one central or fixed point of referral and provides sophisticated consultancy required by generic (and specialized) agencies.

Sociopolitical Community

As witnessed by the preceding comments, the sociopolitical community at the city, county, state, and national levels is aggressively promoting local services for the retarded. There is an ever-increasing amount of legislation being passed that is intended to provide financial support for a variety of programs (see Chapter 9). Similarly, there is considerable action at all levels concerning the rights of the retarded and the establishment of advocacy programs. It is anticipated that funding will become increasingly flexible with a greater emphasis on enabling the retarded to select services of their choice.

PARENTS

Parents today can be divided into two groups: (1) those whose children have been born in recent years and who are receptive to the idea of maintaining their child in the local community; and (2) those parents whose retarded child was born a number of years ago and are now confronted with the prospect of deinstitutionalization. Fortunately, parents in the first group, though they have suffered the traumatic experience of having a retarded child, are finding a variety of services readily available to them in their local community. In most instances, they need not suffer the second trauma associated with placing their child in a residential facility for extended care.

Fifteen years ago this was not the situation. Frequently parents were confronted with one of two choices: either (1) keep their child at home with little or no support; or (2) place their child in a residential facility. As eloquently expressed by one parent: "An institution is only considered by desperate parents. Every parent I have known has moved heaven and earth to find another solution" (Jagar 1974, p. 83).

Other comments clearly illustrate the personal and emotional concerns of parents confronted with deinstitutionalization:

> As to deinstitutionalization plans, it seems to be of utmost importance that this should be done very slowly and with great care. The entire living conditions of a home must of necessity evolve around the retarded member. Parents have already gone through this "Garden of Gethsemane" by parting the first time with the child. Then if a child is returned home from an institution and the situation is again found an impossible one, to have to go through this traumatic experience a second time would likely come very nearly to destroying mentally and physically the retarded child and the parents.
>
> I realize that our institutions are presently overcrowded, and that this situation must be alleviated, but I do not agree with "deinstitutionalization" as it now stands. You can not deinstitutionalize the child without at the same time deinstitutionalizing his family. The child will not continue to develop educationally or emotionally unless the family finds it possible, perhaps with assistance, to make the necessary adjustments.
>
> As a parent my great fear is that many residents now in institutions will be returned home to unprepared and older parents and unprepared communities, and the gains over the years that have been made in institutions will be lost [Jagar 1974, pp. 82-84].

These concerns can not be ignored. No parent should be forced to have his retarded child or adult son or daughter return home if the situation is not appropriate. Although other community living alternatives are becoming available, parents are legitimately anxious about their quality. They are very sensitive to some of the unfortunate experiences associated with deinstitutionalization. Also, they are worried about the potential financial burden of deinstitutionalization. It is not uncommon for parents who are on Social Security or other limited income to express fear about the financial responsibility which they may have to assume. Others are concerned that their savings will be consumed or that they will be unable to leave anything to their other children in the event of death.

While parental counseling during deinstitutionalization is of utmost importance (as is their involvement and participation with their child at all times), parents need a threefold assurance that: (1) their youngster will receive quality services with adequate supervision; (2) deinstitutionalization will not result in an undue personal financial burden; and (3) there will be appropriate backup facilities other than the home in the event that community placement proves inadequate. Parental concerns and fears are genuine and should be so recognized.

THE RESIDENTIAL FACILITY

The need for and future of residential programming has been explored by a number of persons, including Tarjan (1966) and Wolfensberger (1969, 1971*a*, 1971*b*). A complete discussion will be found in Kugel and Wolfensberger's edited volume, *Changing Patterns in Residential Services for the Mentally Retarded* (1969). Since the present consideration will be quite limited, these references should be examined.

There are three widely held diverse opinions concerning residential facilities: (1) they should be "bigger and better"; (2) they should not exist at all; and (3) they should be smaller, tending toward specialization. Of these three positions, only a few persons support the concept of "bigger and better" facilities. These same individuals usually oppose deinstitutionalization.

A slightly larger number of people believe that there is or will be no need for residential services. This point of view is best advanced by Wolfensberger (1971*a* and 1971*b*).

The most commonly advocated position is that residential facilities have and will continue to have a definite role in providing for the retarded. The exact nature of this role is changing. The concept of the residential facility as an isolated "island unto itself" serving all levels of retardation and all types of problems is no longer valid. The contemporary residential facility is decreasing in size, serving a more limited severely and profoundly multihandicapped population, and is becoming just one of many agencies in a comprehensive community-oriented continuum of care.

The future role and responsibility of residential facilities was recently outlined by the National Association of Superintendents of Public Residential Facilities for the Mentally Retarded (1974, pp. 4-6), which fully supports deinstitutionalization. Briefly, their report indicates:

> Residential populations will continue to undergo significant change. With few exceptions, only the most severely and profoundly, multiply handicapped mentally retarded will require extended residential service.

> A number of short-term programs will be established with the intent of ameliorating specific problems and returning the child to his home community as soon as possible.

> Comprehensive developmental programs for several long neglected groups of retarded persons—the sensorially handicapped (i.e., blind and/or deaf) and emotionally disturbed—will be developed.

> Most residential facilities already offer a most welcome service to parents of the retarded—respite care.

> Residential facilities in the future will not function in an isolated capacity.

> Programming will be a shared responsibility between residential facility and community.

> It naturally follows that as communities begin to provide a continuum of care for retarded persons and their families, technical assistance and training will be required. This is especially true when agencies attempt to design programs for the more severely and profoundly multiply handicapped retarded and for those who are making the transition from residential to community living.

Whether or not this role will be realized or, in other words, whether or not deinstitutionalization will become a reality depends upon a number of influences. These have been described in some detail by Scheerenberger (1975). In essence, the primary responsibility rests with the community and society in general rather than the residential facility. Until vital services and programs exist in the community, the traditional role of the residential facility will, of sheer necessity, have to be maintained.

SUMMARY

Deinstitutionalization is desirable and feasible. It represents a goal which recognizes the worth and dignity of each individual and his right to live in as free and independent a society as possible. It is a goal which is increasingly accepted by the retarded, the family, and the community. Various courts and legislative bodies are beginning to provide a firm basis upon which essential community programs can be provided. The trend is well established; it remains for all concerned to insure that resultant programs and services always fulfill the needs of the developmentally disabled.

REFERENCES

Basic Rights of the Mentally Handicapped. Washington, D.C.: Mental Health Law Project, 1973.

Friedman, L. *A History of American Law*. New York: Simon & Schuster, 1974.

Goldstein, H. "Population Trends in U.S. Public Institutions for the Mentally Deficient." *American Journal of Mental Deficiency* (1959): 599-604.

Jagar, E. "Institutional Reform through the Eyes of a Parent." In *Region IV Staff Development Conference on Institutional Reform*. Columbia, S.C.: South Carolina Department of Mental Retardation, 1974.

Jaslow, R. *A Modern Plan for Modern Services to the Mentally Retarded*. Washington, D.C.: U.S. Government Printing Office, 1967.

Kennedy, J. *Message from the President of the United States*. Washington, D.C.: House of Representatives (88th Congress), Document No. 58, 1963.

Kugel, R., and Wolfensberger, W. *Changing Patterns in Residential Services for the Mentally Retarded*. Washington, D.C.: President's Committee on Mental Retardation, 1969

Lauber, D. *Zoning for Family and Group Care Facilities*. Chicago, Ill.: American Society of Planning Officials, 1974.

Lessard vs. *Schmidt* (Judgment). United States District Court: Eastern District of Wisconsin, 1973.

National Association of Superintendents of Public Residential Facilities for the Mentally Retarded. *Residential Programming: Position Statements*. Washington, D.C.: President's Committee on Mental Retardation, 1974.

Scheerenberger, R. C. "Generic Services for the Mentally Retarded and Their

Families." *Mental Retardation* 8(6)(1970):10-16.

______. "A Model for Deinstitutionalization." *Mental Retardation 12(16)* (1974):3-7.

______. *Managing Residential Facilities for the Developmentally Disabled.* Springfield, Ill.: Thomas, 1975.

Tarjan, G. "The Role of Residential Care—Past, Present, and Future." *Mental Retardation* 4(6)(1966):408.

Wolfensberger, W. "Twenty Predictions about the Future of Residential Services in Mental Retardation." *Mental Retardation* 7(6)(1969):51-54.

______. "Will There Always Be an Institution? I. The Impact of Epidemiological Trends." *Mental Retardation* 9(5)(1971*a*)14-20.

______. "Will There Always Be an Institution? II. Residential Alternatives to Institutions." *Mental Retardation* 9(6)(1971*b*):31-38.

Wyatt vs. *Stickney* (Judgment). District Court of the United States: Middle District of Alabama, Northern Division, 1972.

2

Institutionalization

A Perspective for Deinstitutionalization Program Development

RONALD L. THIELE, JAMES L. PAUL,
G. RONALD NEUFELD

DEINSTITUTIONALIZATION is a very complex social institutional issue. In the preceding chapter, Scheerenberger provided an orienting perspective on the complexity and nature of deinstitutionalization.

In the present chapter the authors discuss institutionalization, the process that deinstitutionalization is designed to modify. The purpose of this chapter is to further elaborate the nature of deinstitutionalization by further describing social and philosophical aspects of institutionalization, including the quantitative scope of the problem, and discussing salient issues involved in developing deinstitutionalization programs. The general discussion in this chapter and the one preceding provides an orienting perspective within which the chapters dealing with specific topics that follow can be considered.

The chapter is divided into four sections. In the first section, the process by which institutionalization is accomplished is described and discussed in terms of those characteristics that work in the disinterest of people and those that work in their interest. The examination of the process is limited to those aspects that relate to the developmentally disabled. Deinstitutionalization is defined as the process of countering institutionalization to reduce or eliminate those forces that compromise the interests or the integrity of the developmentally disabled.

The second section describes (1) a model for specifying the scope of the problem, based on a hypothetical incidence distribution of the developmentally disabled derived from a review of epidemiological studies; (2) a framework for matching the needs of the developmentally disabled with components of human service delivery systems; and (3) the organizational network, including local, regional, and state structures, which orchestrates the match between the needs of the developmentally disabled and resources. Much of the institutionalizing process is embedded within and between the components of that service network. The position taken here is that careful planning and program development is one central issue in countering institutionalization. That is, the developmentally disabled are institutionalized, in large part, because there is no appropriate service or support system available when and where it is needed. This results in inappropriate referrals and placements which are a disservice to the developmentally disabled and in the bureaucratization of service systems which drift into custodial and repressive patterns of care.

The third section describes components of exemplary programs organized to deinstitutionalize or otherwise advocate for the interests of the developmentally disabled. The fourth section draws from the material in the first three sections certain themes and conclusions. Potential initiative functions of Developmental Disabilities Councils are used as a focus for this discussion.

THE INSTITUTIONALIZATION PROCESS

Institutionalization may be simply defined as the process of adaptation to an institution. The process represents a method and an attitude by which we deal with human beings. Attitudes shape and dictate methods. Origins, categories, and applications of attitudes toward the developmentally disabled will be emphasized.

The reasons we intervene in the lives of persons to the point of institutionalizing them are based on criteria which fall into two major categories—social and functional. In the social category, the criterion is behavior which is considered inappropriate, unacceptable, or threatening in relation to age, sex, and subculture settings. In the functional category, the criteria are the degree of estimated or perceived competitiveness, productivity, or dependence for age, sex, or subculture setting. On careful consideration, it seems that these are valid criteria upon which to base some form of intervention in the lives of handicapped or dependent persons.

If success is to be achieved in the widespread efforts at deinstitutionalization, it is worth studying the process of institutionalization so we may identify those stages vulnerable to change or modification. The process is outlined here in five steps. It seems logical that these steps would occur in the order presented and they may occur at more than one stage of the sequence. Each of the steps emphasizes the methods and attitudes with which we deal with human beings but does not include discussion of the physical environment in which these events may occur. It will be apparent that the word *adaptation* is not restricted to a time period and that the word *institution* does not refer exclusively to a specific type of residential facility.

Step 1—Identification and Labeling

The formal identification and public labeling of a person as being one of a group of persons with a disability such as mental retardation, cerebral palsy, or epilepsy takes place at different times in the person's life and for varying reasons. This identification and labeling may occur.

In discussing the "clinical perspective" in the study of the mentally retarded, Mercer (1965, 1973) described how the process of identification and labeling had become highly formalized to include an elaborate terminology and classification system and a highly respected group of professional evaluators and labelers. She observed that the more formalized and recognized the labeling procedure became, the more the findings of deviance (from the norms established by the process) were accepted as intrinsic characteristics of the labeled persons.

The burden of the label and its implication on the lives of those identified is well expressed by Edgerton (1967) in his book *The Cloak of Competence*. He states: "It may be that any stigmatized person prefers to verbalize some stigma other than the one which he actually bears. However, one might speculate that no other stigma is as basic as mental retardation in the sense that a person so labeled is thought to be so completely lacking in basic competence. Other stigmatized persons typically retain some competencies, limited though they may be, but the retarded person has none left to him. He is, by definition, incompetent to manage any of his affairs" (p. 207).

Deviance has historically carried negative connotations. The categorical subgroup of deviants know by this labeling process as mentally retarded have stereotypically been perceived as "bad," "inferior," "dangerous," "immoral."

The motivations for the development of evaluating and labeling systems are not being questioned here. The many important contributions to research, treatment, and program development are acknowledged. Many of the prominent categorical programs and forms of assistance that we rely upon today were developed in response to the needs of these "labeled" groups of "deviants."

We have seen special services developed for categorical labels. We have seen persons excluded from those needed services because of the wrong label. We have seen inaccurate labels applied to qualify persons for needed services. This process may not be an inherent evil of labeling but a reflection of the persistent strength of public support generated in behalf of various categorical groups. It has only been with the recent advent of the developmental disabilities movement that we have begun to deliver generic services, and even this effort has been for a tenuous amalgam of a few selected categories.

Mercer (1973), in discussing the "clinical perspective" model of mental retardation, points out the rather awesome authority of the labels and the professional labelers in the assignment of people to services.

That the quality of services reflects the public stereotypic attitude toward the labeled group is best reflected in the history of the residential institutions for the retarded (Wolfensberger 1969). The explicit and compelling writings of Blatt have chronicled the contemporary quality of institutional services and the attitudes which support and condone these conditions. In reflecting on the "back wards" of institutions, Blatt (1970) comments: "What was being demonstrated was that the architects of back wards, the progenitors of the feces-smearers, the culprits of this holocaust are normal men and their public policy" (p. 5). In reasoning on the cruel dispassionate treatment rendered in many institutions he says: "On the other hand, certain human beings have been taught or trained—or this is part of their nature—to conceive of other human beings in ways that most of us think of animals. . . . It isn't that these attendants are cruel or imcompetent people—although all too often they are—but they have come to believe, for various reasons, that those in their charge are not really human" (p. 20).

Obviously the identification and labeling process has not in itself been responsible for the ills of institutional care. The personal and public perceptions of attitudes toward the labeled deviant groups have strongly influenced the quality of caring and service we afford them. Labeling is the first step of the institutionalization process.

Step 2—Destruction of Self-Worth

How well we think of ourselves is largely determined by how we interpret what others think of us. It is a widely and strongly held concept of human development that the level of our feeling of self-worth has a critical effect on the quality of our adaptation to our life situation. The effects of every stage of the process of institutionalization encourage the destruction of self-worth.

The effects of labeling, the burden of the stigma on how one is thought of, have been discussed above. In speaking of the "socialization to the role of retardate" Mercer (1973) postulates that once a person is placed in the status of retardate in a society his behavior is reinforced to play that role until "he will come to perceive himself as a retardate and incorporate the status of mental retardate as part of his concept of self."

The frustrations, disappointments, and personal pain of failure to achieve like one's peers has been widely reported in the literature of education, psychology, and child development. Our society is not geared to regard failure with favor and does not even positively and regularly acknowledge good effort which falls short of success. The process of admission to an institution, whether residential or day, frequently represents a further or even final acknowledgement of failure in the larger society. The special class in the public school, regardless of what euphemistic title it may bear, is known to all as a place for those who have failed in the mainstream of education.

The process of regimentation offers little or no recognition of personal worth and rejects efforts at self-determination or self-expression, thus compounding the destruction of self-worth and effectively preventing its development or repair. Thus this stage of the process is a part of every stage. Its destructive impact is only equaled by its inhibitory effect on development and coping.

Step 3—Admission to an Institution

Admission to a residential institution is a single event of almost unparalleled significance in the life of an individual. It is the "action phase" of the institutionalization process, sharply defined in time and place and recountable in detail of occurrences. The description presented by Blatt in *Exodus from Pandemonium* (1970) is concise, poignant, and deeply disturbing. Those, including the authors, who have been associated with residential institutions can verify the essence of such descriptions if we will be honest. As startling as the implicit brutality and as moving as the pathos of these episodes may be, their real significance lies in the implications of the acts. The individual is stripped of privacy, individual identity, and autonomy of action. The person's separation from family and friends is absolute. He enters a situation in which he effectively is totally deprived of his individual rights. Separation from family and friends, deprivation of individuality, and denial of basic rights are fundamental, inherent, and inescapable attributes of the condition of residential care.

Today, in a few institutions which have established systems of resident advocacy which attempt to protect individuality and human rights, the impact of admission has been blunted and modified greatly. Such achievement, where it has occured, is noteworthy, for it means that the basic attitudes and beliefs of staff members have been modified or altered. After all, staff members of institutions are representative members of the same communities which apply labels and hold stereotypic beliefs about those labeled. Who, more than those who staff institutions, have better reason to hold the belief that the mentally retarded have little or no potential to achieve? They have watched generation after generation of mentally retarded enter instituions and fulfill the prophecy of failure. It is this "institutional attitude" which prevades from the top administration on down, or from the lowest ward aide on up, that creates the climate which wreaks such havoc on those admitted to the institution.

For some, admission to the residential institution is a relief from their community situation and may actually provide real hope for assistance and improvement. Many of these have already suffered the "admission shock" when they entered a community service. Many of our community programs are pervaded with the same attitudes described for the residential institution. Admission to these programs, although not explicit in the separation from family, deprivation of individuality, and denial of rights, does subject the participant to the prophecy of "no potential." Admission to many programs is a further indication of society's perception of the individual as inferior and incompetent and further isolates him or her from the general community.

A uniform and total condemnation of residential facilities and community programs is not intended. It is the intention to indicate that there does exist an "institutional attitude" which is a corollary or extension of the labeling or stigma attitude. The presence of this attitude in the staff of a program will largely determine the quality of experience the participants of that program will enjoy.

Step 4—Regimentation

If construed as meaning the creation of an ordered, structured life routine which insures that basic life necessities are met, then regimentation need not necessarily have a totally negative connotation. Historically, however, for the developmentally disabled, it has exceeded the simple good intentions for guarantee of provision of life necessities.

Regimentation most frequently occurs in settings designed and staffed by people who are a part of that society which has identified and labeled the person. Even in those situations with the most enlightened staff members, demands are usually made that the person adhere to certain policies and procedures of the institution. These include, at least:

1. Being made part of a group whose activities of eating, sleeping, personal hygiene, and recreation are standardized to a rather rigid time schedule. An observed effect of this is that time becomes a meaningless abstraction.

2. Enforced segregation of sexes varying from total and permanent separation to partial separation. Even partial segregation must be interpreted as essentially permanent.

3. Loss or major diminution of the prerogative of personal possessions, individual selection, and style of clothing and grooming.

These and other policies and routines seem to be largely based on the premise that:

1. These provide for the greatest efficiency and convenience of the staff and facility.

2. The residents are incompetent and incapable of making "proper" independent judgments or decisions.

3. The residents are being protected from: (a) the outside world, (b) themselves, (c) each other.

4. The "moral standards" of the individuals and the public are being protected.

The need for some order and routine in the conduct of everyday life is generally accepted by all of us. Regimentation has been most conspicuous in the residential care setting, but community-based programs have not been entirely free of its excesses. In the residential setting, the prevailing and pervasive attitude has been "keep them clean and quiet." We usually attribute responsibility for this attitude to the institutional staff, and in fact they must share in the guilt. It is also true that the public, including families and friends, wishes to see residents in a clean and serene state. This fortifies the fantasy that the resident is living in a state of unknowing, unaware, chronic bliss. Visions to the contrary such as those made famous by Blatt (1966) in "Christmas in Purgatory" and many subsequent local exposés disturb the public tranquility and arouse despair and guilt over this terrible "problem." While we deplore the chaos and filth of the "back wards" we frequently mistake the sterile, sanitized, ordered environment of many of the new glass and stainless steel facilities as a marvelous humane improvement. What we overlook in both situations is the destructiveness of the regimentation process to the human spirit, the self-worth, and the potential for development. It is the reflection of the attitudes and feelings toward the individuals by the society in which it occurs that makes regimentation such a destructive part of the total process of institutionalization.

Step 5—Prophecy Fulfilled

In each of the preceding four stages reference has been made to common attitudes of the general public that underlie their perceptions and treatment of the mentally retarded. Reference has been made to widely held stereotypes of behavior of the mentally retarded. These stereotypes include such judgments as "incompetent," "inferior," "immoral," "bad." The individual who is placed in the mentally retarded group by the labeling process inherits a prophecy as much as a stigma. That prophecy is that he will eventually demonstrate the stereotyped behaviors and characteristics assigned to the mentally retarded.

Mercer (1973) postulates that once a person is placed in the status of mental retardate by the labeling process of the social system, the individual is socialized to play that role: "As his fellows reward and reinforce role behaviors that conform to expectations and punish role behaviors that deviate from expectations, he internalizes the role that he plays. If he is socialized to meet the role expectations for the status of mental retardate, he will internalize the requisite pattern of behaviors. He will come to perceive himself as a retardate and incorporate the status of mental retardate as part of his concept of self" (pp. 33).

Hence, as the person labeled retarded grows but does not achieve personal competency and demonstrates sexuality without appropriate social competence, the prophecy is fulfilled. Institutionalization is complete, and our beliefs and attitudes are justified as is the process itself. In the residential setting, reaching this stage is considered a "good adjustment," for it is usually accompanied by a state of docile regimentation and conformity.

This suggested model of the process of institutionalization may seem to imply that a series of discrete events occur. It is meant to describe a continuum of the expression of attitudes of society toward some of its members which begins with the first stirrings of concern by parents or social peers that the individual is not achieving in accord with expectations. It has its end when parents or social peers are convinced of the permanent irreversible incompetence of the individual. The process may take years or run its course in months.

It is our belief that many effects of the process may be reversed and that alternatives to initiation of the process exist.

SCOPE OF THE PROBLEM

It has already been pointed out that the process of institutionalization is not likely to be reversed without careful planning and program development. Traditionally planning has been viewed as an activity for state-level administrators. The functions of state-level planning are to obtain state and federal resources and to try to coordinate program development. Despite the intent of planning to provide direction for program development, local programs seldom reflect a systematic planning process. In most states communication from local to state organizations is minimal. The result is great variance in local programs. The variance is demonstrated both in the quality of service provision and also in the theoretical or philosophical perspective that underlies the program. Other products of isolated planning activity are file cabinets full of unused plans or perhaps uncompleted plans.

Careful planning starts with need identification. Many plans never move beyond that point. Planning activities are launched, needs assessments are undertaken, and before this first in a series of planning activities is complete, the activity is aborted. Needs assessment activity is sometimes assigned to staff members or groups as a "cooling out" activity. In other cases, new employees may not be able to relate to the work of a previous employee and therefore recycle an activity that is already complete. The point is, planning and needs assessment often occupies more time than it should because of duplicated effort and poor use of resources.

While complete and accurate data is important to sound planning, planners sometimes make the collection of data and information more complex than it needs to be. In this connection, Stedman (1970), using a three-dimensional framework of age, severity, and sociological area, has developed a design for projecting need. The model (see Table 2.1) is based upon a "hypothetical community" of 100,000 population. The conversion ratios presented in the table were taken from 1970 census data. Similar ratios could be developed from current census data in order to bring the information up to date. If a planning mechanism is mired down at the level of needs assessment, and if the development of services is suffering from this problem, it is suggested that this model could be used to accelerate the planning process. The model also has utility for persons or organizations to evaluate the strength, weakness, and gaps that exist in an existing delivery mechanism. According to Stedman, the following services are suggested by the data presented in Table 2.1:

1. Diagnostic and counseling services for all of the 7,000 mentally retarded and their families.

2. Welfare, social, and educational services to enrich the learning opportunities of the 603 mildly retarded preschool children, many of whom live in slums or in otherwise depressed circumstances.

3. Public health nursing and homemaker services to assist in caring for the 96 moderately and 24 severly retarded infants and young children in this population.

4. About 93 special education classes for the 1,610 mildly retarded school-aged children who, with specialized training, could become self-sufficient adult citizens.

5. About 27 special education classes for the 256 moderate or trainable mentally retarded children who, with the appropriate training, could become productive workers in supervised or sheltered work settings.

6. A day-care recreational center for the 63 severely retarded children of school age who would be unable to profit from formal school placement.

7. Vocational counseling, job training, and placement services for the 471 retarded young adults who can contribute to their own and the community's welfare if given an opportunity to work in a supervised environment.

8. Specialized job training for the 3,157 mildly retarded adults over 25 who can take a productive place in our nation's economy.

9. Activity centers for the 578 retarded young adults and adults who may never take their full places as workers in the community, but who are no less important from the social and humanitarian point of view.

10. Residential centers to meet the needs of those 142 retarded young adults and adults with problems requiring supervision, care, and training so comprehensive as to require a 24-hour effort.

TABLE 2.1

Average Incidence of Mental Retardation Based on 1970 Census Figures in Four Populations: 100,000

Estimated Incidence 2% (Suburbia)

I	Pre-school Under age 6	School-age Age 6-10	Young Adults Age 20-24	Adults Age 25 & over	Total All Ages
Mild	172	460	134	903	1669
Moderate	28	73	21	144	266
Severe	7	18	5	35	65
TOTAL	207	551	160	1082	2000

Estimated Incidence 3% (Overall)

II	Pre-school Under age 6	School-age Age 6-10	Young Adults Age 20-24	Adults Age 25 & over	Total All Ages
Mild	258	690	202	1353	2503
Moderate	41	110	32	216	399
Severe	10	27	8	53	98
TOTAL	309	827	242	1622	3000

Estimated Incidence 5% (Rural)

III	Pre-school Under age 6	School-age Age 6-10	Young Adults Age 20-24	Adults Age 25 & over	Total All Ages
Mild	431	1150	336	2256	4173
Moderate	69	183	336	360	666
Severe	17	45	13	86	161
TOTAL	517	1378	403	2702	5000

Estimated Incidence 7% (Inner City)

IV	Pre-school Under age 6	School-age Age 6-10	Young Adults Age 20-24	Adults Age 25 & over	Total All Ages
Mild	603	1610	471	3157	5841
Moderate	96	256	75	503	930
Severe	24	63	18	124	229
TOTAL	723	1929	564	3784	7000

Table 2.1, cont'd.

Conversion Ratios

IQ Distribution		1970 Census—Age Group/Percentage Population			
Category	%	Under 6	6-19	20-24	25 & over
Mild	83.43	10.32	27.56	8.06	54.06
Moderate	13.30				
Severe	3.27				
	100.00				

	Under 5	5-13	14-17	18-21	21 & over	TOTAL
1974	7.7	16.1	8.0	7.5	62.4	101.7
1970	8.4	18.0	7.8	7.0	60.5	101.7

Note: Projections of 1974 population distribution by age indicate a significant trend toward fewer preschool and school-age children in proportion to the total population.

This provides an obvious starting point for planning. The only situation in which this information would be useless is if these services had already been developed for the populations indicated. Since comprehensive planning is sometimes a lengthy process, a state may move immediately toward program development based upon data from a hypothetical community.

Another major problem in planning and program development concerns the lack of vertical communication—communication that extends from local to state organizations. The bureaucracy that has engulfed the entire human service system resembles a gigantic onion. One may be successful in peeling away one layer only to discover yet another layer. In many areas the layers include local, regional (within state), state, regional (multi-state), and federal. In many areas there is limited communication between layers. Table 2.2, developed by the authors, outlines activities that should be undertaken at different geographic levels of the bureaucracy. Communication through geographic boundaries could be accomplished through the process of planning.

Table 2.2 includes two areas that may arouse controversy. The first concerns responsibility in planning, the second service delivery responsibility. First, it is our belief that state planners should look toward service providers and consumers at the local level for statements of needs and assignment of priorities. Persons at the state level who are skilled in planning technology should then compile the plan and have it approved at the local level. This approach to planning would assure communication from the local to the state level and increase the likelihood that plans would be meaningful and relevant documents. The second possible area of controversy concerns responsibility assigned in the area of service delivery. The large majority of residential institutions across the country are state-operated facilities. They are monuments which should remind us that large bureaucracies should not be in the service-delivery business. The actual delivery of service should be left to local citizens. State agencies in turn should develop monitoring capability. The role of state agencies in the service-delivery system should be limited to resource acquisition, the development of standards, monitoring, and training. State agencies along with consumers should participate in the development of standards and the process of monitoring.

TABLE 2.2

Possible Planning and Program Development Activities for Multi-Level Systems

Geographic Area	Planning					Service Delivery	Resource Development	Project Demonstration and Research	Monitor	Standard Development	Training	Public Awareness and Information Dissemination
	Needs Assessment	Priority Setting	Goals & Objectives	Evaluation	Plan Approval							
Local Service-Providers Consumers	X	X			X	X			X	X		
Regional (In-State)						X	X				X	
State			X	X			X	X	X	X	X	X
Federal Regional Multi-State							X					
Federal				X			X	X	X	X		X

An examination of the chart indicates limited responsibility for regional activity both within a state and also the multistate federal regional mechanisms. The principle underlying the development of regional mechanisms was to decentralize authority. It was hoped that this decentralization would result in improved service coordination and communication. Unfortunately, it is beginning to appear that these decentralizing mechanisms simply increase the complexity of communication. We have perhaps simply added another layer of bureaucracy to an already staggering system, each layer being very complex.

DEINSTITUTIONALIZATION PROGRAM DEVELOPMENT

The institutionalizing process described earlier in this chapter is deeply entrenched in the culture of caregiving systems. The purpose of programming for deinstitutionalization is not to stop institutionalization. It is, rather, to minimize the negative impact of institutions and institutional practices. Stated positively, deinstitutionalization is an attempt to revitalize the potential of service-delivery systems for responding appropriately and efficiently to the needs of persons those systems are established to serve.

The things wrong with institutions, and there are many, are the targets for program development. There are two major considerations here: (1) What is the "institution" at which programs are targeted? and (2) What is the nature and source of data on which we act?

The remainder of this chapter will focus on these two questions and primarily on what is involved in deinstitutionalization program development and the topics or themes that need consideration in planning. Engineering questions of how to develop deinstitutionalization programs will not be examined here. These and other technical issues in planning will be considered in chapters that follow.

The Institutional Focus of Program Development

The institution here includes the total culture of the self-contained residential setting plus those activities that either lead to admission or to discharge from that setting. This definition involves (or implicates) the community in institutions, and it involves the institution in communities. It is thinking about and acting as if institutions were islands, set apart, belonging to nothing that contributes to the "institutional" problem. This idea was developed by J. Iverson Riddle, superintendent of an institution, who knows the problems of keeping the institution "connected."

From this perspective, identifying a child with special needs and labeling him without providing services are part of a larger system that may include keeping the child on a ward where there is little or no positive stimulation or education. The larger system, similarly, involves the child discharged from the institutional residence and placed in a public school setting where he may have no relevant adaptive skills to cope and where the school may have no program to teach him. These situations are separated by time and space but fundamentally involve the actions (or inactions) of institutions on the life of the child.

This has significant implications for program development. First, it recognizes the connections between different parts of the institutional system. The ecology of institutionalization, then, requires that any planned deinstitutionalization activity or program anticipates the effects it will have on other aspects of the institutional systems. The activity will surely feel the impact of those other aspects if it is a significant activity for the system.

Any deinstitutionalization plan should include some picture of how the total institutional system fits together. It is ultimately that system which must be changed if the plan is effective. Changing parts of the institutional system should have a calculated, planned impact on the whole system. This is one way to think about impact potential in allocating resources. It is also a basis for thinking about program monitoring and evaluation. That is, if we know the system, we also know or can discover the key indicators of significant change in the system.

Another implication of this view has to do with program coordination and the integration of services. One of the myths in programming is that programs are ineffective because they are unrelated or uncoordinated. "If we can get 'them' connected or coordinated," the fantasy is, " 'they' will become more effective and efficient." We persist in this hope in the face of clear evidence that coordination alone usually will not change anything.

The problem with the coordination myth is that what public human-service institutions and agencies do to people *is* connected. They are frequently connected philosophically, fiscally, and even procedurally. While separated by time and space, human services get welded to each other in a variety of ways over time. Any publicly supported human-service system that has any history at all has found its niche in the institutional system.

It is not, therefore, simply more coordination or "interagenciness" that is needed. What we seek is coordination relative to a set of rules or standards. Our hope is to get services working together to more effectively accomplish certain goals we agree are worthy. We further want to coordinate how we accomplish those ends so that certain values are manifest and maintained in the process. Coordination without standards is like a personality without a conscience or a meeting without an agenda.

The Joint Commission on The Accreditation of Hospitals has developed exemplary standards for residential facilities (1973) and for community agencies (1974). These standards relate to each facet of the total institutional system. Whether or not one agrees with all of the standards, they spcify rules for most critical client-institution encounters. Thus there is a conceptual basis for holding institutions accountable.

Nature and Source of Data

A basis has already been presented for conceptualizing the scope of the problem and projecting program plans. This provides an *a priori* data base for planning, so far as the individual is concerned. Here we need to add two dimensions to the data for planning: (1) experiences and wishes of the consumer, and (2) program data.

EXPERIENCES AND WISHES OF THE CONSUMER

The ultimate source of information about whether a service is working for a person should be the person himself. It is in adapting what we have to offer to meet the needs of each new person what we keep ourselves from the socially infectious institutional inertia. Institutional health requires personal commitment. In order to be creative and responsible, he must listen to a person's question before we offer answers. One of the most anti-institutional responses can be our recognition with the person that we do not have an answer—perhaps we have never heard the question before. This can free up much advocacy potential. Acknowledging the questions and refusing to institutionally strap the person to an answer he does not want is basic advocacy. We know we are wrong—institutionalized in one of its worse senses—when we are organized to treat the experiences of handicapped people as if they were the same, because they are handicapped.

Why should they share the same hopes, the same faith, or the same fears because they share a similar handicap or the same residence? People hurt one at a time—perhaps more so if they are handicapped. Healing cannot be institutionalized. Deinstitutionalization programs must seek to reduce the institutional penchant for erasing the freedom of individual encounter and prerogative.

Some point out the problems of the severely and profoundly handicapped in communicating the fit they experience with our interventions and their unmet needs. There are very few who cannot tell us if we look for as well as listen to their answers. Staff sensitivity here is essential. Staff may need to be taught to listen with their eyes. The handicapped person may need help in identifying and communicating his needs.

This is difficult to maintain. It is the so-called radical counter-institutional orientation that argues it is not possible. It must be possible if institutions are to be renewed and supported.

Communication with the handicapped person is the essence of service delivery. Lack of communication is one way we depersonalize handicapped persons.

PROGRAM DATA

Program monitoring is an essential element in the accountability structure of an institutional system. Knowing what is happening to whom, when, for what purpose, and to what effect enables administrators to make more informed decisions about the service delivery. What is monitored is the ongoing fit between the service and the service consumer. There is no reason for monitoring other than improving the service-client fit.

Monitoring is a complex and difficult activity. What is looked at, when, how, and by whom must be based on several considerations. First, the person's right to privacy cannot be violated. Second, the staff can become paranoid or cynical about monitors and monitoring procedures. Third, people monitors are human too and can develop their own blindness based on their vested interests in an issue or a particular client. There must be a system for keeping monitors honest—with themselves. Fourth, information loss must be calculated in the sampling design for monitoring. That is, things that are wrong and should be known may be saved for unmonitored time and space. Fifth, it is essential to be able to act on information. A monitoring system that has no action potential is worthless.

There are many different types and styles of monitoring systems.

Only two will be mentioned here. One was developed at the Western Carolina Center in Morganton, North Carolina. This was developed and continues as an institution-based advocacy system with a monitoring component. The advocates have responsibility for keeping up with specific residents in the institution, monitoring their progress toward deinstitutional goals. If progress is not being made, the advocates help determine why and negotiate better services. They keep the residents from getting lost.

They also keep track of the quality of environments and activities in the institution. They identify resident-centered issues that need attention in order to improve resident services.

The advocates have direct access to the superintendent, whose office lends credibility and authority to their work. Without strong support from the chief executive, this kind of system would not work. The advocates who, even with the superintendent's support, suffer problems of morale and alienation could not survive. They must move easy, using power discretely and sparingly. Even their "velvet hammer," if swung too often, triggers staff behavior designed to reduce their power. This poses a real problem for the superintendent. He has to support his staff in the delivery of services while he is actively promoting the advocacy (and, at times, agitation) functions. Sometimes reports conflict. Whom does he believe? Most often neither person is willfully lying. Sometimes basic professional values are involved. Examples of conflicts in this area include the maintenance of a token economy, the types of reinforcers allowed, and the use of punishment in research.

There are some clear-cut issues involving, for example, the physical abuse of residents. Here the superintendent can act decisively. Most of the issues, however, are not so clear cut. They require working through relationships and differences in discussion, restructuring a situation, and frequently making moral rather than technical decisions.

A different monitoring system was developed in the Child Advocacy System Project (1974). This project developed procedures for monitoring children in their own communities and for monitoring community services. Two manuals *To Protect and Respect* (1974) and *A Matter of Service* (1974) were produced on child monitoring and service monitoring, respectively.

It has been suggested here that: (1) institutional systems extend from the community into residential centers and from the residential centers out into communities; (2) deinstitutionalization programming must relate to this total institutional system; and (3) the data base for program development must come from (a) a projected quantitative scope of the problem,

(b) the service consumers or their advocates, and (c) the effectiveness of existing programs and services.

In general, there must exist an accountability structure which, at a minimum: (1) keeps information current, valid, available, and flowing; (2) prevents the drift of decision-making upward and pushes it closer to the consumer or his benefactor; (3) provides procedural recourse for correcting abuse or denial of rights of the developmentally disabled, as perceived by the developmentally disabled, his or her benefactor, or other person knowledgeable of advocacy needs; and (4) provides active advocacy for constructive and immediate resolution of problems which seeks neither to embarass nor intimidate. Such an accountability structure is certainly facilitated by, and some would argue probably best accomplished by, third-party involvement in monitoring, information flow, and advocacy activities.

There are other major topics that must be considered in developing deinstitutionalization programs. First, the deinstitutionalization program efforts must include attention to the legal and human rights of the developmentally disabled. This must include making such rights known as well as correcting their denial. Second, there must be a decision-making philosophy and the accompanying machinery to effectively involve consumers or their representative in the decision-making process and keep consumer-relevant decisions made as close to the consumer as possible, rather than higher in the bureaucratic service structure. Third, there must be a benefactor or advocate system of some type. Heber (1970) found the presence or absence of a benefactor to be the most crucial variable in successful deinstitutionalization. Fourth, deinstitutionalization activities must penetrate the attitudes, morale, and competencies of the staff who work directly with the developmentally disabled. In large institutions, for example, the direct-care staff may be a source of some abuse. They are also a source of enormous advocacy potential which is frequently buried under bureaucratic messages of meniality and general lack of regard. Transformation at this direct-care level is essential. Fifth, there must be an information system that provides data *on clients* regarding needs, and *to clients* or benefactors regarding resources. This system, as already suggested, must also include evaluative data on programs. Sixth, community alternatives to institutionalization must exist. Group living, foster home, and sheltered work arrangements are a few of the essential community resources that prevent the need for institutionalization and make possible the re-entry of the institutionalized person into the community. The development of effective community alternatives is certainly a cornerstone to the success of the total deinstitutionalization effort. Seventh, there must be specific attention to the budget system and the process by which budgets are renewed or changed. If money is going primarily into institutionalization, substantial deinstitutionalization will not occur. Eighth, there must be a free flow of information to the public about services and needs. Public education should be structured within a psychology of constructive involvement of those receiving the information.

REFERENCES

Accreditation Council for Facilities for the Mentally Retarded. *Standards for Community Agencies*. Chicago, Ill.: Joint Commission on Accreditation of Hospitals, 1974.

______. *Standards for Residential Facilities*. Chicago, Ill.: Joint Commission on Accreditation of Hospitals, 1974.

Blatt, B. *Christmas in Purgatory: A Photographic Essay on Mental Retardation*. Boston: Allyn and Bacon, 1966.

______. *Exodus From Pandemonium*. Boston: Allyn and Bacon, 1970.

Edgerton, R. B. *The Cloak of Competence*. Berkeley: University of California Press, 1967.

Heber, R. F., and Dever, R. B. "Research in Education and Habilitation of the Mentally Retarded." In *Social Cultural Aspects of Mental Retardation,* edited by H. C. Haywood. New York: Appleton-Century-Crofts, 1970.

Holder, H. D.; Pelosi, J. W.; and Dixon, R. T. *A Matter of Service: How to Monitor Agencies that Serve Children*. Durham, N.C.: Learning Institute of North Carolina, 1974.

Kugel, R. B., and Wolfensberger, W. *Changing Patterns in Residential Facilities for the Mentally Retarded*. Washington, D.C.: President's Commission on Mental Retardation, 1969.

Mercer, J. R. *Labeling the Mentally Retarded; Clinical and Social System Perspectives on Mental Retardation*. Berkeley: University of California, 1973.

______. "Social System Perspective and Clinical Perspective: Frames of Reference for Understanding Career Patterns of Persons Labeled as Mentally Retarded." *Social Problems* 13(1)(1965):18-34.

Pelosi, J. W., and Johnson, S. *To Protect and Respect*. Durham, N.C.: Learning Institute of North Carolina, 1974.

Stedman, D. J. "The Hypothetical Community; A Template for Planning Mental Retardation Programs." *North Carolina Journal of Mental Health* 4(3)(1970):26-29.

II Theory

3

Stigmatization and Labeling

PAUL R. DOKECKI, BARBARA J. ANDERSON,
PHILIP S. STRAIN

AMONG THE MORE FORMIDABLE OBSTACLES to deinstitutionalization are social processes associated with the interrelated concepts of stigma, stigmatization, and labeling. The world of handicapped and deviant persons can often be characterized as involving a vicious cycle as follows: (1) stigma gives rise to negative social reactions (stigmatization), often leading to the identification and labeling of a person as deviant; (2) stigma enhances the likelihood that the labeled deviant person will be institutionalized; (3) stigma negatively affects the institutionalized person's opportunities to receive adequate intervention programming; (4) stigma thus magnified reduces the probability that deinstitutionalization will be recommended for the person; and (5) stigma increases the probability that deinstitutionalization and related intervention efforts will fail, if attempted, because of negative social reactions in the community.

We may say (after Goffman 1963) that *stigma* is any information which potentially disqualifies an individual from full social acceptance. The information does not inhere solely in the individual but rather in the juxtaposition of a person's actual and virtual social identity. *Actual social identity* involves the past and current attributes (physical, emotional, intellectual, political, economic, social, etc.) that an individual can be proved to possess. *Virtual social identity* refers to the normative expectations or assumptions made about an individual which, in effect, become demands to be and behave as society expects. Within the context of this personal attribute-societal expectation system, *stigmatization* (and its special case, *labeling*) is a negative social reaction, the actual act of socially disqualifying the potentially disqualifiable person, the strength of which is directly related to the perceived degree of violation of normative social demands. Thus, for the stimatized individual stigma involves "an attribute that makes him different from others in the category of persons available for him to be, and of a less desirable kind—in the extreme a person who is quite thoroughly bad, or dangerous, or weak. He is thus reduced in our minds from a whole and usual person to a tainted, disoriented one . . . by virtue of a special discrepancy between virtual and actual social identity" (Goffman 1963, p. 3).

In the remainder of this chapter we pursue issues relevant to Goffman's "thoroughly bad, or dangerous, or weak" people, particularly the more severely and profoundly retarded, within the context of the recent push for deinstitutionalization. While we view the problems of the to-be-deinstitutionalized retarded person as transactional (Dewey and Bently 1974; Dokecki and Strain 1973; Dokecki, Scanlan, and Strain 1972), involving both the person and the political, economic, and social environment, the stress on stigmatization and labeling in this chapter leads us to emphasize the environment. Moreover, in our analysis of most social problems we caution against the too-prevalent tendency to overemphasize the individual and to blame the victim (Ryan 1971) while ignoring broader social environmental factors.

HISTORICAL ISSUES

Construction of deinstitutionalization policies and programs in the mid 1970s without consideration of historical issues is foolhardy and dangerous. Rhodes and Sagor (1974) have pointed out that social institutions originally develop in response to very real social problems and value conflicts; however, after a time we lose sight of these motivating factors despite the fact that they often continue to influence societal and institutional practice. Rhodes and Sagor refer to this institutional amnesia as "mystification" and caution that service-delivery systems can become ineffective or even destructive unless we understand fully their historical, political, economic, and social context. This is especially true regarding the role of stigmatization and labeling in deinstitutionalization.

Is the current deinstitutionalization movement reinventing its own variation of the wheel? In 1857, Samuel Gridley Howe (cited in Kirk and Lord 1974) wrote:

> Being called upon lately to give advice about the establishment of Institutions for the Blind and the Deaf Mutes in a new state, I have counselled a course different from the one I myself followed many years ago. It is to dispense with any great costly building, having common dormitories, dining rooms, chapel, and the like. To make no preparation for any great common household at all; but to build a simple building, with all the conveniences for structuring classes, and make provision for boarding the pupils in private families. In a word, to reduce the Institutions, as we would any machine, to the simplest form.

Farber (1968) has suggested that the recent deinstitutionalization proposals for mentally retarded individuals contain only minor elaborations of Howe's position and that a general negative societal attitude toward the institutionalized mentally retarded as persons to be feared, ridiculed, and "treated" in such a manner which insures their lack of future participation in the larger community has impeded humane progress.

Rainwater (1970) has presented a framework for conceptualizing the perspectives which people use to understand and deal with individuals who are labeled deviant and who are not part of society's mainstream. This scheme is presented in Table 3.1. The user of each perspective levies a diagnosis, presumably based on some evidence or stigma, speculates on "underlying" causes or etiology, and proposes a "cure" or therapy. The institutionalized retarded person has been viewed from a variety of perspectives over the years, including the moralizing, medicalizing, and naturalizing (especially the biological determinism variety). However, the position we wish to advance in agreement with Farber (1968) is that our society has always fundamentally believed, and continues to believe, that retarded persons can best be viewed within the moralizing perspective wherein they are seen as evil (possessing a moral flaw), and potent (threatening the well-being of the community).

Dokecki *et al.* (1975) showed how the history of such social institutions as the family (cf. Aries 1962) and public welfare (cf. Piven and Cloward 1971) have involved the use of the moralizing perspective in viewing and dealing with deviants. Economic issues have been centrally involved. In a related view, Farber (1968) has suggested that an important negative consequence of modern economic systems is the situation of the mentally retarded. Retarded citizens are part of technological society's surplus population, and society requires such a surplus to permit the best fit between people and positions in the rational selection process in situations involving education, economics, politics, and marriage. The surplus population is made up of those lacking needed competencies related to these institutions. The poor treatment accorded retarded citizens is hy-

TABLE 3.1

Perspectives for Explaining the Existence of Deviant Individuals

PERSPECTIVE	DIAGNOSIS	ETIOLOGY	THERAPY
1. Moralizing (oldest approach)	"Sinner"— evil & potent	Moral flaw in person or environment	Punish-control/ redeem-save (e.g., fundamentalist churches, Black Muslim)
2. Medicalizing (replaced sin with sickness)	"Sick"— evil & weak	*Pathology in person:* apathetic orientation; disturbed child-rearing; trained incapacities; absence of certain experiences	Psychotherapy; compensatory education; importance of clinical approaches and individual diagnosis
		Pathology in environment: disorganized community with deviant goals	Build new community infrastructures; community involvement; remove children from disorganized environment
3. Apotheosizing	"Natural Man" "Heroic Culture" —virtuous & potent	Special capacities; life of beauty and virtue (as compared to sterile suburbs)	Natural man and heoric culture adapted as symbols (in dress, slang, etc.); attack rest of society & join disinherited for new power base
4. Normalizing	"Ordinary People" (although mistreated and poor)—virtuous & weak	Conditions of disinheritance have only superficial effects on personalities	Debunk other perspectives and their policy implications; emphasize "opportunities rather than radical alterations in the system (e.g., training, counseling, better coordinated services)
5. Naturalizing	a. Biological determinism	Inferior internal structures	Benign totalitarianism; eugenics
	b. Cultural-relativistic	Valid, functional way of life; different but with inner coherence	Cultural pluralism (liberal policy) Do-nothing (conservative policy)

Based on Rainwater (1970) and appearing in Dokecki, Strain, Bernal, Brown, and Robinson (1975).

pothesized to be a function of society's need for maintaining the surplus. This hypothesis is consistent with Piven and Cloward's (1971) assertion that "capitalism makes labor conditional on market demand, with the result that some amount of unemployment becomes a permanent feature of the economy. In other words, change and fluctuation and unemployment are chronic features of capitalism" (p. 5).

An early and interesting chapter in American history related to stigmatization of the retarded involves the Puritan settlement of New England. In a book entitled *The Wayward Puritans*, Erikson (1966) studied the history of the identification and treatment of deviance in the seventeenth-century Massachusetts Bay Colony and subjected the historical data to sociological analysis. Of particular interest was the extremely harsh and cruel treatment, extending even to branding and mutilation, of those classified as deviant. Erikson found that the operation of the Puritans' society corresponds to a general theory of deviance in which "the deviant is a person whose activities have moved outside the margins of the group, and when the community calls him to account for that vagrancy it is making a statement about the nature and placement of its boundaries. It is declaring how much variability and diversity can be tolerated within the group before it begins to lose its identity" (p.11). And "deviant forms of behavior, by marking the outer edges of group life, give the inner structure its special character and thus supply the framework within which the people of the group develop an orderly sense of their own cultural identity" (p. 13).

Having proposed that deviance functioned to help define and maintain the Puritans' social structure, Erikson documents that the harsh and brutal treatment of deviants grew from moral and religious concerns, specifically from the belief in predestination—people are either saved or damned. Further,

> the New England Puritans assumed that most men would sooner or later give evidence as to whether they were chosen or not. Persons who had felt grace would be so touched by the experience that they would develop a new sense of responsibility toward the community and slowly move into positions of leadership: persons who remained in doubt would stay in the middle ranks of the community and pursue their honest callings until they learn more of their fate; persons who had reason to fear the worst would drift sullenly into the lower echelons of society, highly susceptible to deviant forms of behavior. Thus the social structure of the Kingdom of God closely resembled that of the English nation, and it was obvious to the dullest saint that confirmed deviants belonged in the lowest of these ranks. (p. 189)

Dokecki *et al.* (1975) agreed with Erikson that the moralizing perspective as applied to deviants is seemingly still with us. Erikson (1966) comments that

> The theological views which sustained . . . the ways of dealing with deviants . . . have largely disappeared from the religious life of the society, but the attitudes toward deviation which were implied in the pattern are still retained in many of the institutions we have built to process and confine deviant behavior as the product of a deep-seated characteriological strain in the person who enacts it, rather than as the product of the situation in which it took place, and we are still apt to treat that person as if his whole being was somehow implicated. (p. 198)

Consonant with Erickson's analysis of deviance, we suggest that mentally retarded people are viewed by American society as "modern wayward Puritans," as individuals who (1) are viewed as morally lacking, (2) are to be blamed for their plight, and (3) are to be treated harshly (for example, by being institutionalized). These modern wayward Puritans, however, fulfill important functions in our society in helping the majority group to define its boundaries (Aries 1962; Erikson 1966), and to operate its economy efficiently and in an orderly fashion (Farber 1968; Piven and Cloward 1971).

As Dokecki *et al.* (1975) point out, it is as if our society operates according to the principle of *social Darwinism with a conscience*. (See Hofstadter 1944 for an account of the role of social Darwinism in American history.) Social Darwinism, reinforced by Puritanical attitudes, leads us to view those who do not make it in our society as unfit, unworthy, and immoral. This is seemingly our society's predominant view of mentally retarded people. In some respects they are seen as less than human, as savages and barbarians (Ryan 1971), as nonpersons. Confinement and institutionalization are therefore appropriate and not unreasonable.

We speak, however, of social Darwinism *with a conscience*. While probably motivated by the need to guarantee their controlled and limited participation in the labor force (Farber 1968), there is something in the modern American conscience which rejects open and blatant brutal treatment of the mentally retarded. There is, as it were, a governor or a civilizer placed on the underlying primitive moralizing perspective.

But has our conscience overcome our Puritanically tinged, economically oriented Darwinistic attitudes? The persistent fear we seem to have of the mentally retarded and the virtually permanent stigma of being classified and labeled mentally retarded suggest that our conscience has not won the day. We aim at institutional reform but we fall short.

Farber and Lewis (1972) commented regarding compensatory education that American society plays a half-hearted and seemingly devious game which is ultimately harmful to the situation of the mentally retarded and other powerless and deviant groups:

> Thus, in terms of the social meanings and needs which it serves, the compensatory strategy is *successful* in its failure to realize its explicit intentions. The absence of demonstrable success itself keeps us interested in the strategy. Believing as we do in the viability of its basic assumptions, failure is taken to mean only that we have not yet found the right technique or program. Thus we persist in our search for the right way to intervene educationally and in doing so we guard against these hard questions which might upset the status quo interests we seek to protect. We persist in the service of an illusion—an illusion necessary to resolve the conflict between our values and our interests where the surplus poor are concerned. The compensatory strategy is our cultural legerdemain. By means of it we have been *successful* in *failing* to address the problem of unequal access to opportunity—in maintaining the disadvantage of the surplus poor—while at the same time we have convinced ourselves that we are attempting to maximize equal access to opportunity. Our overt failure is our real success and for this reason we do persist. (pp. 93-94)

Will the same be said for efforts at deinstitutionalization? What kind of an effort will be required to deal with the barriers to effective current efforts wherein historical, political, economic, and social factors maximize the negative effects of stigmatization of the retarded?

Consonant with this historical anaylsis, Farber (1968) suggested a multi-leveled program for the retarded which involves: (1) the effective use of resources to enhance the competence of individuals; (2) resources to help the family become a human development enhancing system; (3) rearrangement of society's institutions to permit the surplus population to escape from nonperson status and more fully participate in America's social institutions; and (4) attempts to shift America's value system toward more concern with the importance of human growth and development. On this fourth point Farber comments that "this program would be a comprehensive strategy to incorporate the surplus population into the major institutions and public cultural patterns in the society; to be effective, it requires a profound modification of the social structure" (p. 269).

In effect, Farber's scheme ranges from the individual and the family to the whole of American society. The progression is also from the relatively easy solutions to the vastly more difficult, but in the long run, more successful ones. "Naturally, the value-modification solution with regard to surplus populations is the most difficult to accomplish. The program most immediate and most amenable to manipulation is, however, the least successful. Just how serious we are in wanting to solve social problems relating to surplus populations . . . will determine exactly how much effort and sacrifice we are willing to undergo in order to revise modern society" (Farber 1968, p. 270). Dokecki *et al.* (1975) cited with approval Farber's program as applied to low-income and minority group children and families, and we advance it here as having relevance for those concerned with deinstitutionalization policy and programs. Up to this point we have been building the case that the negative effect of stimatization on deinstitutionalization is essentially a problem of societal values. Farber's "value-modification solution" must be attempted, therefore, or program and policy efforts will have little more than cosmetic effects.

STIGMATIZATION AND LABELING OF THE
MENTALLY RETARDED

We have just seen that the label "mentally retarded" is a formidable stigma, with deep historical roots, in our society. On the other hand, it has been pointed out that there is nothing "inherently evil" (Haywood 1971) in the classification and categorization with respect to intellectual levels. Edgerton and Edgerton (1973) have similarly pointed out that "labeling is a continuing interaction between labeler, the labeled, and many other significant persons. This interaction is akin to a negotiation and thus while the label has great potential for destructive self-fulfillment, this fulfillment is not inevitable" (p. 231).

What has been inevitable in the assignment of the label "mental retardation," and to a great extent in the label "institutionalized as a mental retardate," is the assumption of homogeneity and the simultaneous disregard of important differences among labeled individuals. As Edgerton and Edgerton (1973) have empirically demonstrated with public school children, the illusion of a homogeneous group ignores and conceals the heterogeneity of assets and disabilities among the labeled just as it blocks individualized solutions for rehabilitation and education.

Finally, if the label "mental retardation" can perhaps be nonpunitive in some interactions (to recruit funding; to secure access to needed community services), the information that an individual has been institutionalized elicits unequivocally discrediting and disqualifying societal reactions (Edgerton 1967; Farber 1968). As Goffman (1961) has described the institutionalization process:

> Often entrance will mean for the recruit that he has taken on what might be called a *proactive status*. Not only is his relative social position within the walls radically different from what it was on the outside, but as he comes to learn, if and when he gets out, his social position on the outside will never again be quite what it was prior to entrance. . . . When the proactive status is unfavorable, as it is for those in prisons or mental hospitals, we popularly employ the term "stigmatization" and expect that the ex-inmate may make an effort to conceal his past and try to "pass." (p.472)

Heber and Dever (1970) have suggested that institutionalization results from having been "convicted" of mental incompetence. And as will become clear, incarceration as a criminal and as a mental retardate provides many parallel experiences, both during and after confinement.

Who are the individuals currently institutionalized as mental retardates? Since World War II the admissions rate of the mildly mentally retarded has been declining with a corresponding increase in institutionalization of the severly and profoundly retarded (Balthazar and Stevens 1975; Farber 1968). However, institutions continue to admit the mildly and moderately retarded, primarily because of lack of acceptable and accessible service alternatives (Dennis 1972; Rosen 1974). Currently the majority of individuals labeled mentally retarded are not institutionalized (Balthazar and Stevens 1975). Therefore, our concern is understanding the process by which this minority of labeled mental retardates come to be incarcerated and are thus doubly stigmatized by society.

In a scholarly and comprehensive clinical study of changes in the incidence and prevalence of mental retardation, Stein and Susser (1970) have documented: "Sometimes the social role of mental handicap is assigned to individuals who have neither impairment of the brain nor intellectual disability. Their social roles are inadvertently acquired by their admission to 'treatment' because of a combination of behavior disorders and lack of social support. Thus a proportion of the inmates of many institutions for mental deficiency have neither detectable clinical lesions nor IQ scores below the normal range" (p.308).

What is the explanation for institutionalization, then, if not mental incapacity? Bernard Farber (1968), as we have seen, has proposed a sociological analysis of mental retardation and the institutionalization of a minority of those labeled mentally retarded. Mental retardation has been conceptualized as deviant behavior from some perspectives and as incompetent behavior from others (Mercer 1971). Farber has integrated both perspectives into a theoretical view of the mentally retarded as one segment of the "organizationally surplus population," those individuals who have failed in some way to perform adequately their social roles in basic societal institutions such as the economy, the family, and the public schools.

Farber has discussed a class of "life-chance-indicators," factors upon which the probable success of individuals in our modern society depend—race, religion, age, physical deformity, communication inadequacy, economic privation, unstable family relations, as well as perceived intellectual competence. Farber documents that mental retardation is *not* "the stigma that projects itself into an otherwise normal situation" (1968, p. 223) for the mildly retarded and seldom for the severely retarded.

In summarizing several major studies in which the presenting problems on admissions records were accounted for, Farber (1968) has concluded: "Mental retardation alone does not account for admission to residential institutions. Persons admitted to residential institutions tend to be characterized by physical disabilities, little prior schooling even at older ages, low socioeconomic level of the families, high rates of family instability, many behavior problems and a high rate of delinquency, membership in minority groups, the presence of health and emotional problems in the family, and much contact by the families with social welfare and legal governmental agencies" (p. 217).

Thus institutionalization for reasons of "mental retardation" is used to legitimate the individual's inclusion in the surplus population, and we should recall the section on historical issues to be reminded how long standing and deep seated are the attitudes toward the surplus modern wayward Puritans.

Institutionalization

It should be noted from the outset that residential facilities for the mentally retarded do not represent unitary phenomena (Balthazar and Stevens 1975). Institutions vary in size, funding pattern, and programs.

Our discussion here focuses upon those settings, usually large public institutions, which reveal the characteristics of "total institutions."

According to Goffman (1961), the basic character of "total institutions" is marked by physical and psychological barriers to social intercourse with those outside the purview of the institution. Goffman has further described "total institutions" in terms of four basic operating principles. First, all aspects of daily life, such as working, eating, and sleeping, are conducted in the same geographic location under a common authority. Second, these daily activities are carried out in large groups, where deviation from the prescribed routine is considered detrimental to the operation of the institution. Third, these activities occur in an invariant sequence at prearranged times. Finally, the imposed structure of institutional life and the concomitant routines are justified as practices necessary to fulfill the official aims of the institution. As White and Wolfensberger (1969) and Wolfensberger (1969) have stated, the inevitable outcome of living within such a system is dehumanization, or the stripping away of civil rights and personal autonomy.

Goffman (1961) has referred to the dehumanization of institutional residents in terms of the "mortification of self." According to Goffman, mortification is accomplished by several interrelated processes. First, the elements of one's personal identity are removed. For the incarcerated mentally retarded, this is expedited by a legal declaration of incompetence. This "stripping" process includes the removal of civil rights and all other possessions with which the person may have identified himself. Additionally, strictly enforced institutional routines are substituted for those activities which the inmate previously performed with more autonomy.

The experience of institutionalization may be conceptualized as promoting highly stereotyped and limited opportunities for acquiring behaviors which would be deemed "appropriate" beyond the walls of the institution. As Goffman (1961) has implied, opportunities for learning within "total institutions" are restricted to those which result in the acquisition of "institutionalized" behavior. The tragic cycle is thus set into motion, whereby the inmate adopts those behavior which are evoked and maintained by the institutional environment and which inevitably reinforce the imposed stigma of incompetence.

Deinstitutionalization

We conceptualize deinstitutionalization as a broad range of living alternatives which increase the civil liberties and personal autonomy for present or former inmates. This definition implies that deinstitutionalization, to some degree, may be accomplished within the institution as well as beyond its walls and jurisdiction. The movement of residents to the "least restrictive setting" (Wyatt v. Stickney 1971) is but one example of the possibilities for intra-institution restoration of civil rights and autonomy. Furthermore, we see deinstitutionalization outside the residential setting as an exit and re-entry process. Clearly, as Rosen (1974) and Edgerton (1967) have stated, deinstitutionalization does not simply result from exiting the institution. If successful community adjustment is to be accomplished, the former inmate must be accepted into a new social system. It is at this point or re-entry into the community that the liabilities of stigma particularly take their toll.

An examination of deinstitutionalization programs today reveals an almost exclusive concern for developing a more adaptive behavior repertoire on the part of the inmate prior to his exit from the institution (Rosen 1974). Such a perspective reflects a lingering bias among professionals to ascribe the condition of mental retardation to factors of personal defect or malady. Regrettably, little attention in the form of research and program development has been addressed to deinstitutionalization as a process which requires adjustment on the part of both the former inmates *and the mainstream society*. Farber (1968) has suggested that for remediation to be effective, ameliorative strategies must deal simultaneously with the multiplicity of "life-chance-indicators" which characterized the institutionalized mentally retarded prior to being incarcerated.

Heber and Dever (1970) have voiced a similar criticism regarding the limited focus of remedial programs for the institutionalized mentally retarded:

> Recent follow-up studies do not suggest that the contemporary institution or special education program provide him [the resident] with that ability [to adjust to contemporary society]. He enters adult society as it presents itself in our slums, and if he works at all he is quite likely to earn an income below any reasonble level of subsistence. It is hard to believe that those retarded who have not had the benefits of special education are any worse off. We believe that this is not difficult to understand when one considers the nature of our traditional programs of institutional rehabilitation and public school special education in relation to our contemporary society. (pp. 409-10)

Moreover, the process of re-entry into the community has, for the most part, been the responsibility of the former inmate. He is to find his own way and acquire some means to minimize the stifling effects of his stigma as he begins to interact with individuals and agencies in the community. His chances of successfully escaping the surplus population are poor. Edgerton (1967) conducted comprehensive psychological and ecological investigations of the lives of discharged institutional residents. The most critical problem which faced the individual in his struggles to secure and maintain employment, find a marital partner, and manage his material possessions and leisure time was the stigma of his former institutionalization: "The label of mentally retarded not only serves as a humiliating, frustrating, and discrediting stigma in the conduct of one's life in the community, but it also serves to lower one's self-esteem to such a nadir of worthlessness that the life of a person so labeled is scarcely worth living" (p. 145).

These two central problems, of "passing" with others and of "denying" to one's self the adjudgment and confinement by society as a mental retardate, consumed the energies of the former residents. Management of these needs for coping with the threat of disclosure in everyday demands of living and for increased self-esteem was successful to the extent that the former resident independently secured the aid of an informal "benefactor." Clearly the burden of "making it" in a society hostile to the stigmatized retarded person was borne solely by the former residents. If future deinstitutionalization efforts persist in emphasizing the former resident to the exclusion of dealing with the community stigmatization process, they are doomed to failure.

TOWARD EFFECTIVE DEINSTITUTIONALIZATION POLICIES AND PROGRAMS

In the Project on the Classification of Exceptional Children (Hobbs 1975) one of the recommendations regarding institutions was as follows: "The large congregate residential institutions for children of all categories (retarded, delinquent, emotionally disturbed, dependent, blind, and so on) should be closed and the children cared for in community-based programs." In elaborating this recommendation it was cautioned that "returning children to communities is not a panacea. It can lead to neglect and abuse quite as serious as that which occurs in large institutions.

There is no easy solution. . . . The argument for community-based programs rests on the assumption that it is better to make the normal socializing agencies (the family, school, church, neighborhood) work than it is to have special agencies take over their function.''

This last statement raises many issues, and stigmatization is central to most of them. Institutions were founded precisely because the "normal socializing agencies" were unable and/or unwilling to deal with the stigmatized. Why should they be any more willing or more able today? Why should the fiat of the courts or the proposals of the social engineers (our own peer groups) be expected to bring about Farber's value-modification solution in some automatic or magical fashion?

The practical implications of our assertions that negative societal reaction and prejudice stand as the principal barrier to successful re-entry of the stigmatized individual into the community are not readily apparent. Exhortations to change the structure and priorities of our governmental and social institutions and to alter the value system of our normal socializing agencies and the public-at-large are counsels of perfection. Yet some effort must be expended in these directions or deinstitutionalization as a social movement will surely fail.

Another point to be recognized is that the very existence of total institutions exacerbates the condition of mentally retarded people by reinforcing the societal stigma of personal incompetence assigned to inmates. In essence, the existence of institutions make deinstitutionalization most problematic. While one aim of the deinstitutionalization movement may be to exert pressure to improve existing institutions, this strategy may in the end prove self-defeating. And yet, it is hard to imagine an America without institutions in the very near future. We are probably unwilling as a society to make the efforts and sacrifices to deinstitutionalize totally; moreover, present and impending world economic crises will threaten to end even the minimal efforts we are now making.

The stigma of mentally retarded, deviant, and handicapped people are many; however, we must reject exceptionalistic approaches which overemphasize these individuals' attributes and lead us to blame the victim. We must look toward more universalistic solutions which place the majority of the blame where it belongs, on the stigmatization process in which our society too easily engages (Dokecki and Strain 1973; Ryan 1971). Immediate and long-term efforts at deinstitutionalization must not fail to include major resources for influencing community perceptions and values and the ways in which service delivery and the normal socializing agencies structure their priorities and values.

REFERENCES

Aries, P. *Centuries of Childhood: A Social History of Family Life.* New York: Vintage, 1962.

Balthazar, E. E., and Stevens, H. A. *Emotionally Disturbed Mentally Retarded: A Historical and Contemporary Perspective.* Englewood Cliffs, N.J.: Prentice-Hall, 1975.

Dennis, F. Legal Implications of Decentralization of Institutions for the Retarded. Unpublished paper, George Peabody College, 1972.

Dewey, J., and Bentley, A. *Knowing and the Known.* Boston: Beacon, 1974.

Dokecki, P. R.; Scanlan, P.; and Strain, B. A. "In Search of a Transactional Model for Educational Intervention: Reactions to Farber and Lewis." *Peabody Journal of Education* 49(1972):182-87.

Dokecki, P. R., and Strain, B. A. "Early Childhood Intervention 2001: Transactional and Developmental Perspectives." *Peabody Journal of Education* 50 (1973):175-83.

Dokecki, P. R.; Strain, B.; Bernal, J.; Brown, C.; and Robinson, M. E. "Low-Income and Minority Group Children and Families." In *Issues in the Classification of Children: A Sourcebook on Categories, Labels, and Their Consequences,* edited by N. R. Hobbs. San Francisco: Jossey-Bass, 1975.

Edgerton, R. B. *The Cloak of Competence: Stigma in the Lives of the Mentally Retarded.* Berkeley, Calif.: University of California Press, 1967.

______, and Edgerton, C. R. "Becoming Retarded in a Hawaiian School." In *Sociobehavioral Studies in Mental Retardation,* edited by D. E. Meyers. Los Angeles: American Association on Mental Deficiency, 1973.

Erikson, K. T. *Wayward Puritans: A Study in the Sociology of Deviance.* New York: Wiley, 1966.

Farber, B. *Mental Retardation: Its Social Context and Social Consequences.* Boston: Houghton Mifflin, 1968.

______, and Lewis, M. "Compensatory Education and Social Justice." *Peabody Journal of Education* 49(1972):85-95.

Goffman, E. *Asylums: Essays on the Social Situations of Mental Patients and Other Inmates.* New York: Anchor, 1961.

______. *Stigma: Notes on the Management of Spoiled Identity.* Englewood Cliffs, N.J.: Prentice-Hall, 1963.

Haywood, H. C. Labeling: Efficacy, Evils, and Caveats. Paper presented at the Joseph P. Kennedy, Jr., Foundation International Symposium on Human Rights, Retardation, and Research. Washington, D.C., 1971.

Heber, R. F., and Dever, R. B. "Research on Education and Habilitation of the Mentally Retarded." In *Socio-Cultural Aspects of Mental Retardation,* edited by H. C. Haywood. New York: Appleton-Century-Crofts, 1970.

Hobbs, N. R. *The Futures of Children.* San Francisco: Jossey-Bass, 1975.

Hofstadter, R. *Social Darwinism in American Thought.* Boston: Beacon, 1944.

Kirk, S. A., and Lord, F. E., *Exceptional Children*. Boston: Houghton-Mifflin, 1974.

Mercer, J. R. "Sociocultural Factors in Labeling Mental Retardates." *Peabody Journal of Education* 48(1971):188-203.

Piven, F. F., and Cloward, R. A. *Regulating the Poor: The Functions of Public Welfare*. New York: Pantheon, 1971.

Rainwater, L. "Neutralizing the Disinherited: Some Psychological Aspects of Understanding the Poor." In *Psychological Factors in Poverty,* edited by V. L. Allen. Chicago: Markham, 1970.

Rhodes, W. C., and Sagor, M. "Overview." In *A Study of Child Variance. Vol. 3: Service Delivery Systems,* edited by W. C. Rhodes and S. Head. Ann Arbor: The University of Michigan Press, 1974.

Rosen, D. "Observations of an Era in Transition." *Mental Retardation* 12(1974): 61-65.

Ryan, W. *Blaming the Victim*. New York: Random House, 1971.

Stein, Z., and Susser, M. "Malleability of Intelligence and Epidemiology of Mild Mental Retardation." *Review of Educational Research* 40(1970):29-67.

White, W. D., and Wolfensberger, W. "The Evolution of Dehumanization in Our Institutions." *Mental Retardation* 7(1969):5-9.

Wolfensberger, W. P. "The Origin and Nature of Our Institutional Models." In *Changing Patterns of Residential Services for the Mentally Retarded,* edited by R. B. Kugel and W. P. Wolfensberger. Washington, D.C.: President's Committee on Mental Retardation, 1969.

Wyatt v. Stickney, 325 F. Supp. 781, 784 (M.D. Ala. 1971).

4

Politics, Political Structures,

and Advocacy Activities

DONALD J. STEDMAN

ANY CONSIDERATION of either the concept or the procedures of deinstitutionalization must immediately confront the need to understand and successfully negotiate state and local governmental structures. If deinstitutionalization is to be effective, laws, legislation, policies, procedures, ordinances, and governmental habits must be shaped and implemented which will assist in the generation of community-based comprehensive services for persons with developmental disabilities. No advocate can be successful for very long without a road map of state and local government and some idea of how to develop alternative strategies for negotiating the various routes between the influence and the power centers. This means that advocacy must be a political activity which involves political structures and some persistent advocacy activities in order to develop the landscape of services necessary in the community to pave the way for successful deinstitutionalization programming.

The organization of government, especially state government, was originally developed with advocacy in mind, but formal and informal political structures are oriented toward promoting or containing economic conditions rather than developing and delivering human services. Popular government is designed for the pursuit of *property*—the early meaning of "happiness." Human services—preventive, interpreventive, protective, or remedial—are not easily developed, maintained, advanced, or implemented through the bureaucracy. However, the bureaucracy is all we have, and we should neither destroy it nor ignore it. We should attempt to understand and work through it in order to enhance the development and delivery of services to individuals in need.

The basic difficulties or barriers include the following elements.

POLITICAL vs. REAL NEEDS

The needs and objectives of the advocate or the person with developmental disabilities are not always the same as those of the politician or the bureaucrat operating within political and governmental structures. It is important to understand that a reasonable match between political priorities and real priorities is the best that can be obtained. They are seldom in 100 percent agreement. Political decision-makers use professionals and disabled constituencies in order to develop appropriate issues, legislation, and resources that are of great importance and value to both the politician and the advocate, but often for different reasons. There is often a fundamental discrepancy or barrier constituted by a real difference between political and real needs. In times of economic hardship these differences and lines are easier to see.

LEFTOVER BARRIERS

The primary obstacle to effective advocacy activity in the handicapped field is the residue of twenty-five years of political activity on behalf of the handicapped. Advocacy requires depoliticization of the handicapped field. This fact alone may defeat any substantial plans or actions by advocates over the next few years.

In the course of achieving gains and recognition for the handicapped, the huge bureaucracy, a powerful lobby, and an unholy consumer-legislator-bureaucratic complex have been spawned. They now may impede change, confuse planning, retard the setting of priorities, and foster continued competition between categories of handicap at a point when the public is ready to respond effectively to clearly articulated needs and advocacy activity.

We are ready for a time to do what is *right*, not what is politically possible or expedient. The question is, do we have the nerve?

POLITICAL-PROFESSIONAL TRUST

It often takes a great deal of trust in politicians with a good sense of timing to initiate or release pressures for change at times when it may seem to the advocate that activities should go the other way.

There has been an uneasy alliance or interdependence between politicians and professionals in the handicapped field. Each needs the other since change is a political process. The professional is needed to provide reliable information on research, economic conditions, service alternatives, planning schedules, and a touch of scientific authenticity. The politician is needed to gain entry to resources and to the planning and policy structures of government in order to implement or to try out new ideas. Either side is often duped in the process, for there are both self-serving politicians and egocentric professionals. The advocate should realize that he dons some of this image of the professional when dealing with the politician. The advocate should understand the occasional skepticism encountered. The needs of the advocate and the needs of the politician do not have to be identical, provided the goals are the same and the strategies are sufficiently compatible as to be congenial.

COMPETITION BETWEEN AGENCIES

The political structure is such that competition between local, state, and federal agencies is reinforced by differential rewards from legislators and congress for those agencies which have new or unique approaches to problems. Oftentimes agencies will secretly develop new approaches or unveil new programs at the time of budget hearings. This amounts to a competition between agencies reinforced by the budgetary process which, in the long run, yields duplication of programs and costly, uncoordinated development. It fosters a serious barrier to the effective integration of human services at the local level. Advocates, in their attempt to develop information from agencies or to cause agencies or organizations to share information, must be aware that the possession of special information is a source of power. Asking that information be shared is similar to asking that power be given away. Methods must be devised to make it "safe" for agencies and organizations to disseminate and share information, especially about new strategies or information tied to new budgetary requests.

POVERTY OF INFORMATION

We have yet to develop a satisfactory information base that would provide data for effective management information systems, adequate planning, and sufficient effective program evaluation to develop cost-benefit or other types of displays of program effectiveness.

The advocate will encounter not only difficulties in gaining information from the political and bureaucratic structures but extreme difficulties in marshaling information that can be adequately interpreted either in the program-development phase or in the program-evaluation phase. A data base is required for advocates to work effectively to develop new programs.

TRANSIENT PRIORITIES

Social priorities at the community, state, and national levels are often "here today, gone tomorrow." Advocates must be aware of the fact that priorities are transient and that the community is fickle with regard to the attachment of importance to community issues, especially as they relate to human services. Advocates must be able to seize on the presence of priorities which support a thrust for programs and services for the handicapped and not wait long periods of time assuming that priorities will continue. The priorities of communities are tied to political variables, and politicians frame their behaviors and their approaches to their perception of the priorities of their constituency. It is important, therefore, for the advocate to develop and communicate priorities for the handicapped to the political and bureaucratic structures on a continuing basis, although they will be treated as transient and the advocate must be aware of the possibility of the shifting ground of priorities.

FRAGMENTATION OF EFFORT

There is a continuing debate on whether programs for handicapped individuals should be centralized in the political and bureaucratic structures with a "lead agency" or organization which is responsible for developing and delivering services to handicapped. The alternative is a distribution of programs across the various structures—health, education, social services, mental health, rehabilitation. The latter situation requires some type of cross-cutting organization such as an Office for Children or Office for Handicapped Individuals which will allow for a coordination of the efforts undertaken on a broad-based strategy throughout the state or federal government. The situation in the mid-seventies is one in which there is severe fragmentation of effort and a distribution of activity broadly throughout government with little effective coordination at the state or national level. This fragmentation is due in part to the lack of clear national goals and objectives to which a federal or state comprehensive strategy could be tied. However, the advocate can better relate to and help remedy the situation of fragmentation of service if this situation is known ahead of time.

THE KAMIKAZE ROLE OF ADVOCATES WITH THE SYSTEM

Advocates must realize from the start that effective work within the system, if it results in high visibility for the advocate and necessary criticism of the organization, might result in the release of the advocate from employment in the organization. The point at which advocates within the system usually falter is the point at which the commissioner or director or head of the organization in which the advocate works casts a cautionary finger in the direction of the advocate for a too-active role on behalf of the persons to be served, rather than on behalf of the apparent integrity of the organization within which the advocate is working. Advocates may have to be willing to change jobs frequently if they want to be active on behalf of the handicapped.

THE AMBIVALENCE OF PROFESSIONALS

Advocates who marshal the support of professionals to build a case for new or improved programs for handicapped individuals must be aware that professionals often shift their directions in midstream. It is important to realize that data from research can be interpreted in several ways. For each professional available to interpret the data in one way, there will be another professional who will emerge to interpret it in a different light. This may be perceived as ambivalence among professionals. In fact, it is not ambivalence but a clearly acceptable situation in which data, especially social sciences research data, can honestly be interpreted in more than one direction. Advocates must beware too much smugness when data seem to be available from social sciences research which support their point of view.

THE WEAKNESS OF SPECIAL INTEREST GROUPS

Most special interest groups, especially state organizations, do not carry the amount of clout that they first appear to have. The fact that a large percentage of the population should be seen as a constituency for the handicapped is a situation of unsure ground. Organizations, particularly parent groups, often claim more strength than they are able to deliver in a pinch. The poor coordination of special interest groups, specifically at the state level, can turn well-integrated attacks into Custer-like debacles unless a great deal of prior organization, coordination, and awareness of timing are brought to bear on the situation.

THE COATTAIL POLITICIAN

Many aspiring politicians have learned that a bright political future may lie in the direction of catering to the increasingly large constituency for the handicapped. Many federal-level officials as well as state government executives have successfully turned the need for services for handicapped persons into winning campaigns and successful attainment of public office. In some instances these politicians ignore the needs of the handicapped after they have gained office. The advocate must be careful to distinguish between those politicians who will indeed follow through on their campaign promises and those who are merely seeking the support of those who want to advance the fortunes of handicapped persons.

THE CHAOS OF GAINING ACCESS TO RESOURCES

Gaining access to resources for the development of local programs has become one of the greatest hide-and-seek games in the United States. The difficulties of discovering the doors to large pots of money, especially complicated programs such as social security programs, has led to an urgent need for resource development centers and activities on the part of advocates. Engaging in the "legitimate hustle" is something advocates must learn. Discovering ways to move available financial and human resources to local programs to serve the handicapped is an important aspect of advocacy. Often a great deal of time and effort must be spent in studying the organization of state government, current federal and state programs made available through legislation to develop services for the handicapped, and the pathways within and between agencies that have resources, often unadvertised, that can make services possible.

The resistances to advocates are strongest at the lowest level of government—in the mayors' councils, school boards, and county commissioners' groups. Change made at this level will endure longer and have more effect on state and federal behaviors than efforts conducted exclusively at the national level. The basic building block in our society is the county government. At that level, real action is taking place at a quiet but persistent rate.

There are several principles to adhere to in order to work successfully at this important level.

PRINCIPLE 1—BOTTOMS UP!

Advocates must keep in mind that their development of issues and their gathering of data and their advancement of points of view should always be moved from the bottom to the top. One cannot go directly to the governor to expect change on a statewide basis over a short period of time. Governors just do not have that kind of power and certainly do not have the inclination to operate in that fashion. Advocates must work at the community level to develop adequate understanding and cooperation from other persons in order to effect change at the local level and to develop the constituency necessary to make blips on the political screens of members of the state legislature. Working from the lowest level toward the top level is a more effective, although more time-consuming, strategy than attempting shotgun propaganda or direct approach at the top. Strong and lasting program development and positive change for the handicapped takes place through persistent work at the lower levels.

PRINCIPLE 2—IDENTIFY REAL TASKS

Since there are many issues at all levels of politics and government, it is important that the advocate identify only the real and the most important tasks with the clearest priorities upon which work will be accomplished to develop services for handicapped persons. There are often apparent tasks such as the need for public awareness. This task can be a time-consuming and energy-burning effort with no immediate, concrete outcome which will lose the interests and often the cooperation of persons who are helping the advocate. Specific, concrete, and immediate tasks must be identified in order to gain attention and to demonstrate that immediate advances can be made in the direction of human-service program development.

PRINCIPLE 3—PICK WINNERS FIRST

When a number of tasks needs to be accomplished, the advocate should pick a task or a program which appears to have the best chance for success. This will help build some momentum and make the second and third tasks easier to accomplish. It will also make it possible to get more help for the later tasks. Advocates will often pick the most difficult program at the local level, and the consequent frustration or lack of success slows down the kind of community-based enthusiasm and momentum required to build toward a more comprehensive set of programs for the handicapped.

PRINCIPLE 4—COMMUNICATE LATERALLY

While it is important to communicate upward it is of greater importance to keep your colleagues apprised of what you are doing. Also, information between organizations, between agencies, and between people is the best glue in any comprehensive attempt to build programs and to mount an effective advocacy activity. Lateral communication is often the weakest loop within and between organizations since people tend to set their sights toward higher levels or the "highly visible people." It is frequently the case that advocates arrive at a situation or point where a specific priority is being considered only to be shot down because lateral communication and support have not been successfully built among other constituencies that need to be aware of the advocate's goals and objectives.

PRINCIPLE 5—KEEP IT SIMPLE

The advocate must be aware that it is frequently necessary to reduce a one-hour lecture to a ten-minute agenda item. The advocate must also keep in mind that, while the public is reasonably well educated and well read, it gets bored quickly with long-winded and apparently complicated people. It is important to keep presentations, written documents, and other communications at the simplest, tightest, clearest level possible in order to get ideas across. Nothing will bore a politician or a legislative subcommittee more quickly than a highly academic, complicated, abstract presentation on a program or program need. Keep it simple.

PRINCIPLE 6—COLLABORATE

The advocate cannot afford a free-lance, hit and run, highly individualized style. Collaboration and cooperation are necessary to advance ideas and programs. It is part of the lateral communication need and requires trade-off activities such as working on the issues of other organizations in order to get similar cooperation from them at a later date. Collaboration is part of the political process often called horse trading. The advocate must be skilled in this behavior and unafraid to use it.

PRINCIPLE 7—THINK SHORT TERM

Nothing will bore a group that is elected to a two-year term more than a plan which calls for a five-year program development at the local level, which must be built and presented as short-term activity. Ten and twenty-year plans, while important facets of long-range program development, will not attract local attention and will not gain the support necessary to build service activities. Short-term programs and programs designed to provide immediate service are more attractive and will be more effective over the long run in building a comprehensive community program.

Advocacy is a form of political behavior. It rests on values, a predisposition to change, an ability to maintain a broad perspective, a tolerance for ambiguity, and the ability to delay gratification. Advocates without those characteristics are doomed to frustration and disenchantment.

Those advocates who would establish a successful deinstitutionalization activity must be aware of these facts. Those competencies which must be developed or taken on by advocates in order to engage in appropriate political behaviors to negotiate the political road map will be the successful ones. Success will be measured by the amount and quality of human services delivered to persons in need.

5

Consumerism

RONALD WIEGERINK, REBECCA POSANTE-LORO

SINCE THE MID-SIXTIES the rights and the needs of the disabled and handicapped have received recognition as never before. Both litigation and legislation have confirmed their rights to services, treatment, and education. Partially because of this growing recognition, human services and specifically services committed to the handicapped have received the highest proportion ever of the United States gross national product. Unfortunately, this growing recognition and resource allocation has come at a time when our nation has been experiencing the realities of limited natural and financial resources and the likelihood of a moderate if not stabilized, GNP growth. Because there is still a significant gap between the needs and rights of the handicapped and the actuality of services, we must seek to close up the gaps. There is a need to develop services which are cost effective and carefully selected in order to avoid duplication. To do this, we must examine current human-service problems facing the handicapped and develop solutions with both short-range and long-range benefits.

Consumers—those who are themselves handicapped or their next of kin who represent them—should have an important role in the identification of priority needs and the planning and acquisition of resources to meet these needs. The history of consumer involvement in the development and provision of services is beginning to come full circle. Thirty to forty years ago families of the handicapped and the retarded were forced by circumstance to provide for their own needs. There were few if any public services, except for large institutions which were often of last resort. In some cases, parents drew together to help one another with emotional support and exchange of care. In some instances, this led to more formal

63

groups which developed day care, respite care, and other services. Such groups for the retarded led to the development of such organizations as the National Association for Parents and Friends of the Mentally Retarded, later to become the National Association for Retarded Citizens, to be discussed later.

Such formal organizations soon began to contract with professionals for services they earlier provided—such as day care and education. Their directions changed over time, and the push during the 1950s and 1960s focused on establishing services to provide professional-quality care. This push soon separated the families from participation in the direct services, which they turned over to paid staff. The parents served on advisory boards and boards of directors which, over time, included more and more professionals from the community. This in turn led to pressure on the schools, social services, and public health agencies to provide services. When they did, as in the case of setting up public classrooms for the retarded, the parents were to play little or no role in the delivery or monitoring of services. Parents and families of the retarded were forced to take what the professional community had to offer.

In most instances, parents were satisfied with these services—perhaps simply pleased to have them at all and to be free from the day-to-day concerns of developing or providing their own care. However, over time, just as the professional community began to examine the quality of their own sevices (Dunn 1968), parents became concerned about the quality of services and their own exclusion from them. By this time, their exclusion from services was almost complete. Besides the parents' willingness to place services into the hands of professionals, professionals had developed a supporting logic for separation. It was thought that parents needed to be separated from caregiving to provide them with therapeutic respite care and to keep them from interfering with their children's professionally designed and implemented programming.

The results of this separation were often unsatisfactory. Parents needed to know what was happening in their children's lives and needed to help themselves in coping with their children's handicaps. Professionals began to realize that day programs alone could not accomplish educational and social goals for their children. They needed the continuity of care 24 hours a day; they needed the parents' knowledge of and input about their children to assist in developing individualized programs. Since the mid-1960s, parents began to be recognized for what they really are—a child's first and foremost teachers. With this growing recognition, local, state, and federal programs began to suggest and then require the involvement of parents and families in services for the handicapped. This chapter will outline and highlight the development of this trend and attempt to forecast its future.

HISTORICAL BACKGROUND OF TWO ORGANIZATIONS OF NATIONAL SIGNIFICANCE

Consumers historically have played a part in obtaining services for the handicapped in their families. Their role has been increasing in scope throughout the years, leading to the present situation of powerful consumer groups, active in advocacy and deinstitutionalization. As early as 1933, small groups of parents were meeting to discuss possible solutions to common problems with their retarded children. In 1936 and 1939, groups in the states of Washington and New York, respectively, were forming unbeknownst to each other. A network of parent groups had not yet developed, but isolated pockets of consumers were beginning to organize over common problems. By 1950, thirteen states participated in forming the National Association for Parents and Friends of the Mentally Retarded, which was the forerunner of the National Association of Retarded Children or National Association for Retarded Citizens (NARC), as it is now titled.

The early local chapters of what was to become NARC directed their attentions toward procuring direct services for the mentally retarded. Parents and other concerned citizens needed schools, preschool centers sheltered workshops, and the like which were not being supplied by the usual public agencies. NARC chapters actually undertook operations of education and diagnostic services themselves since none were available for their children. As NARC grew, the members began to question how best to serve the needs of the mentally retarded. In 1965, at its national convention, the members made a policy decision to lead the way in demonstrating and initiating services; that is, its primary role was to obtain, and to provide services.

In the early 1950s, NARC developed a model of mental retardation which was based on the concept of the total person. This called for coordinating assistance of a variety of agencies to meet the needs of the entire person, including all aspects of his or her life and experiences. This concept has shaped much of the thinking of today, having led in the 1960s to the comprehensive approach to mental retardation of the Kennedy administration. Kennedy was the first consumer advocate in the executive branch. Parents had found a friend in the White House. The President appointed the President's Panel on Mental Retardation which was given the mandate to lay out the nature of the mental retardation problem in this country. Their work culminated in a report entitled *The National Strategy to Combat Mental Retardation* (1961).

THE IMPACT OF LEGISLATION AND LITIGATION

Legislation

The President's Panel on Mental Retardation, through its recommendations, led the way for passage of the Mental Retardation Mental Health Construction Act of 1963 (PL 88-164), the largest piece of federal legislation ever enacted until that time. This law led to the development of twelve mental retardation research centers, more than thirty university affiliated facilities designed to provide interdisciplinary training, more than two hundred community mental retardation centers, and the development of mental retardation councils in each state and territory. While consumers played no significant role in the development of the first three, the latter, the state MR councils, included at least a one-third membership of consumers and consumer representatives. The former three, designed to meet the research and service needs of the retarded, were destined to begin a long struggle for financial survival.

In 1969, the Handicapped Children's Early Education Act (PL 91-230) was passed. Through regulations promulgated by the Bureau of Education for the Handicapped consumers were to play an important role in the development of model preschool services for the handicapped. The regulations made it clear that each model center receiving funds under the act was to involve parents and families significantly in the program. They were to take part in planning as members of the advisory board, as volunteers, as direct receivers of services, and as service monitors. The law and the regulations fully recognized the importance of parents as the primary caretakers of their children.

The passage of the Developmental Disabilities Assistance and Construction Act of 1970 provided an even broader role for consumer participation. The law established developmental disability councils (DD councils) in every state and territory with the express role of developing state plans for the provision of coordinated, comprehensive services for the developmentally disabled. The DD councils were to be composed of state agency heads, providers of services, and at least one-third consumers or consumer representatives. For the first time the consumers role as co-partner in the assessment of needs and the planning of services was to be recognized publicly. The law was extended and amended in 1975 (PL 94-103) and continued this recognition and through regulations specified that a consumer was a handicapped individual and/or family member of a handicapped person. These councils with their consumer members have played a significant role in the deinstitutionalization movement through the development of community alternatives and their public awareness efforts. At present, these councils provide the best forum for consumer input on the development of future direction in deinstitutionalization.

Another type of forum was provided by the Social Security Amendments of 1975 (PL 93-647), specifically Title XX, which is set aside to provide social services funds for the handicapped among the vulnerable populations. This act called for a process of state plan development for bloc funds which involved public disclosure of the planning process, public hearings, and input from consumers and other interested persons. During a six-month period in 1975, consumer advocates for the handicapped had opportunities to present their needs and priorities along with other groups. While not a notably successful effort for the handicapped, the process is likely to become more commonplace in future decision-making regarding state-federal programs. Consumers would do well to learn the process.

The most recent piece of federal legislation affecting the role of consumers in the provision of services is the Education for All Handicapped Children Act of 1975 (PL 94-142). The law is designed to assure that all handicapped children are served through public education by 1980. It provides massive amounts of money to the states for such programs. The law also specifies that each child will have an individualized program and that due process procedures involving the child and parents are required. Thus, parents and handicapped children would become part of the decision-making process in determining what types of education services would be provided.

While legislation alone cannot insure or command active consumerism, it can set the stage for such involvement and can serve as a symbol of its acceptance. Just as current legislation more and more reflects a bias toward deinstitutionalization and normalization, it is reflecting a bias toward consumer involvement and consumerism. Consumers have been active in the creating and the passage of legislation. They have been active recipients of the benefits and disbenefits of it. And now, more and more, they are being identified as partners in decision-making, monitoring, and service delivery. Legislation both endorses and highlights this notable trend. Legislation is actively characterizing the role of consumers in deinstitutionalization.

Litigation

The assassination of John F. Kennedy was an untimely blow to advocates for the mentally retarded. After this, their focus shifted from the executive branch to the judicial branches of government. This switch has led to a number of cases which have altered the legal framework of this country regarding education and services to the handicapped. Historically, the judgment against segregation in the school system (*Brown* v. *Board of Education* 1954) precedes other litigation concerning mainstreaming, deinstitutionalization, and the rights of the developmentally disabled. It is the basis for many later suits.

In 1971 perhaps the most significant recognition of the rights of the retarded was made as a result of the *Wyatt* v. *Stickney* suit in Alabama. This judicial decision outlined the rights of the mentally retarded, including the right to the "least restrictive" conditions necessary to achieve the purpose of habilitation. At about the same time, a landmark case was being settled in Pennsylvania which established the right to education for all children (*Pennsylvania ARC* v. *Commonwealth of Pennsylvania* 1971). As a result of this case, the state was ordered to take responsibility to insure that *all* children obtain adequate educational programming. Included in the decision was the establishment of a hearing board and revision and clarification of the school code in order to insure adequate protection for the handicapped. A rallying point for the deinstitutionalization movement was *New York State ARC, Inc.* v. *Rockefeller* 1972. Charging inhumane conditions at the Willowbrook State School, the suit asked for a set of minimum standards for treatment and habilitation of the mentally retarded. The suit provided fuel for the fire in the cases against large institutional care. These cases have set precedents within the legal framework for future litigation. It is almost certain that in the future consumers will have an active part in this trend toward legal rulings against inhumane institutional care and segregated unequal education practices. There are already direct consequences of this legal action apparent in programs that have been developed in the last few years. More changes are certain for the future.

At the same time legislation and litigation actions were establishing the rights of and an important role for consumers, numerous models for service delivery were being developed and implemented that reflected parent and consumer involvement. These service models, in many cases, responded to the current movement toward deinstitutionalization and educational mainstreaming. It is our purpose here to briefly describe some of these models, highlighting the roles of parents in each. They reflect a continuum of deinstitutionalization from early intervention to educational mainstreaming to community alternatives.

EARLY INTERVENTION AND PREVENTION

One of the most promising approaches to deinstitutionalization is to prevent the need for institutionalization in the first place. This is one of the many goals of early intervention and prevention. By providing for high-risk pregnancies, infants, toddlers, and preschoolers at an early age, the likelihood for later services improvement and institutionalization will be reduced. This goal is reflected in the many nutritional, genetic counseling, and early intervention programs which have developed across this country since the mid-sixties. Most of these have sprung up as a result of a federal legislation initiative. For example, more than two hundred early intervention programs have been developed under the auspices of the Handicapped Children's Early Education Act of 1968, which called for the development of model preschool programs to provide comprehensive educational services for handicapped children and their families.

Three of the most successful programs of the first group funded in 1969 are the Regional Intervention Program (RIP) of Nashville, Tennessee, the Early Childhood Education Program of the University of Washington, and the Home Visit Program of Portage, Wisconsin. The RIP serves a twenty-six-county region in central Tennessee. It provides services for children with all types of handicaps and their families on a zero-reject basis. Any family with a handicapped child that desires the services will begin receiving the services offered within forty-eight hours. The program actively serves on a day-to-day basis more than sixty families, ninety new families each year; more than 350 families receive some ongoing service each year. The small central staff of five professionals is able to do this because all direct services are provided by trained parents of the handicapped children.

Upon entering the service system, the parents agree to work with their own children from six to nine hours a week until they and their children are making substanial progress on a program. After that, the parents devote the six to nine hours a week for a six-month period in volunteer help to other families and children in the program. With backup support from the professional special educators, the parents conduct intake services, train parents in individual tutoring and parent and child interaction techniques, run the day care program, teach the four classrooms (toddler class, intake class, language class, and community class), and perform liaison with community services. The parents and professionals of RIP have been able to demonstrate that together they can provide quality, low-cost services in a carefully designed system which utilizes the best of both groups.

The Early Childhood Program for Exceptional Children at the University of Washington is located in the University Affiliated Facility. It is a model demonstration program that has helped in the development of many preschool and Head Start programs around the nation. The children served are in most cases both physically and mentally handicapped and cover a wide range of conditions. Like RIP, it highlights the feasibility of a cross-categorical educational approach at the early childhood levels. The program is parent oriented in that it provides direct parent training, parent and staff meetings, and a parent-to-parent support program, and it involves parents in direct services. The parents serve as volunteers in the classroom, as data technicians in recording child behavior, and as behavior modifiers in the homes. The variety of roles for parents provides for consumer involvement at many levels.

The Portage Project of Portage, Wisconsin, is a home-visit program that provides parent training in the homes of rural parents. Families with multiply handicapped children from birth to six years of age in a regional area are served. Teachers visit the homes weekly to work with the children, train the parents, and develop home programs. Working closely with the public health nurses, the teacher provides consultation to the parents on parenting, educational and behavioral programming, and assistance in gaining access to other services. When the children reach school age the teacher from the Portage Project continues as consultant to the families as needed. The services are exclusively based on the needs of the family, directed toward them, and ultimately conducted by them. This type of consumer involvement will be necessary to assure quality services to all handicapped preschool children by 1980, as in the goal of the Bureau of Education for the Handicapped. Should this goal be reached, our nation will be a great step closer to a quality deinstitutionalization program.

MAINSTREAMING

If early education programs meet their objectives in providing a substantial foundation upon which schooling can build, our schools must be prepared to use this foundation. In part, mainstreaming will go a long way toward addressing this need. It also goes a long way toward addressing the needs of handicapped youngsters of school age who have for so long received less than adequate services apart from regular education in the same special education or have received no services at all. In some areas of the country, as many as 40 percent of school-age handicapped children are not in schools and 60 percent or more are not receiving any type of special education. Professional, consumer, and court actions have been needed to begin to redress these grievous conditions.

A direct result of many consumer court cases involving the schools has been the mainstreaming movement which has entered the public school system like a bolt of lightning. (Some of this litigation, e.g., *Brown* v. *the Board of Education* and *Pennsylvania ARC* v. *the Commonwealth of Pennsylvania*, has been discussed above.) Education systems throughout the country have attempted to meet the specifications of these court rulings and consumer complaints with innovative mainstreaming plans. In effect mainstreaming means integration of exceptional children into the common flow of the educational system. It seeks an end to segregated special classrooms for the special children and a beginning of provision for their special needs in the regular classroom.

One school system with a mainstreaming plan is Madison, Wisconsin. The Madison Plan removes from the educational vocabulary the traditional categories of exceptionality (EMR, LD, ED) and recombines these categories along a dimension of classroom readiness. The system provides for the training of educable mentally retarded, emotionally disturbed and learning disabled children in a setting allowing for an increased flow of children between regular and specialized resources, regardless of their previous labels. This is accomplished by grouping students according to learning *needs* rather than diagnostic *labels*. In this manner, it eliminates the traditional labeling and grouping and, therefore, the need for self-contained classrooms. The children are placed in a classroom at the level which addresses their behavioral needs. As these needs are met, the children move up to the next level, eventually spending all or most of their time in a regular classroom. The assessment which allows the child to move from one class to another is based on academic and behavioral functioning with the final goal an increase in the time spent in the regular classroom.

In Fountain Valley, California, a somewhat different approach to mainstreaming has been taken. The program, Children Without Labels, is based on district-wide restructuring of the school's physical facilities. Each school is organized so that six to eight classrooms are clustered around a learning center which is fully equipped with diagnostic and instructional materials. The classrooms are clustered in more ways than the physical arrangement alone. Each learning center has a learning coordinator who is responsible for the center and for the six to eight teachers in the cluster. The learning coordinator plans and coordinates instructional activities for the teachers. Also, he or she is responsible for small groups and individual instruction in the learning center for some children. In addition, each school has auxiliary staff, including a school psychologist, speech clinician, and a special education resource teacher to provide additional help with individualized programs. With this program, individualized planning is done for all students, including the handicapped. It has abolished the necessity for labels in planning and implementation.

There is yet another track taken by an elementary school in Lawrence, Kansas, to mainstreaming. Faculty from the University of Kansas and from the Pinckney Elementary School worked together to devise a mainstreaming format which would offer a full range of services, similar to Deno's (1970) cascade of services in theory, which is well-defined at each level so that teachers and resource persons are aware of what is needed and provided by each of them at certain instructional levels. This hierarchy also assures that a variety of services are available to meet the particular needs of each student. Children are placed in an option level (e.g., resource room regular or tutorial in regular class) after the regular classroom teacher contacts a resource person for help. The resource person acts as a consultant to the teacher initially and may then place the child in one of the levels of the hierarchy of services for service above and beyond consultation to the teacher. Weekly reports and instructional service plans (ISP) are kept on each child to provide an ongoing evaluation of the child's program. In this way, other levels in the hierarchy may be found to be needed in a particular case, and the child is assured of the most appropriate placement throughout the program.

Staff in the Pinckney Project include the regular classroom teachers, consulting teachers, half-time physical education, music, and remedial reading teachers, and one-day-a-week school psychologists, learning disability teachers, and a counselor. These persons work together under the hierarchical setup to provide services to the handicapped which meet each student's personal needs. The philosophy is that the services should be instructionally based and the alternatives for exceptional children should be designed within the building level. The goal is to provide whatever services are needed within the school itself so that the students do not need to go elsewhere for their needs. The Pinckney Project is fulfilling its goal and offers full services except for the self-contained classroom option. This option is not available within the Pinckney School.

A SUPPORT MODEL FOR MAINSTREAMING

In some areas of the country, integration of special students into the mainstream of the classroom has not been the major problem in the education of exceptional children. For example, in Vermont it was estimated that 80 percent of the handicapped children of the state were already in regular classrooms. The problem was that these children were not receiving the special help they needed beyond the regular classroom work. Utilizing resources and personnel from the University of Vermont, Vermont developed a program in 1968, to train consulting teachers to assist regular classroom teachers in the elementary schools. This assistance took the form of training a group of selected teachers in the education and management of handicapped children in their classrooms. The plan included two years of intensive one-day-a-week training of a group of regular elementary teachers in the techniques and theories of behavior modification. These consulting teachers were taught basic behavioral techniques, including counting and charting of behaviors, parent and teacher training procedures, and consultation techniques for giving assistance to the regular elementary teachers. After their training was complete these teachers consulted to and trained the other teachers in their districts. The program has been in effect since 1969. Consulting teachers are being hired full-time and the University of Vermont has set up a master's degree program for consulting teacher training.

The programs that have been described represent attempts by school systems and educators to meet the needs and demands of the consumer. Mainstreaming is their offering for equality to the handicapped in educational settings. These particular programs did not include direct consumer input as far as planning and implementation are concerned, but they were indirectly influenced by the entire consumer movement, via litigation and legislation.

In response to the myriad of consumer complaints and legal cases (e.g., Willowbrook School in New York) leveled against institutionalized care of the handicapped, many communities have devised alternatives to institutions for their handicapped populations. These alternatives have been developed at various state and local levels. One example at the state level is the Connecticut Plan, which calls for transfer of the mild and moderate mentally retarded residents from institutions to group homes. The plan includes training the residents for socialization and re-entry into the community prior to the move. The plan also calls for citizen advocate participation to support former residents and to help protect their rights. In addition, through provision of group and foster homes the state plan attempts to prevent institutional enrollment from increasing. Campaigns to educate the public have been effective in explaining the role the retarded person can perform in society and in describing the services available. Paraprofessionals have also been trained to implement treatment so the most severe cases can remain in the home.

In some states, plans have been developed on a regional basis. In Nebraska, legislation was passed establishing six regions within the state, each with responsibility for developing services and programs for its own mentally retarded. One of these regions, the Eastern Nebraska Community Office for the Retarded (ENCOR), has answered the deinstitutionalization problem with a move to a wider view of services. This view has shifted the focus from the traditional group home or group living arrangement. The ENCOR staff found the usual deinstitutionalization services small-scale institutionalization rather than a solution to institutionalization. Normalization is the standard the staff has against which to judge the product of their programs. In their plan, the most effective and the most normal deinstitutionalization program is the one which allows the child to remain in the home in the first place.

The philosophy behind the ENCOR system is that the home is the normal, most efficient, most humane setting in which to raise a child. With this in mind, the coordinators have designed a flexible system of supports for the family, based on individual needs, to facilitate keeping the child in the home. The range of services provided is nearly unlimited. Services include provision of materials that can be installed in the home to aid the parents in handling the child (such as support bars in the bathroom and hallway or behavior-shaping equipment for example, a bedwetting alarm) or appliances that simply ease the work load of a harried mother to give her time to tend to the child (e.g., dishwasher, clothes-dryer). Besides the physical accoutrements necessary to outfit a home for a mentally retarded child, ENCOR may provide service employees to do handy work around the home, to babysit, or to provide respite care. The basic idea is to determine what element is missing that would enable a parent to care for his or her own child and to then provide it.

The ENCOR staff is aware that the natural home is not always the best or most feasible situation in which to place the mentally retarded. There are complications like rejecting parents, which cannot easily be overcome regardless of the support available. For this reason, there has been an alternative track developed to serve the population which cannot remain in the natural home. This is called alternate living units (ALU) and in actuality is not a single plan or design but an umbrella term for a wide variety of individualized living arrangements. These ALUs are designed with the particular needs of the individual in mind. Apparently, there is no limit to the types of arrangements possible. For instance, one option is apartment dwelling for two or three retarded adults, or another is a long-term foster home for a single mentally retarded child. This ALU program retains the more traditional group training residence (group home) but with additional functions. The ALUs are satellites of group training residences which in turn are part of a larger network of group homes and ALUs. The nuclear unit is the training residence which may care for a number of children in the residence and then several more who have moved on to ALUs. The staff of the residence provides training and consultative services to those persons who are in charge of the various ALUs under the residence's jurisdiction (e.g., foster mother in a private home or an advocate at an apartment dwelling). They also recruit and train home teachers. The ENCOR staff has attempted to answer the problems of deinstitutionalization in what they consider more normal fashion.

The capital district of New York State has also initiated a regional plan for deinstitutionalization. Briefly, this region is moving away from direct service provision by one large regional institution toward support to regional structures that allow the region to develop its own resources. The emphasis is on the prevention of institutionalization. As of 1976, there were fewer than six hundred of the original fourteen hundred residents in the institution, and by 1978 these will be home also. The region has opted to spend the money appropriated for a new facility for the retarded on programs for deinstitutionalization.

An even more basic unit, the institution itself, can initiate deinstitutionalization. One unit which has retrenched its forces to move in this direction is the Macomb-Oakland Center in Michigan. This institute, covering a two-county area, has begun to develop a network of community-based services including 140 foster homes, ten large group homes, and a number of developmental training centers and nursing homes. The center's staff directs the services provided by this network. In 2½ years, more than one-half the formerly institutionalized persons were in the community. The purpose of the center's deinstitutionalization program is to reduce the number of institutionalized persons by deploying resources available in the community.

The Western Carolina Center in Morganton, North Carolina, an institution for the mentally retarded, has developed an innovative within-system advocacy program aimed at institutional reform. It has an active consumer component in the role of watchdog to the entire effort. Theirs is a somewhat different approach to deinstitutionalization, but basically the goal is the same as that of other programs already mentioned: The center's staff hopes to prepare the residents for re-entry into the community. At Western Carolina Center, however, the task of deinstitutionalization begins with the center itself. The advocacy program was begun a few years ago as the result of a study completed in the center. This study revealed that residents were not being prepared to live in the community or to leave the institution. It indicated that a large percentage of residents were not enrolled in programs geared to their socialization and educational needs. The small percentage that were receiving help were receiving so little (less than three hours a day) that it was almost useless. It became obvious that, for the most part, residents were not being deinstitutionalized but were headed for permanent institutional placement.

The study prompted officials of the center to devise a system whereby each resident was assigned a spokesman familiar with his case to advocate for his needs within the institution. This was the first step toward Western Carolina's curent advocacy program. Initially, all personnel in the center, from laborers to high-level staff, were assigned four residents to represent. In essence, the function of the advocate was to become familiar with the "clients" case histories and, based on that information, to insure that they were receiving adequate care and training. If re-entry into the community was indicated, the advocate was to insure that the client was being prepared for such a difficult transition, and that the community was preparing to receive the client. Then if existing programs did not meet these needs, the advocate was in the position to argue on behalf of the resident for the creation of an appropriate program. This advocacy system had many positive consequences for the residents in the overall institutional framework. However, as a within-system advocacy program, it also had its drawbacks, the major one being that the system created a conflict of interests in the institutional hierarchy. This conflict dulled the impact that an independent advocate might have had, especially to the extent to which an advocate could argue a case for his or her client.

In response to these problems, the decision was made to go one step further in the advocacy movement—hiring full-time advocates whose sole responsibility was to represent the residents assigned to them. The role of advocate was moved from that of an amorphous part-time assignment to that of a full-time staff position. This system solved the problems of the original system in many respects. However, these advocates also were staff of the center, hired by the superintendent and answerable to him. The criterion of full independence, so essential a part of an advocacy system, remained compromised. The staff then realized that such independence could only be achieved with the help of persons outside the institution. It was at this point that the development of a human rights committee was considered. Members of the committee—consumers (mostly parents of the residents) and interested citizens—would meet the criterion of full independence but just as importantly would have a vested interest in bettering the lives of the clients and in improving the overall functioning of the institution. This committee is the watchdog of the advocacy program. The committee members are not salaried or answerable to anyone at the center. They can argue an issue at any or every level within the institution; and if need be, they can take their ''case'' to the public, through the media, courts, etc. In this way, they extend the accountability for the center beyond the institution itself.

The human rights committee serves yet another function beyond the advocacy issue. As a group of consumers and interested citizens the committee is able to serve as advisors to the superintendent and to the advocates. Also, the advocates have used the committee members as resources within the community. For example, an advocate for a certain child might seek help from a parent on the committee to find a home for the child for the holidays when the child has nowhere else to go.

CONCLUSION

Deinstitutionalization as discussed in this book and as exemplified in the programs described in this chapter may be a fortuitous human-service movement. It has a strong foundation in legislation, litigation, purpose, action, and philosophy. On the other hand, it can also be simply another permutation of a service system that is too large, too complex, and too depersonalized to care. In too many instances, deinstitutionalization has simply meant ''out of the beds, into the streets.'' Without the adequate preparation of handicapped persons, support from the institutions, and the development and nurturing of the community's human-service systems, "deinstitutionalized" persons become victims rather than consumers. One significant force that can make the difference between what is, what should be, and what should not be is the consumer advocate movement. Just as consumers have had a significant impact on the foods prepared for their consumption and on the very environments in which they live, so can consumer advocates for the handicapped have impact on qualities of future life for the handicapped.

To accomplish this goal in a positive way, consumers must take purposeful action at a number of important levels. They must become actively involved in presenting their needs within the framework of governmental policy-making. For example, they must take action on Social Services Title XX planning, on the spending of general and specific revenue-sharing funds and on public hearings and other forums held to determine and set priority for the needs of the handicapped. The White House Conference on the Handicapped in 1977 may provide a national forum for such expressions of need.

Consumers must continue their struggles for new legislation and for increases in appropriation to support for current legislation such as the Developmental Disabilities Act and Education for All Handicapped Bill. They must also continue their battles in the courts for clarifications and expression of their rights to fair treatment, education, privacy, and mobility. These actions must be followed by action on standards for care or their implementation. The Joint Commission Standards for Institutions and Community Agencies go a long way toward specifying improved conditions but they need applications through use and resource support.

Consumers will also be finding new and expanded roles in planning, monitoring, evaluating, and providing services. The Developmental Disabilities and Bill of Rights Act of 1975 goes farther than any other piece of national legislation in giving consumers a role in such functions. Making up more than one-third of the membership on the fifty state and six territorial developmental disability councils, consumers have the important function of assessing their states' service needs for the handicapped, both the service gaps and the unnecessary duplications. They have a role in taking these needs and generating program goals, objectives, and action plans to meet them. These in turn are to be used by the state and federal service agencies (health, education, and welfare) to guide their programs. In turn, the consumers on the councils and in the consumer organizations of which many of them are members are needed to monitor and evaluate the outcomes of implementation leading to new objectives and program goals. From this level of activity, consumers can actively affect policy decision-making.

Perhaps most of all consumers can have impact at the local or service levels. By requiring parent involvement in planning, monitoring, delivering, and receiving services, programs are much more likely to meet the needs of the handicapped and draw on the potential and strengths of those they have to serve. This type of involvement was demonstrated in the many service programs described in this chapter. Each exemplified the adage, "Give a person a fish and he will eat today, teach him to fish and he will eat always." Service providers and consumers must teach one another to fish if deinstitutionalization is going to amount to anything more than the current soup du jour of services for the handicapped.

REFERENCES

Deno, E. "Special Education as Developmental Capital." *Exceptional Children* 37(3)(1970):229-37.

Dunn, L. "Special Education for the Mildly Retarded—Is Much of it Justifiable? *Exceptional Children* 35(1968):5-22.

Holder, H. D.; Pelosi, J. W.; and Dixon, R. T. *A Matter of Service: How to Monitor Agencies that Serve Children.* Durham, N.C.: Learning Institute of North Carolina, 1974.

Pelosi, J. W., and Johnson, S. *To Protect and Respect.* Durham N.C.: Learning Institute of North Carolina, 1974

President's Committee on Mental Retardation. *The National Strategy to Combat Mental Retardation.* Washington, D.C.: U.S. Government Printing Office, 1961.

6

The Transformation of Caregiving:

A Proposal

WILLIAM C. RHODES

DEINSTITUTIONALIZATION as a movement has emerged in public consciousness at a time when much new thinking about human services is taking place. It is a single mosaic in an intricate pattern of altered views about caregiving. This changing climate invites in-depth analyses of institutional processes and practices. The process of deinstitutionalizing is certainly more intricate than releasing inhabitants of closed institutions into the open community. Older models of thinking entertained such simplistic solutions. Our present awareness of interdependent chains of social units and social processes teaches us to approach the problem from a more comprehensive perspective. It cautions us to look for total patterns of events which have to be altered if the powerful inertia of institutional history has any hope of being turned around.

Burton Blatt's *Christmas in Purgatory* (1974) is a compassionate visual statement about institutions. It focuses very clearly upon the fact that, despite deepening care and concern, confinement and containment facilities can still become human zoos. This is certainly not the intent of society. Yet, despite generations of best intentions, the practice of "indoor" care has had a disturbing history in western civilization (Foucault 1973). In the United States, the history of "asylums" (Rothman 1971) has been one of periodic peaks and troughs of hope and resignation about institutions. There have been recurrent phases in which some compellingly hopeful idea or strong charismatic figure emerged to re-energize asylums as places for the transformation of people and their society. Then, gradually, the weight of inmate numbers and growing disenchantment of the populace creates a cycle of despair and pessimism. In some of these deepest troughs, pessimism has deteriorated into retaliation and

80

punishment for the differences observed in asylum inmates.

The facilities themselves are social libraries of this whole gamut of images and attitudes toward those who need help. It is a living museum of the range of community emotions and movements associated with human charity and care.

THE CRISIS IN CARE

In the current period of history, the interest in institutions seems to be part of the larger social hope expressed in positive slogans of change such as "mainstreaming," "advocacy," "litigation," and "accountability." We seem to be borne upon a rising tide of good will toward our fellow man and to be searching for ways out of an impass in the arena of human care.

Some modern interpreters of public caretaking see a crisis in the emotions and structures of social service and try to analyze what has occurred. Jean Vanier (1971) views this situation as a crisis of caring in our society and sees our youth as being in despair over the crisis: "I am certain that this state of affairs cannot continue. Our society will be transformed through the fire of revolution or through the stagnant waters of decadence or *through the fire and peace of true love*" (p.18). As Vanier examines our institutional forms of social care, he says:

> Facing the seriousness of our present crisis, we should not be afraid to present a high ideal implying love and self-giving. The days of the lord of the manor, of benevolent and charitable ladies and welfare committees organizing fairs and sales for the poor are over, even if they were bearers of authentic values in their time. I *would even say that the extreme devotion of professional men—doctors, lawyers, government officials, professors, teachers, social workers—but who seek at the same time to augment their material wealth, and to live comfortably, is insufficient today.*
>
> The crisis is now much more profound and serious. To meet it we must follow our logic to its ultimate end. *The gift of oneself to others can no longer be simply on the level of giving "spare-time" during leisure hours or on a professional level. It must be on a deeper, more personal level.* (p. 17, italics added)

One of the critics of the present caregiving enterprises in society sees part of the problem as lying in the comingling of unified power and social care:

> The ideology of power I am concerned with is to be seen in other and frequently decisive areas of modern society—in city government and planning, business enterprises, public housing projects, churches, great universities and school systems. . . . From the ideology of unified power and total power has come all too often a conception of human organization not very different, at bottom, from a military post. No relationship must exist that is not contemplated by central command and assimilated into formal hierarchy of external administration. We see this in school systems today, especially in large cities. (Nesbit 1971, p.xv).

Ivan Illich (1973) feels that mass production of services lies at the bottom of our dilemma: "Our analysis of schooling has led us to recognize that mass production of education as a paradigm for other industrial enterprises, each producing a service commodity, each organized as a public utility, and each defining its output as a basic necessity. . . . We had to face a set of limits to growth in the service sector of any society as inescapable as the limits inherent in the industrial production of artifacts" (p. xii). He says that the growth of these human services has reduced rather than increased our capacity for care: "As the value of services rose, it became almost impossible for people to care" (p. 3).

NEW VOICES OF CRITICISM

It does seem that there are profound social forces at work which could make our situation of today quite different from other historical periods. Deinstitutionalization, as a movement, occurs in the context of deep stirrings in parts of the public consciousness about our social needs and social bonds.

Institutionalization, as a social process addressed to the solution of special human problems, is not a one-dimensional function. It is embedded in a multifaceted network of reactive efforts being woven around the arena of social care. The complexity of this network is being expressed in simple reactive slogans such as those mentioned earlier—de-categorization, de-bureaucratization, de-professionalization, and de-centralization of human care. Each term, in and of itself, speaks about seemingly independent efforts occurring in our intricate systems of social sevice. Yet, they can be viewed as a composite pattern, the whole of which must be grasped in order to understand the social forces at work in the field of care. Deinstitutionalization is only a part of this wave of forces and will occur only when the composite wave is woven into the central pattern of society.

The above terms are reactive terms rather than guideposts to the future. As reactive forces, however, we must examine them one by one to see what they stand for as a criticism of prevailing practices and traditions of caregiving.

"De-categorization," for instance, is a reaction to the underlying classification system which has grown up in this society to separate individual differences into specialized categories of alienation. This system of categorizing differences has been accompanied by differentiation and social specialization of types of asylums which accompany the segregating titles. Institutions for the "retarded," "mentally ill," "disturbed," "delinquent," etc., are the outcome of such specialization. A successful attack upon the categories themselves would pull out the perceptual underpinnings of the facilities. It would radically alter the reality-consensus of the general public with regard to institutions. Breaking through this perceptual bubble surrounding individuals who are different would awaken the society and raise questions about the practices and processes of institutionalization as a means of maintaining social order. Within the public mind, it would challenge the sorting-bin process as a way of showing care. For these reasons, we cannot look upon the concept of "hardening of the categories" as independent of the criticism of institutionalization.

Alongside "deinstitutionalization" and "de-classification," another term which takes issue with prevailing traditions of caretaking is "de-bureaucratization." Bureaucracy is merely a particular organizational form in which resources, customs, and practices are bound together in a vertical structure, with authority organized in a pyramidal form, which is directly a part of the body politic of the state, where roles are strictly defined and circumscribed, where exchanges among roles have specifically prescribed defined behaviors, and where practices throughout the total apparatus are uniform and standardized by legislation and state regulation. Presentday asylums are an intricate piece in this overall bureau pattern. They do not function independently and cannot be understood or operated outside this state-related system. Laws and administrative guidelines bind them as part of the whole. The facilities exist not only as holding centers for human beings but also as subsystems of a supersystem which feeds and is fed into the institution.

"De-bureaucratization" is a rallying cry against this particular organizational form and function. It is a higher-level statement of the first-level term "deinstitutionalization." It is a synonym for deinstitutionalization which is broader in scope and boundaries, but offers the same critique of prevailing traditions of caregiving. However, where "de-classification" is a demand for an alternative perception of the consensual reality which maintains institutions, "de-bureaucratization" is a demand for an alteration of the institutions themselves through a reorganization of resources, control, and functions. It asks for some type of alternative to "state" control and "state"-binding of these components.

"De-professionalization" is another term rising on the horizon. At first blush, it appears to be unrelated to "deinstitutionalization," but upon closer examination it becomes a full member of the same family.

"De-professionalization" addresses itself to the other side of the caretaking relationship. As usually considered deinstitutionalization is focused upon the client side of the helping dyad. It talks about changing the life situation of the target population. However, caretaker and care-receiver are bound together in a single unit in our caretaking society. The role of one cannot be altered without altering the role of the other. The social contract binds them together into a psychological unit, requires that re-conceptualizing one party affects the conceptualization of the other. The re-socialization of inmate roles implied in deinstitutionalization finds correspondence in the helping role in de-professionalization.

Such an analysis would suggest that deinstitutionalization could not succeed without some alteration in the caretaking role to reciprocate with the alternatives in the inmate role.

"De-centralization" or "community control" is another battle cry for change in the caretaking enterprise. The attempt to return programs to the neighborhood is a part of this effort. Attempts to deinstitutionalize usually focus upon a neighborhood or community dwelling such as half-way houses and group houses for institutional inmates. the slogan for neighborhood control of schools or mental health centers, etc., is part of this move toward de-centralization of structures and programs, and toward locating the caregiving and caretaking energies in the natural habitat of givers and receivers. De-centralization also focuses on breaking up huge self-contained institutions through unitizing the institution itself, so that there are natural "catchment" areas for each unit, through an attempt to supplant the institution with smaller living units in various communities, or through some type of "cottage" plan which decentralizes the focus of institutional life.

De-centralization is also directly related to de-bureaucratization. The attempt to decentralize huge institutions into smaller dwelling units is an attempt to change the centralized, hierarchical organization of institution life. The press for community control is an attempt to relocate decision-making away from pyramidal chains of authority and to break out of the organizational form of state-directed, role-specific, absentee-landlord, caregiving. The move toward community-based dwellings is a move away from bureaus of service which operate like public utilities. The attempt to unitize institutions on the base of catchment areas has been a move both to open the institution into the community so that it has greater relevance to community life and to change the organizational environment from that of a bureau to that of a "natural" residence.

Thus we see a direct interrelationship between social-change slogans such as deinstitutionalization and de-categorization, de-bureaucratization, de-professionalization, and de-centralization. De-categorization calls for a change in the consensual reality which enclosed individual differences in impermeable perceptual compartments that alienate those who are captured in them. De-bureaucratization is a challenge to our present organizational form of caregiving which turns over the perceptually separated populations to artificial state structures. De-professionalization is focused on the converse role of the care-receiver-caregiver contract. It insists that deinstitutionalizing residents of state facilities requires alterations in the perceptual bubble surrounding the caregiver just as de-classification is focused on the care-receiver. Finally, de-centralization calls for changing the center of control and influence, as well as the focus of care, from the state to the community or neighborhood.

Each of these terms, although oriented to social change in the field of human care, is couched in the philosophical framework that has existed since the early days of our Republic. These terms take issue with current attitudes and views, current organizational forms, current practices, and current authority. They do not point the way to altered social realities of care. Altered social realities can occur only when the social experience of care occurs in totally new modes and when these modes are stabilized in the ongoing flux of everyday life.

It is not possible to draw detailed bluebrints for these altered modes of experienceing social care. It is only possible to communicate part-experiences or momentary states which break through the current bubble of reality surrounding caregiving. Eventually, the current reality must be fragmented before new modes can enter the arena and be stabilized in the day-to-day, socially shared experience of care. The process must begin, however, in a shared consciousness of care which differs from the current consciousness.

ANOTHER REALITY

In the general consciousness of differences which permeates the society, we have no way of breaking out of the social alienation from those we see as different. However, in a small segment of the population there has recently grown up a different consciousness of normality and abnormality which does break through our current reality and takes us into another realm of experiencing differences in people. In this new consciousness, the social reality of a person is not reducible to any category we can apply to him or her. Within this reality, to call an individual mentally ill, retarded, criminal, alcoholic, etc., is not to know him as he is. Knowledge that is founded on detached observation of person as "other" with an eye toward locating him in a pre-established conceptual framework is, within this reality, a distortion. Real understanding arises in and from the unmediated relationship in which the would-be knower gives himself as a whole being rather than an observer. The attempt at understanding is fulfilled in a precious awareness of the reality that the other presents. There is a considerable difference between allowing the individual to reveal himself to me as my being is revealed to him, and assuming, a priori, that his experience must fit neatly within the conceptual framework that I bring to bear on him.

Within this new consciousness, allowing the individual to present himself to us in his own way, stripped of the categories in which we confine him, can be a disconcerting and unpredictable experience. Yet, such revelations help us to be alive to ourselves as well as to him, help us to know the depth of feelings he arouses in us—joy, sorrow, revulsion, ecstasy—which mirror things in ourselves. It is greater than the stereotyped experience of criminal, insane, or feebleminded. Furthermore, to treat an individual as a particular case of a general category, to recognize him only as a participant in a "syndrome," is to deny him reality, his own agency in determining his life.

Within this new consciousness, what we call "normality" may be a profound masquerade in which we hide from ourselves what we are, and the masks we use to hide ourselves are those we call abnormal. We have focused our view upon explaining, understanding, and treating abnormality. What may need explaining, however, is the profound masquerade we call normality. Normalcy is the condition of being out of touch with one's own existence, one's own experiences. As Ronald Laing (1966) has said: "The condition of alienation of being asleep, of being unconscious, of being out of one's mind is the condition of normal man. Society highly values its normal man. It educates children to lose themselves, and to become absurd, and thus to become normal. Normal men have perhaps killed 100,000,000 of their fellow normal men in the last 50 years'' (p. 24).

As Berger and Luckmann (1967) have said: "[It is] much less shocking to the reality status of one's own universe to have to deal with minority groups of deviants, whose contrariness is ipso facto defined as folly or wickedness, than to confront another society that views one's own definition of reality as ignormant, mad, or downright evil. . . . Therapy entails the application of conceptual machinery to insure that actual or potential deviants stay within the institutionalized definition of reality" (pp. 107-108, 113).

This new alternative consciousness believes that if all the privately alienated should expose their condition to each other there would not be enough machinery available to insure the institutionalization of the conventional reality. Therefore, we publicly alienate a few among ourselves and place them in the machinery of public services which funnels them into real institutions, thus hiding from our own view what they mirror inside ourselves.

There is a possibility that this new consciousness, this new perceptual view, of differences and deviation may spread rapidly across society. Prevailing social definitions of reality have been profoundly shaken in the last few years. Momentous human events have undermined our unitary world view. Since the 1960s our society discovered the "generation gap," "gay liberation," "women's lib," "black power," and "sexual freedom." The unified reality shared by the populace had suddenly exploded into multiple universes of reality—a psychedelic carnival of realities—a variety of private inner visions spilling out into the social scene like a dazzling light show of colors and forms, a veritable kaleidoscope of changing life experiences and life patterns. Against this mitotic universe any single view of deviance becomes difficult to maintain, difficult to re-stabilize. "Normal" man is propelled into himself. His private alienation is publicly exposed; and the seeds of insight, long dormant, slowly begin to sprout.

Laing (1967) has said: "There are forms of alienation that are relatively strange to statistically 'normal' forms of alienation. The 'normally' alienated person, by reason of the fact that he acts more or less like everyone else, is taken to be sane. Other forms of alienation are labeled by the 'normal' majority as bad or mad" (p. 24).

Within the new consciousness of deviance the variant person, alienated or not, emerges as a hero. He is heroic in this recalcitrance. Although all the socialization pressures conspire against him, he refuses to participate in the official version of reality. Within this new consciousness of differences what emerges on the other side of the burst bubble of conventional normality is a celebration of "being" in the multivaried forms in which it reveals itself. Although deviance itself is not "being," to affirm and celebrate deviance in the current situation is to negate the ultimacy of the existing definition of being and reality. Just as the "normal" man views deviance as a symbol of non-being, the new consciousness finds in it the one glimpse of being that is available to us.

The deviant may not recognize that, in his uniqueness, he is the author of his own being. In fact, the very state of his existence may not fulfill him, and may not add to the world around him. Nevertheless, in his differences, he presents himself honestly, while normal man hides inside a shell of convention, unaware that he does not present himself at all. The way he handles the negation of his shell posed by the self-presentations of the deviant is to deny the threat to his established symbolic universe by reference to special niches for those who are "out of touch with reality," "too stupid to handle a reality," or "at odds with reality." Variance is placed in a special class in which a rule prevails that variant experience is not to be treated as real.

Foucault, in his preface to *Madness and Civilization* (1973), writes: "We have yet to write the history of the other forms of madness in which men, in an act of sovereign reason, confine their neighbors and communicate and recognize each other through the merciless language of non-madness."

The new consciousness of care breaks through the merciless language of non-madness which has reigned so long, to bring back together again the alienated normal and the exiled abnormal. It strikes the chains from the symbol universe which fetters us to modern institutions in the same way Pinel struck the chains binding inmates of ancient institutions. To free ourselves from this present symbol universe would be to free ourselves from the madness of sovereign reason which confines our neighbors and allows us to recognize each other only through our alienation. Communication would be restored, barriers removed, and the need to confine would vanish. We would no longer need to shield ourselves from our differences, or be on guard against the differences of neighbors. Categories would dissolve.

With the bursting of the perceptual bubble surrounding differences, with a full revolution of the symbolic field from "categorizing" to "celebrating," care could break the locks of professional institutions. Care could be freed from storage in social services and replanted in the vital soil of community. In state service systems, valuable resources are often diverted in order to maintain bureaucratic power structures. Communities might be better able to avoid such energy and resource diversion and to devote themselves to true care giving.

Although to replant the seed in the community and re-expose it to the chemistry of man is to chance again that the progeny may be uncertain—either care of power—in doing this the regeneration of care gains a new possibility which does not exist in state-serviced structures.

If, further, the symbol universe surrounding differences gives ground more extensively than it now has, then the new community could be a soil richly nourishing to care. The world-view of differences, disability and deviation, can change just as the view of blacks or women or gays is subject to change. By a full turn of the wheel, the celebration of differences or deviance could overturn convention and open the way to transplant care back into its natural habitat.

If care itself should be transplanted from its bureaucratic housing back into the community, then community could be revitalized as real places for people to live rather than places to hide from each other. If communities become places to live there would be no need for walled off areas in which to conceal defects in the porcelainized picture of reality that we struggle so hard to maintain. Institutions and their social equivalents would no longer be viable solutions to deviations from the conventional symbol universe.

Already, cracks are beginning to appear in the universal shell. Pluralism and self-identity have gained a profound hold on our imagination Although self-identity is in its reactive state—women reacting against the male world, blacks against the white world—a new pluralism is growing up in which a new sense of community and self is taking root, the community of women, of blacks, the counter-culture community, the new conservative community. If such communities reconstitute themselves, then care will have to become central to their existence, because such communities, in heightening their difference as the essence of their being, are encompassing their difference in care. Thus, they are communities of individuals established to celebrate their difference rather than leashing or confining them. The affirmation of identities previously negated by society is the symbol base for new realities. It is the rallying point for new communities.

A powerful solvent to existing institutions is to transform them into such communities. Remove the sense of an occupying force of state agents. Foster a celebration of uniqueness and encourage a sense of identity. Allow a gradual construction of an indigenous governance structure, with declared independence from state structures. Dissolve the inmate status and restore citizenship. Invest care mechanisms in the hands of the citizens, as, for instance, does Synanon. Remove the walls and containment forces and regulations. Surround the enterprise with dignity. Such would be the essence of deinstitutionalization. In very concrete terms, such rallying flags as de-categorization, de-bureaucratization, de-professionalization, and de-centralization would all fly together in a single transfiguration.

To accomplish this form of deinstitutionalization the elements at hand could be woven together into a whole. Vanier (1971) has demonstrated that a group of individuals with a special consciousness of social contribution is available in the general population. Such individuals can and will enter into a covenant with those in need of such support. Their own reality and the commitment that follows are consonant with mutuality in the face of differences. In these settings a sense of occupation forces would be quite out of character. In certain specialized institutions (such as facilities for the retarded), where the range of resident skills has to be expanded, nuclear cadres of such people could be called on to transfer from communities they now occupy to bring their attitudes, ways of working, and styles of life into the institution. In other specialized institutions, such as training schools for "delinquent," the expertise and personnel of such self-help communities as Synanon could contribute routines, philosopy, and self-change mechanisms.

To foster self-identity and transpose categorization into a celebration of differences, the psychology of the feminist movement and the Black movement is a potential model. The reverence for life, in all its manifestations, in all its wide variations, can be appealed to in both the internal and external community.

Probably the most difficult and yet the most central part of the transformation is a decided shift in governance. Much work has to be accomplished within state bureaus themselves. This would be the most critical test of voluntary deinstitutionalization. The perceptual bubble surrounding both professionalism and state caretaking seems to be most intact and toughest in the climate of state care. Those trapped within the bubble are surrounded by a mirrored surface. Each time they try to break out the mirror reflects back to them their own socialized reality. In such a mirror-world, the suggestion of separating service and state is unbelievable, incomprehensible. A deep concern for survival of the individuals and their living habitat is strongly stirred. But this would be the test of the possibility of moving from the current reality of institutions to new living communities.

There is a strong tradition in American history for the community form of intentional living. The Amana (Fairfield 1972), the Oneida Community (Carden 1969, Robertson 1970, 1972), and the Bruderhof (Zablocki 1972) are examples of the older tradition. Synanon (Yablonsky 1972), Daytop (Casriel 1971), and the Farm (Stephen 1970) are examples of the new tradition. Camphill Village (Fairfield 1972) is an example of a homogenous community of specialized differences. These could be helpful blueprints and cautions to state planners.

The restoration of citizenship and dissolution of inmate status may not be far off. Litigation is blanketing institutions like a heavy snowfall. "The Right to Treatment," "Restoration of Rights," "Violation of Civil Rights," "Equal Protection," and "Equal Rights" are levels inserted under the heavy rock of institutional convention, which may bring about a decided shift in our current views.

Investment of care mechanisms in the hands of the residential community may be the most difficult stroke of all. All the conceptual models, the symbol worlds of professionalism, would be challenged by such a bold move. In good conscience, the professional cadre of caretakers would raise strongly reasoned objections. They would marshal a vast solid literature of caution or outright opposition. The established tradition in Alcoholics Anonymous or Synanon would arouse powerful debate. And yet, such a possibility is conceivable. Such an alternative to the present convention is possible. Synanon has a method, Camphill Village does exist. Vanier (1971) is spreading his gospel across the world. Member-directed change, growth, modification, and care, do have a tradition.

The removal of walls surrounding institutions is part of the current resurgence of care. Opening into the community and uniting the organizational structure are efforts in this direction. A composite effort at transformation of the total institution into intentional communities of care might begin to open the iron curtain separating "us" and "them." This will never be a universal fact, however, until the walls in our minds are dissolved.

Essentially, then, what is being suggested here in outlining a process of transformation of institutions into communities is that the methods, models, and ideology are at hand. What is needed is the mobilization of psychic energy and the determination to bring about such a transformation. Communities of care would be a break with the historical tradition of institutions in our society, but no more than exploration of the moon, or a revolution in sexual mores. The deinstitutionalization which would be required is in the conventions of care which have been institutionalized in the public mind, in its representative agencies, the bureaus, its state agents, and the professionals. Furthermore, the residents of the facilities would have to be helped to transform their own psychology into a celebration rather than a condemnation of their own differences.

The earlier part of this chapter suggested an alternative symbolic universe as a way out of the one-dimensional reality surrounding caregiving. It tried to show that the way is being paved for such an alternative by sweeping social events which are shattering the conventional reality which we have accepted so long. The latter part of the chapter has suggested a specific way of deinstitutionalization through communizing institutions. The major ingredients of such a community transformation are a separation betwen state and human services, the institution of covenants of mutual dependency in place of professional caretaking, breaking down the psychic and physical walls which separate "normal" and "abnormal," and the institution of self-generated and self-maintained growth forums in place of externally imposed treatment techniques.

If we could take action on these multiple, related fronts, the somber psychology of plague surrounding caretaking should yield to its internal opposite—a psychology of celebration.

REFERENCES

Berger, P., and Luckmann, T. *The Social Construction of Reality*. Garden City, N.Y.: Anchor, 1967.

Blatt, B. *Christmas in Purgatory: A Photographic Essay on Mental Retardation*. Boston: Allyn and Bacon, 1966.

Carden, M. L. *Oneida: Utopian Community to Modern Corporation*. Baltimore, Md.: Johns Hopkins Press, 1969.

Casriel, Daniel, and Amen, Grover. *Daytop: Three Addicts and Their Care*. New York: Hill and Wang, 1971.

Fairfield, R. *Communes USA: A Personal Tour*. Baltimore, Md.: Penguin, 1972.

Foncault, M. *Madness and Civilization*. New York: Random House, 1973.

Illich, I. *Tools for Conviviality*. New York: Harper and Row, 1973.

Laing, R. D. *The Politics of Experience*. New York: Ballantine, 1967.

Nesbit, R. *The Quest for Community*. London: Oxford University Press, 1971.

Piorel, P. "A Treatise on Insanity in which are Contained the Principles of a New and More Practical Nosology of Maniacal Disorders." From D. Davis. London: W. Todd, 1806. Nutley, N.J.: Roche Laboratories, Reprint, 1966.

Robertson, C. N., ed. *Oneida Community: An Autobiography, 1851-1876*. Syracuse: Syracuse University Press, 1970.

———. *Oneida Community: The Breakup*. Syracuse: Syracuse University Press, 1972.

Rothman, D. *The Discovery of the Asylum: Social Order and Disorder in the New Republic.* Boston: Little, Brown, 1971.
Stephen. *The Monday Night Class.* Santa Rosa, Calif.: Book Farm, 1970.
Vanier, J. *Eruption to Hope.* Toronto: Griffin House, 1971.
Yablonsky, Lewis. *Synanon: The Tunnel Back.* Baltimore, Md.: Pelican, 1972.
Zablocki, B. D. *The Joyful Community: An Account of Bruderhof, a Communal Movement.* Baltimore, Md.: Penguin, 1972.

III. Structures and Strategies

7

Accountability

JAMES L. PAUL

INSTITUTIONALIZATION, once viewed as a positive intervention into the lives of handicapped people, has become one of the more serious problems in the delivery of services to the handicapped. A major problem arises with the integration of the handicapped person into the mainstream of the society's life and law.

The institutional movement has stimulated many procedural and substantive innovations in the identification and treatment of the handicapped. Some of those innovations have become malignant, compromising the personhood and citizenship of the handicapped.

Since the mid-sixties attention has been focused on those aspects of our system of caring for the handicapped which jeopardize his integrity or violate his rights and preempt his opportunity to exercise normal obligations. This attention has been more concerned with the legal implications of providing services than with the technical aspects of the professional services provided.

One of the central issues to emerge has been that of accountability. Deinstitutionalization may be viewed as one aspect of the effort to make services for the handicapped more accountable to the needs of the handicapped.

While the present writing is concerned with the handicapped, it should be noted that both deinstitutionalization and accountability are concepts that extend into the structures of the total society and the foundations of all human services. Accountability, for example, is one of the most important concerns in American education.

Accountability is a useful way of thinking about relationships. In the present chapter we are interested primarily in the relationships between handicapped persons and institutional systems that serve them. More specifically we are concerned with the accountability of those systems to the handicapped persons.

The chapter includes, first, a discussion of deinstitutionalization. The view presented is that deinstitutionalization is a movement to counter the structures and effects of institutionalization, a process by which institutions reduce their accountability to clients. The second and primary section of the chapter discusses elements of accountability, certain models of accountability that exist in the educational system, and the information problem. The educational system was selected for study and the development of examples because (1) it illustrates the major issues and problems in accountability, (2) it cannot be regarded as a special case of problems removed from the concerns of most people, (3) it is the basic institution outside the family in the "open" society with responsibility for teaching and providing educational services for *all* children.

Deinstitutionalization and mainstreaming are different stirrups on the same saddle. Accountability, it is argued, is a complex problem having to do with the way we look at and get information about people and the ways we make decisions relative to that information. The rights of a person to know and to decide in matters that relate to his own life are central to the problems of institutionalization and the appropriate framework within which to discuss accountability.

This is not a programmatic essay describing the specifics of how to make institutions more accountable. It is, rather, a conceptual discussion that offers some analysis of the definitions and issues and suggests a perspective from which action plans may be developed.

DEINSTITUTIONALIZATION: A PERSPECTIVE

Ours is a society of institutions. Institutions are social structures that give form and constancy to the wishes and intentions of people over time. Institutions are gestalts of social behavior and structure. They are only approximations of what any one or group of us would have them be. They rarely if ever represent our creeds exactly. Institutions mediate and, themselves, give witness to our values. We are more proud of some of the values than of others. We are more aware of some than of others. While individuals or groups may despise certain institutions or institutional consequences—for that is the source of dissent and revolution—as a society we are our institutions and we value what is manifest in our institutions.

There is usually some resistance to institutions because there is never a perfect fit between institutions, those supporting institutions, and those served by institutions. People relate to the future—needs, hopes, and expectations. Institutions have no dreams of things to come. They are more or less stable structures rooted in history—the way things have been. This balance maintains order and, indeed, protects the more vulnerable citizens. The tension, however, of what has been and what now seems right and socially appropriate motivates institutional change. Deinstitutionalization is a good example.

Institutionalization is a basic social process. It is comprised of the educating, recruiting, coercing, regulating and shaping activities, rules, and physical arena of institutions. It is also comprised of the adapting behaviors of those participating in the institutions. Institutionalization is the successful adaptation of individuals to institutional requirements.

We are all institutionalized in this most basic sense and seek to maintain most of our successful institutional adaptations. Problems arise when an institution makes unacceptable demands on its participating members or when the institution ceases to serve an acceptable social purpose. That is, the institution does too much of a wrong thing or it does not do enough of the right things.

Doing too much of the wrong things can, perhaps, be best characterized by the bureaucratization of the institution. Bureaucracy in this sense would be counterproductive or destructive. An example in the bureaucratization of human-service systems would be a proliferation of demonstrably undesirable institutional practices such as the labeling and removal of mildly retarded children from normal child environments because of the mild retardation. Social roadbeds such as those tracks which run out from and alongside the normal child situations are dug by bureaucratic machinery. This machinery runs at the level of collective behavior, the institutional gestalt, not the individual wishes or intentions of those who participate in it and ultimately keep it working.

The inappropriate uses of special classes is an example of how difficult it is to modify deeply bureaucratized institutional practices. It has taken the judicial system, citing some practices illegal, to change some aspects of the too many wrong things in institutions. Many people, professionals and laymen alike, knew logically and empirically that special classes were being misused. Many of them would have changed the system if they had known how. The cases had to be taken to court.

The other side of the problem, the institution's not serving an acceptable social purpose, can be a case of institutional insufficiency. An example of an institution's not doing enough would be its failure to provide enough social stimulation to institutionalized babies. It can also be a problem of institutional inappropriateness. This results from the institution's not serving its original mission or from its preoccupation with its original mission, which is no longer supported by the society. For example, institutionalization, as it is thought of in its most hard-core physical manifestations in caring for the handicapped, is the removal of the handicapped from the community to remote institutions. At one time this was seen as appropriate and humane. Now the morality of integration, the ethics of individual freedom, the constitutionality of human rights, the plurality of acceptable value systems, and the sensitivity to individual life style have forced new attention to the institutional mission or separation and segregation. The basic rights denied, such as the right to due process, have attained new focus. There are many aspects of the phenomenon of institutionalization.

Sociologists have helped us recognize that institutions serve many social functions. While they may be geographically remote, they are nonetheless inseparably connected to the character and the economic structure of society.

For whatever purposes, institutions for the handicapped are maintained, and, for whatever social needs they now satisfy, institutions were originally established to care for the disabled. They were established to improve the lives of the handicapped. They were established to get the handicapped out of chains, out of jails, and out of poor houses.

When a society assumes responsibility in an area of social life, it institutionalizes the means by which that responsibility can be implemented. The institutional movement for the handicapped has two major consequences with which we are dealing today in trying to deinstitutionalize the handicapped. First, it institutionalized the caregiving function. Some now argue that personal caregiving cannot be institutionalized and remain personal. Institutions, they contend, are impersonal and lack individual human concern. A less radical view of institutionalized caregiving would be that it is exceedingly difficult to maintain a responsive human environment in a large, complex, bureaucratic, institutional system. Bureaucratization and institutionalization tend to shift activity in the direction of the systematic, routine, mechanistic, and impersonal. The needs of the individual must be carefully considered in programming and in the kinds of environments that are permitted to exist in institutions. One of the major recent developments in deinstitutionalization has been that of normalization. Normalization could be thought about as programming (curricular, environmental, and interpersonal) for the modification and correction of institutional drift in the direction of the impersonal which "normally" occurs when the caregiving function is institutionalized.

The second major consequence of the institutional movement which deinstitutionalization is now seeking to modify has to do with the structure and focus of accountability. That is, it directed accountability away from the person served. In taking over some responsibility for providing care to the handicapped, government had to develop a delivery system, in this instance institutions. It also had to develop a structure for being accountable for the responsibility it assumed and the money it spent. Government commonly develops bureaucracy to accomplish these functions. The bureaucracy, both for and of the institutional caregiving system, has been considerably elaborated over time and has successfully installed the basic attitude that the direction of accountability in a bureaucratic space is upward.

This basic attitude and the structure that maintains it have many implications for the institutional careers of the handicapped. The basic attitude toward "my boss," the boundaries fixed for "my job," and the policy and regulations governing "the place where I work" do not always work in the best interest of the handicapped person we claim to serve. There are many examples of the problem and the conflict created for the person who faces apparent contradiction or paradox in being a good employee and being a good servant of the handicapped person. A teacher who wishes to work with some parents but is not allowed to do so because it is not in the job description; a maintenance worker who wishes to take a child fishing but is not allowed to do so because it is against institutional policy; a superintendent who wants to establish a new role or to reclassify an old position but is unable to do so because the state personnel agency, which may know little or nothing of the needs of the handicapped, does not see the sense of it or cannot reconcile the request with other positions in the system—these are examples of accountability directed away from the handicapped person and at that person's expense.

OVERVIEW OF ACCOUNTABILITY

Accountability is a social concept, understood according to certain values which obtain in the situation in which it is practiced. It is the flow of responsibility in a particular organizational culture. It is neither good nor bad; it is an organizational manifestation of a set of values.

Accountability may, in a basic sense, be examined in terms of the accounting or accountable agent and the direction of the accountability. Both the accountable agent or unit and the direction of accountability may be further divided into either individual person or organizational considerations.

From this perspective, accountability may be related to issues of organizational balance or equilibrium, style, and character. These issues would vary according to the purpose and goals of the organization, its size, or its openness.

Accountability can be further analyzed in terms of its cognitive or substantive domain in contradistinction to its structural or organizational domain. The substantive content domain would include ethics and the nature of information processed, for example, which would in turn be concerned with theory, concepts, and data. The structural domain involves the implementation and maintenance issues. This is primarily a matter of the exercise of accountability over time in a particular organizational context.

The following sections deal with three major topics on accountability related to the broad perspective outlined above. The first topic explores the nature and elements of accountability. The second topic is the exercise of accountability, including a description of certain accountability models. The third accountability topic is the constraints on concepts and knowledge in being accountable, including an examination of decision-making and validity.

ELEMENTS OF ACCOUNTABILITY

Three questions always exist when the development of a valid system of accountability is considered seriously: (1) Accountability to whom? (2) For what? (3) How will it be exercised? One can think of these questions in terms of moral, professional-technical, and organizational accountability.

Whether for performance or money, accountability is a complex phenomenon, deeply rooted in the culture of the arrangement in which it is being considered. To be able to account for something one must know what that something is, to whom he is to account, and how. The following section discusses these elements of accountability and their moral, professional-technical, and organizational implications. A view of history is presented and a micro-system is described to illustrate the content, direction, and structure of accountability.

Historical Perspective

In the simplest order of things, man on the frontier could clearly account to himself and his immediate family. The basic need was to survive—food, water, and protection. The need served and for whom was sufficiently explicit that he could arrange his time and energy around it. His own body and the bodies of his family would register and resonate his failure.

This was only part of the picture. Labor was divided and, to that extent, responsibility was shared. If he brought meat home, his wife had to process it for eating. This constituted an elementary contract. All members of the family shared responsibility for another basic need, that of tolerable social interaction among themselves. The affiliative need is also basic.

A social microsystem, in this example the family, emerged as an interaction of the needs, the conditions, and constraints imposed by the habitat in which those needs were to be met and by the resources available to meet them. A culture of life style, values, beliefs, rules developed constituting the organizational, moral, and social basis for understanding and judging performance. The *content* (for what), *direction* (to whom), and *structure* (how) of accountability could not be understood apart from the culture of and the needs being met in this microsystem.

Later, when this family moved closer to other families, the picture became more complex. Another system developed as the individual family systems were brought together. Boundaries between the families (physical, social, psychological) had to be negotiated so that the integrity of the individual family culture was protected and the survival needs of the new collective could be met. The contracts became more elaborate relative to division of labor and behavioral expectations.

The commitment to monitor one's own behavior and delay or deny gratification for the collective good is based on the implicit assumption and promise of reciprocity—that is, others will similarly deny themselves. (Theories of personality have evolved from this elementary concept.) This is one framework for viewing deception and, hence, accountability. That is, you are accountable to me according to the terms of our social contract, which requires something of both of us. If I do my part and you only pretend to do your part, I am being deceived. To this point accountability had primarily survival and efficiency connotations. When social contracts became more complex, the terms less explicit, and the control of those contracts by individuals reduced, accountability took on more specific moral meanings involving the character, will, motivation, and responsibility of people. I can see if you fed your family. I cannot see the lie you told. I cannot even see the "good" intention you had in deceiving me.

Society developed elaborate and complex means of protecting itself from deception and insuring honesty. This insurance, over time, was institutionalized in a system of checks and balances and collective recourse. The collective behavioral and attitudinal axioms became law, and procedures were established for purging the offender, the offended, and the collective. A legal system emerged.

Collective rituals and myths were developed to cement the social order. In time other needs and collective functions such as education were grouped and institutionalized. Initially the school was a natural extension of the family, sharing the same beliefs, myths, values, rituals, and attitudes toward the management of children. Family and school were different parts of the same cultural fabric. The parents and teachers shared responsibility for mediating the culture of the collective.

Current patterns of behavior, divisions of labor, and relationships are considerably more elaborate and complex. The agreements or contracts, for example, which used to be sufficient to insure the orderly flow of life are now negotiated and managed in very different ways. They now frequently have to incorporate inconsistent or even conflicting value systems. They rely on subtle signals such as hinting as well as on formal legalistic boundaries to work satisfactorily. The following is a description of one small segment of life which illustrates some of the dimensions of such contracts.

A Contemporary Microsystem

Most people have a line item in their budget for transportation because transportation is a personal need. The car is a program for meeting that need. The car requires several things to run—gasoline, oil, mechanical integrity. If the car's needs are not met then the person has no transportation and, therefore, the basic need for transportation is not met.

There is a system to monitor and maintain the program (car) that is meeting the person's need (transportation). The person drives the car and knows the high correlation between the reading on the gas gauge and the distance the car can be expected to run. He monitors two things as the car is used: (1) gas, and (2) the general well-being of the car (absence of alarming sounds or movements, presence of normal motor sounds, workability of steering, braking, gearing, and accelerating mechanisms, and their correlations).

The driver needs transportation and the car needs gas, which the driver knows where and how to obtain. When gas is asked for, the attendant usually checks the oil. If the car needs oil, the attendant sees that the oil is put in. This is an automatic decision, based on knowledge of the relationship between oil, the running ability, and the life of the motor. If the windshield is dirty, the attendant cleans it. This has to do with another dimension of the transportation system. That is, the car does not need a clean windshield to run better but the driver needs it to see where to drive.

The attendant also checks the tires. If one or more needs replacing, the attendant tells the driver about it. This is a more subjective decision with additional implications. First, the safety of the driver and others is involved in the decision about tires, which is not the case, for example, with gas. Second, tires cost more than gas. Third, the criteria for judging and making the decision are not quite as clear cut. This is a shared decision. If the decision is to replace the tire(s), another set of decisions gets involved regarding the type of tires that will be bought.

Notice the car's regular need for gas and the driver's ability to monitor that need to maintain a system for transportation bring the car to another monitor—the station attendant.

The other need the driver monitors is the general well-being of the car He then makes preliminary decisions about the nature of those needs and how to meet them. Being a layman, the driver usually decides to refer to a professional mechanic for a diagnosis. The treatment (repair) prescribed must be weighed in terms of several criteria, the largest of which is usually cost. Although other opinions and estimates can be obtained, a decision must be made. The equation is—given the need for transportation and the driver's decision to meet that need with a certain type of car—what are the costs (losses) and benefits (gains) of (1) repairing the car as compared to (2) trading it for another. The decision has subjective criteria, such as esthetics, as well as objective criteria, such as money.

This is a description of a common situation in which there are identified needs, alternatives (programs) available for meeting those needs, monitors for the alternative selected, criteria for monitoring, and decision points for maintaining the program to meet the need. Figure 7.1 outlines the elements of accountability as described in this situation.

This is an interesting and instructive system to observe for the purpose

FIGURE 7.1. Elements of Accountability.

of comparison to other, more complex, systems such as education. There are obviously some basic differences, however, between the system described here and the educational system. First is the explicit, objective, universal (within the system) nature of the need. Second is the clarity with which most of the success criteria can be stated. Third is the location of the monitors. Fourth is the locus of decision points about (1) the nature of the need, (2) how to meet the need, (3) how to monitor the program, and (4) when and how to change the program. Fifth is the implicit direction of accountability.

The program (car) and all asked to become involved with the car are accountable to the consumer, the person with the need. That person is satisfied so long as the need for transportation is met with the type vehicle that is wanted at a cost the person can afford and is willing to pay.

Accountability today is tremendously more complex than in the simple frontier nuclear family culture. More people are involved and their relationships are infinitely more difficult to understand. What it means to be accountable is closely related to what it means to be responsible. This is basically understood in terms of the beliefs, values, purposes, and roles of people in certain environments or situations.

There now exist many environments for each person. Books have been written on situational ethics suggesting that rules are time and place specific. Ecological theory has obtained considerable visibility in the social sciences, in part, at least, because it relates conceptually to the issues of the pluralistic and fragmented environments of human beings. It views human behavior as a function of the total network of a particular setting. That is, *who* one is and *how* one behaves *vary* from setting to setting.

Models of Accountability

Historically we have attended more to the structural arrangements for serving handicapped children (institutions, special classes in public schools) and the economic survival of these arrangements than we have to the philosophical premises and payoff for children in those arrangements. Theory, to the extent it has existed at all, has been mostly a matter of the particular professional orientation of the persons in charge of the arrangement. As money has become available we have *added* services and staff with different theoretical orientations. The end result in many instances has been a shoddy theory and practices which have no apparent internal integration.

Several general theoretical orientations vie for prominence in our current programming, including the behavioral, psychodynamic, biogenetic, sociological, and ecological. These orientations are manifested in different service or departmental organizations. We have departments of training and education, medicine, social service, rehabilitation, cottage life; special programs such as engineered classroom and resource centers; and specialized individual treatments such as psychotherapy and tutoring. We have classrooms, sheltered workshops, and halfway houses, projects to stimulate babies, and projects to provide models for children. We have elaborate psychometric systems to detect and quantify differences which we expect to become disability. We have much, and money for more. How do we assess where we are, the utility of what we have, the gaps?

The following discussion reviews several models to illustrate the development of our thinking about programs for children and the evaluation of these programs. The models are examined in terms of the purpose, nature, and uses of evaluative data in order to clarify the issue of accountability.

From the mid to late sixties it was popular to try to apply the "medical model" to education. The way in which a physician diagnoses the medical needs of a child and makes decisions about the treatment to be given to the child is shown in Figure 7.2. Figure 7.3, the linear mediation model, shows the medical model applied to education. The educator acts as a broker for the child. Given funds (resources) for the child, the educator makes decisions about the nature of the child's educational needs and how best to mediate the resources to meet these needs.

There are basic differences between medicine and education, however, which make general application of the medical model difficult. First, in medicine the flow of money is more directly linked between the person receiving the service and the person giving it. The service provided by the physician is paid for by the recipient or by someone directly responsible for the recipient (family or guardian). The service provided by the physician is monitored by the patient or those responsible for him over time, and the continued use of the service is related to its efficacy. Thus the physician is accountable to the patient and/or the patient's family. Second, the medical model has a more objective, scientific base. The indicators of the problems (symptoms), the diagnosis, and the treatment are more objective in their determination and assessment than those encountered with educational and social problems. Both educators and physicians approach a child with certain perceptual filters which are a product of their personal philosophical orientations, their training, and the data they collect about the problem. The physician, however, has a more objective basis on which to evaluate

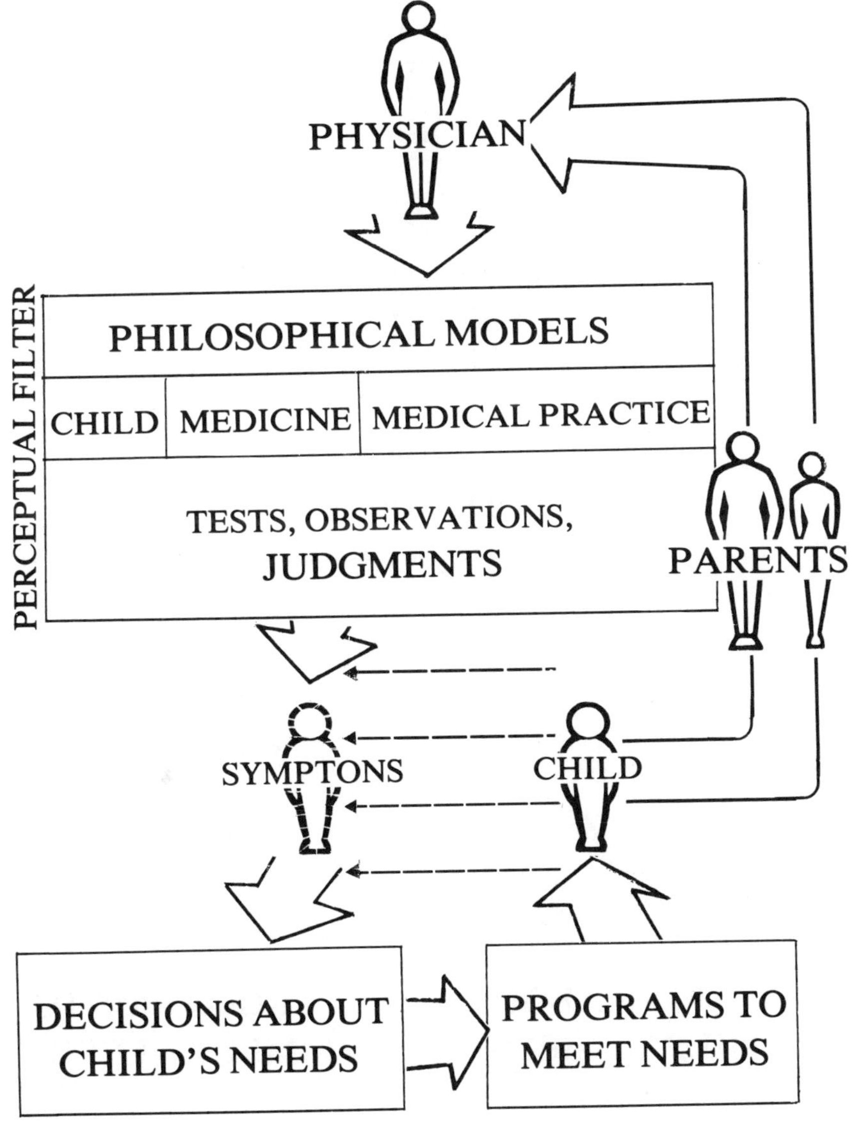

FIGURE 7.2. Medical Model.

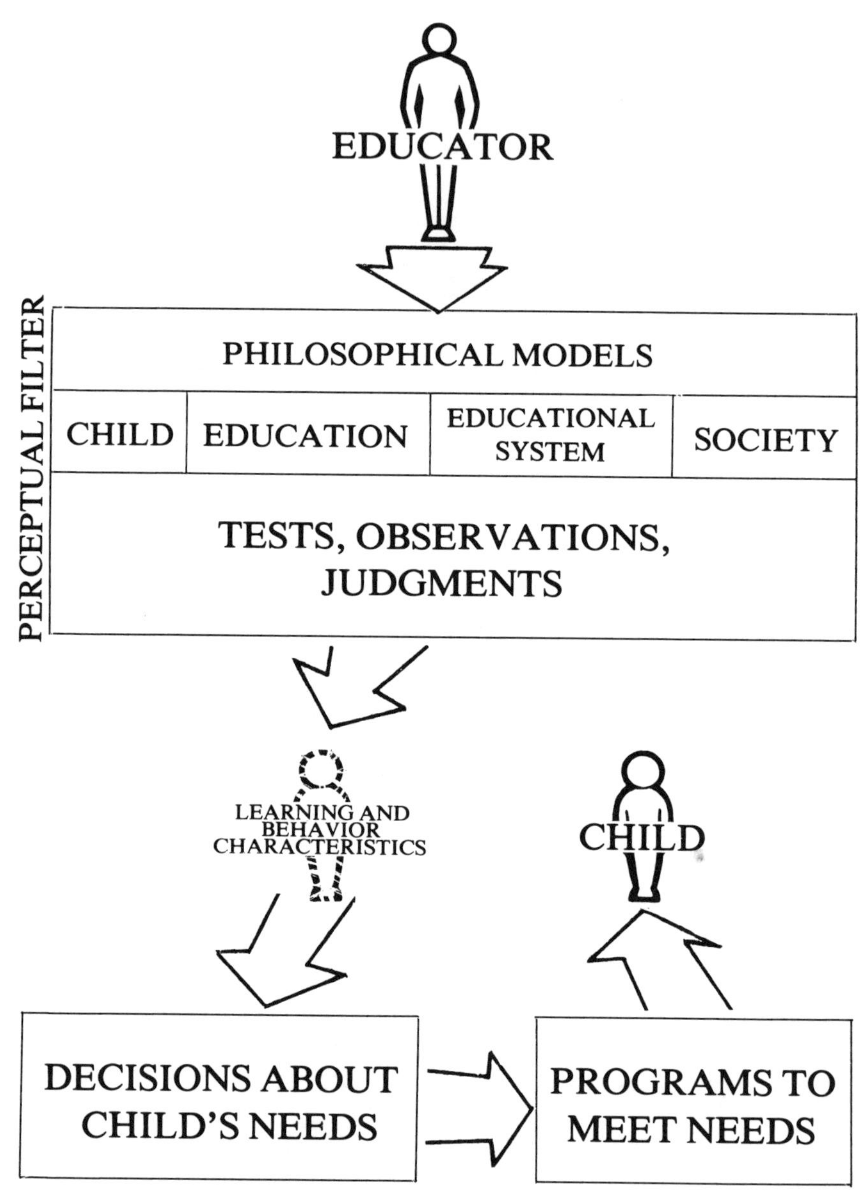

FIGURE 7.3. Linear Mediation Model.

his or her program for the child. We have already seen how the various theoretical orientations in education produce different programs for the child.

There is, then, a fundamental difference in the task implied by the two models. The problems and needs that the educator wants to uncover usually cannot be reduced to organic terms. The existential question of "who is man" cannot be reduced to "what is man." The linear mediation model is oriented to changing the child/environment encounter.

In retrospect we can also see that when the medical model is applied to education there is no evaluation, no provision for determining the validity of the program decisions. There is a large margin for error in the philosophical model of the educator. The needs of the child are not given but are derived from the educator's model. The translations of needs into programmatic response are assumed to be valid, an assumption we now know cannot be accepted without question.

The line administrative model as shown in Figure 7.4 is useful in examining accountability structures. The local school is accountable for the child's progress, reporting to the school system, which then, in some manner, reports to the state, which in turn has some accountability to the federal government. Funds flow downward from the higher levels. Accountability is articulated upward, away from the child, directly in terms of the administrative system administering the funds.

When guidelines for the expenditure of federal funds are added, the accountability structure changes only slightly, as shown in Figure 7.5. The administrative structure becomes a conduit for the exchange of funds and data relative to the guidelines. Again, accountability is away from the child.

Figure 7.6 elaborates on the decision-making process which stems from funding guidelines or criteria. There is evaluation and feedback, but the program is accountable to the assumed needs of the child, as articulated in the guidelines. Accountability will be closer to the chld *if* the guidelines represent his interests. But the evaluation itself does not question the criteria set down in the guidelines and their fit with the needs of the child. Once again, accountability is away from the child and toward the guidelines.

Figure 7.7 represents the structure that would exist if we could direct accountability toward those who pay the bill—the taxpayer. This is essentially the same accountability structure as that represented by the medical model. The parents, as the taxpayers, provide money for services to their child. As in medical care, the taxpayer has a right to expect a return on his investment. However, complex bureaucracy makes this accountability link difficult to establish and experience.

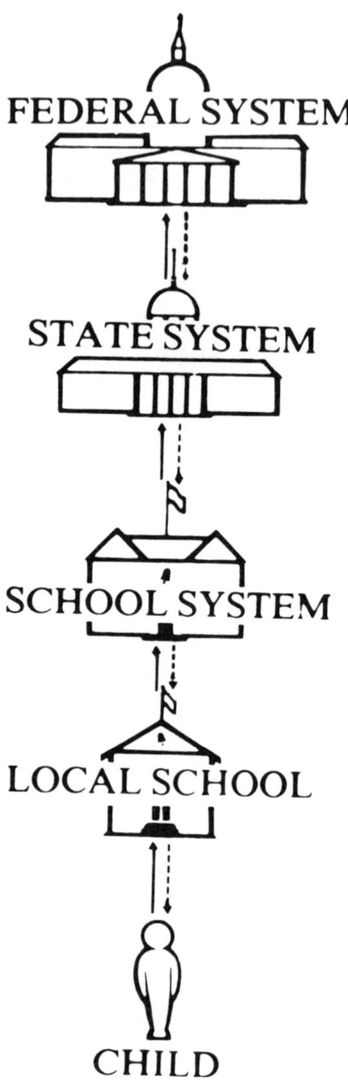

FIGURE 7.4. Line Administrative Model.

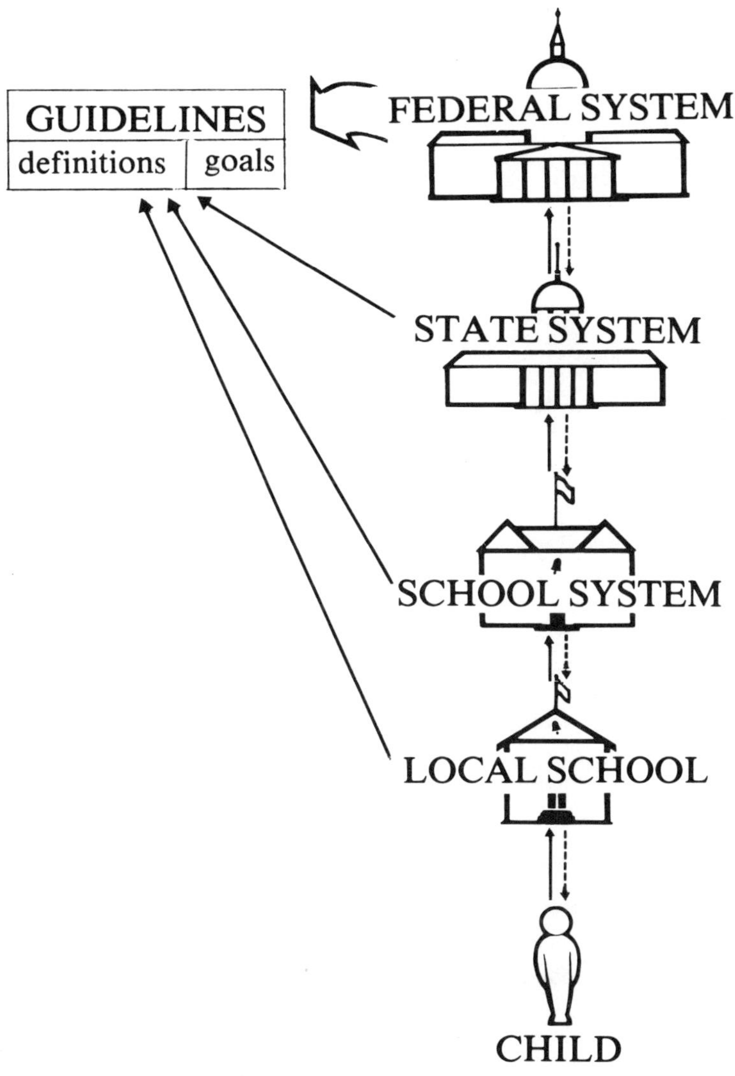

FIGURE 7.5. Guidelines for Accountability and Federal Expenditures.

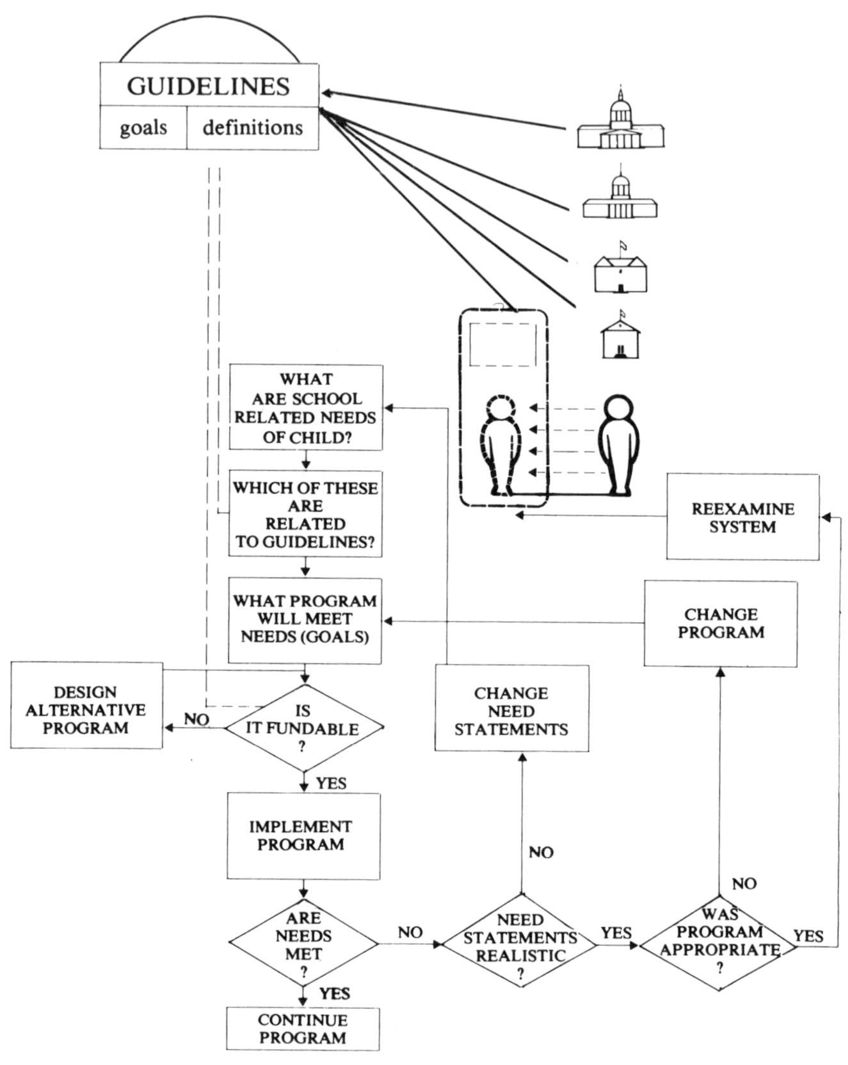

FIGURE 7.6. Decision-making Process and Funding Guidelines.

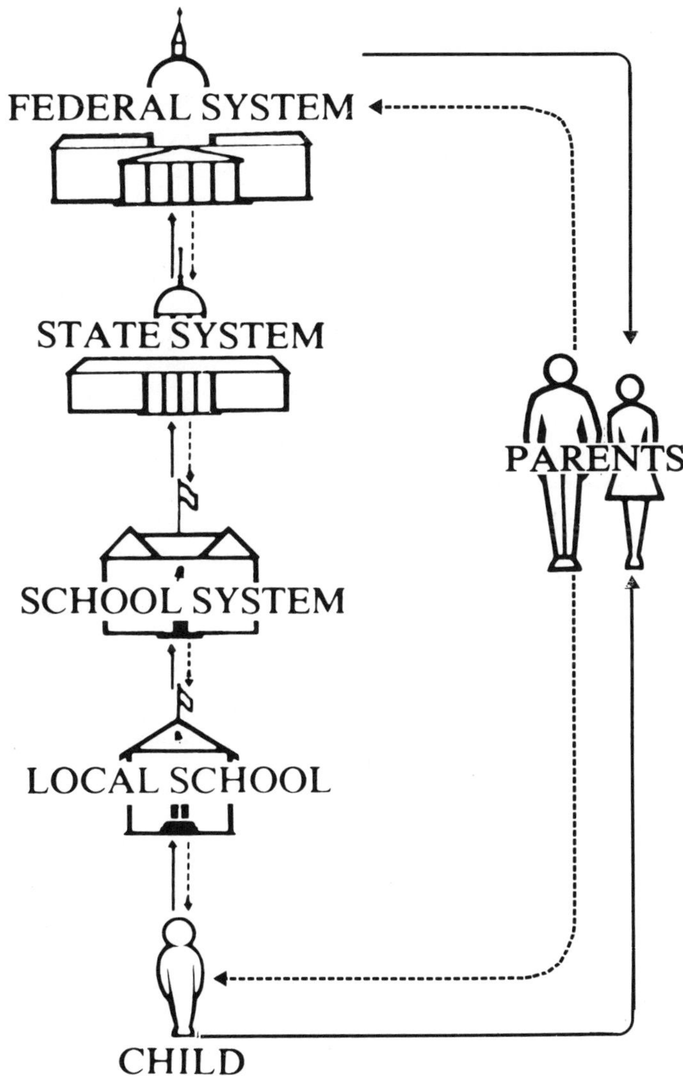

FIGURE 7.7. Taxpayer Model.

Figure 7.8 represents the line administrative model adapted to provide accountability in the direction of the child for whom the funds are available. This accountability structure represents the intent of consumer-oriented human-service law. The line administrative model, however, does not suggest a perspective that facilitates effective evaluation.

Figure 7.9 suggests the kind of view of the child and educational program needed for honest evaluation. Effective evaluation must monitor the child as he interacts with his environment and his educational or therapeutic program. The child should be a part of the goal setting and monitoring process. Evaluation must consider the child's goals as well as the goals of the environment and of the program.

Figure 7.10 suggests the kind of decision-making process that evaluation, within the framework of Figure 7.9, would follow. The child's goals are a part of the program criteria. Note that there is constant examination of the fit between the child's goals, the environment's goals, and program. This accountability structure differs from others in that problems outside the immediate program—problems with the child, the environment, or the child-environment interactions—are conceptualized and considered as part of the evaluation.

Accountability structures built around this kind of understanding of the interaction of the child with his or her environment acknowledge the problems involved in educational programming in a pluralistic society. An understanding of the ecology of the individual child can insure some measure of validity in interventions into that child's life.

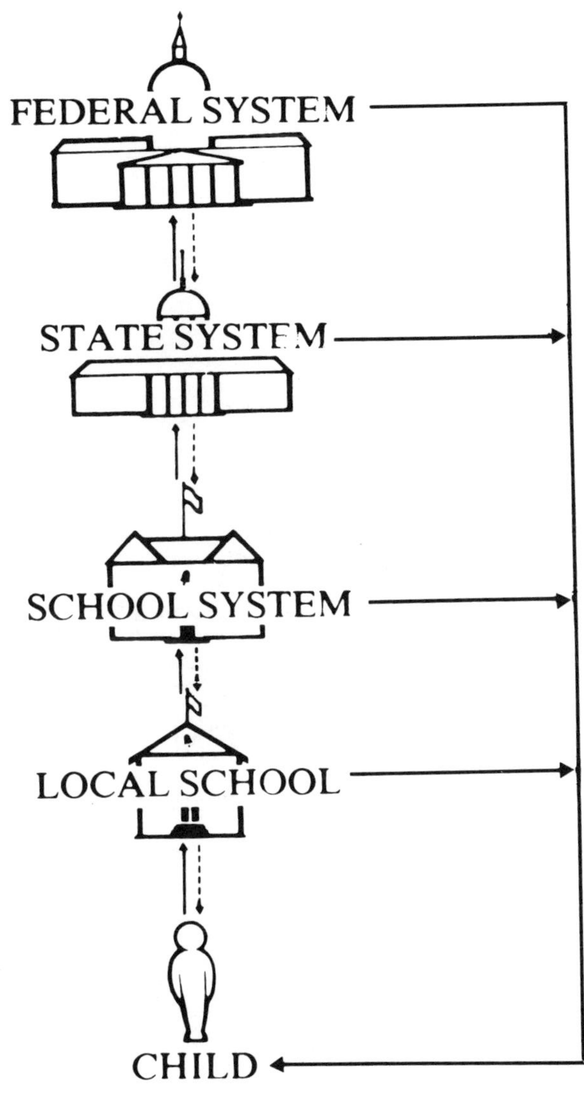

FIGURE 7.8. Line Administrative Model With Accountability Toward the Child

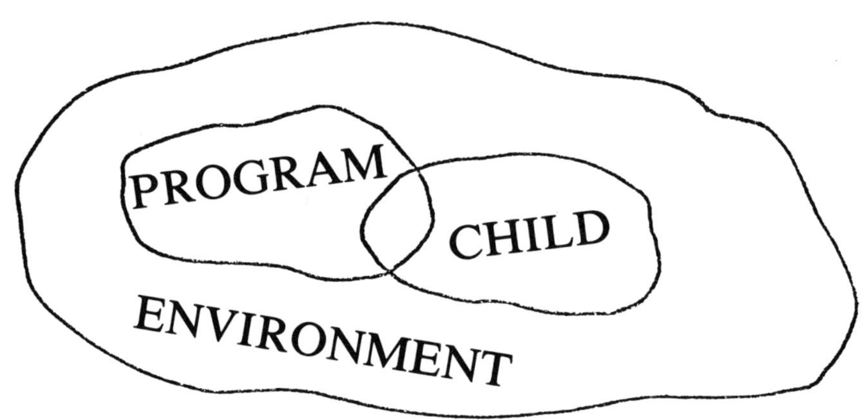

FIGURE 7.9. View Necessary for Effective Evaluation.

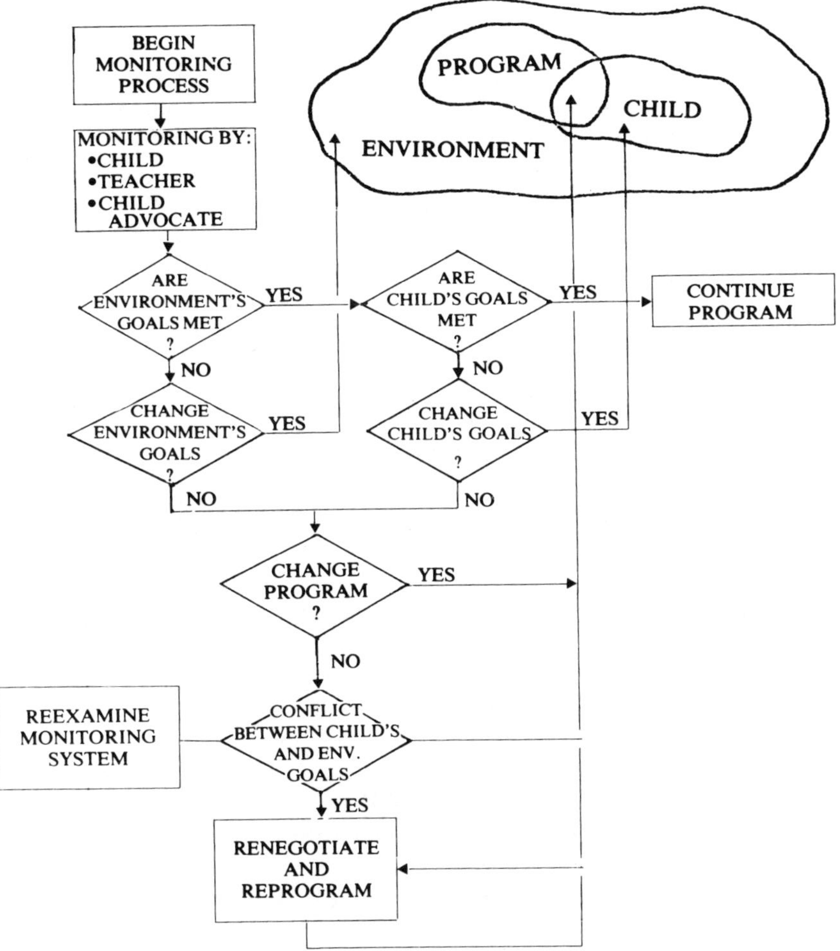

FIGURE 7.10. Decison-making Process.

The Information Problem

One aspect of the accountability issue concerns the *validity* of the information available to those who, in good faith, make decisions that affect other people's lives. Validity, in this case, has to do with two questions: (1) is the information accurate? and (2) is the *apparent* meaning true?

The question of accuracy is based on methodological considerations: Is the data on hand observed, recorded, and reported without error? Does the data, technically, justify the inferences made by those who use it? There are rules for determining the technical accuracy of data.

The question of apparent meaning is very different and is concerned with the theory being used for "making sense out of" or organizing the data. It has to do with the nature of the variables and their relationship to each other. Is what the data "says," according to the assumptions made about the reality being sampled, reasonable? The truth of the assertions or inferences is related to how responsible the sense is we make out of it. The *sense we see* is the basis on which we make decisions. Is that sense, as we see it, reasonably consistent with the experienced sense of the other whose life is affected by our decisions?

The question of validity raised in this context goes beyond, but is not totally distinguished from, the appropriate domain of science. The use of information has both technical and ethical implications. Ethics, then, should be a basic topic in considering the question of accountability.

The meaning of social data cannot be separated from the setting in which that data was observed or collected. Data are the events that occur in settings. As the events become regular and predictable, they become programs. Programs and settings become associated with a regularity that is observable and is perceived as routine, "the way things should be," or normal. The regular activity or programs associated with a place in the way people think about it may be considered institutional. This view of institutions is helpful in considering the nature and meaning of the data we collect for the purposes of accountability.

The following material describes a framework for examining behavior which illustrates conceptual and empirical issues involved in understanding behavior. The theory of behavior used in the analysis views individual behavior as a segment of a transaction in a collective. This ecological view of behavior argues logically that removing behavior from its transactional context is to effectively lose the meaning of the behavior. Behavioral excess or behavioral efficiency relative to the role of student, for example, must be understood in the setting where the role of student has specific meaning; otherwise, the excesses and deficiencies have no specific meaning. Not only is there space-specific cultural meaning to the behavior which has explanatory utility relative to the occurrence of the behavior, but there is also time-sequence-across-space meaning. The following discussion provides a framework for analyzing transactions.

The critical time frame for understanding child behavior in ecological terms is not an entire childhood, but rather a 24-hour day which can be repeated. The time frame, a boundary for transactional opportunity, and not the content of the transactions, is replicated. Within the 24-hour time frame, there are several critical time units which may be isolated on the basis of the place in which behavior occurs and the directionality of the behavior. Some of the time-space-directionality units are child specific in their orientation; that is, they occur because the child is there. Others are more generally understood relative to the microculture of which the child is a part. The following classification seems useful for ecological analytic purposes: (1) time frame, (2) space culture, (3) directionality or purpose, and (4) interactions.

Using this frame of reference, then, one would examine the purposes and spacetime transactions starting when the child wakes up in the morning. The analysis would follow until the child left that home setting. The time frame might be from 6:30 to 7:45 A.M. The purposes, for example, would be generally to prepare to leave that setting to move into another. In order to accomplish this, other goals must be accomplished, such as, getting out of bed, getting dressed, eating. In addition to these behaviors in preparation for leaving the home setting, there would be other behavior relative to affirming and maintaining the physical space according to the standards of that setting such as making beds and washing dishes. Talking and kissing goodbye would be other categories of behavior. It should be clear that all of these factors would vary among home settings. The child coming out of the home next door in the morning would probably have experienced a more similar ecology than a child coming out of a home across town.

For some children the transaction over time *between* settings, such as between the home and the school, represents a unique ecological setting in his day. A school bus would be such an example.

A next major place with its own set of purposes in which a child interacts over time is the public school. The six or seven hours a child spends in the public school could be further divided into smaller time frames relative to activities and the interactions around those activities to accomplish more specific goals of that institution.

This type of time-space-interaction-purpose analysis could be extended over an entire 24-hour period. There would be some consistency over days in each unit analyzed relative to a particular child. That is, the 6:30 to 7:45 time frame for any particular child would have some consistency over days because it is the integrity of that particular microculture that is being examined. After there is some basic understanding of the workings of each unit relative to a child, it would then be possible to examine these units for other children for purpose of comparison. It would further be possible to examine a flow through these units on any given day for one child and then make comparisons of such flow for other children.

The framework for analysis proposed here provides some basis for collecting data on and understanding behavior in ecological terms. It provides some empirical basis for examining, for example, the way in which exchanges in one setting are "wired" into or related to exchanges in another setting by means of the person who moves across those settings. It provides some basis for examining culture-specific or institution-specific deviance. It provides some basis for examining the culture of child development. It may provide some clues as to what arrangements work best for which children and why. This shifts the deficit camera from the child to the arrangements with which the child conducts his or her daily developmental business.

Obviously this type of data is not easily obtained. There are several existing data collection strategies that might be considered useful in supplying the type of data required for the framework proposed. Participant observation would be one obvious strategy. This certainly would not be ideal because of the invasion by the participant observer, which has serious ethical and legal as well as methodological problems. Theoretically, over time it should be possible to develop microculture time frames and purpose statements. The difficulty would be in obtaining accurate transactional data. One interesting possibility is to develop sufficient understandings of transactional nets or patterns so that limited behavioral samples would be sufficient for constructing the transactional patterns through inferential procedures. We do not yet know enough about discrete behavior or about transactions or the relationship between the two to make such inferences based on such limited data. There are several interaction models and data collection procedures which seem, on the surface, to fit the transactional model criteria proposed above. The development of such a model would be crucial to this ecological framework. The most parsimonious approach to the problem, given the enormous amount of data involved and the model construction work to be done, would probably be through computer simulations.

SUMMARY

In this chapter deinstitutionalization has been discussed in terms of the problems of institutional accountability. An interaction perspective was presented as a useful way to conceptualize the situation from which data is collected for the purpose of making program decisions. The total ecology of the person was described as the appropriate perspective from which conclusions are drawn regarding the well-being of a person or the nature of difficulty. Neither legislative guidelines nor static philosophical models can provide an analysis of problems that fit all persons in all settings. Rather, decisions should be made close to the person involved and reviewed regularly as to how well the person-program-environment fit is working.

Deinstitutionalization must be viewed as a process that counters existing institutional processes. Here it has been suggested that a major part of the acountability problem is embedded in: (1) philosophical perspectives that define people and problems, (2) the structures that give us data consistent with those perspectives, and (3) the processes by which decisions get made based on that data, apart from the people, or benefactors, affected by those decisions.

8

The Law

H. RUTHERFORD TURNBULL III, ANN P. TURNBULL

A NEW AND MAJOR GOAL in the field of mental retardation is deinstitutionalization. As used here, this term refers to the return of persons residing in centers for the mentally retarded to community or home environments.

A compelling impetus in the deinstitutionalization movement is the assertion of legal rights on behalf of institutionalized retarded individuals. While the movement and this impetus are commendable and worthy of society's best efforts, there are unresolved implications in the deinstitutionalization process. Some of these are raised below, not as objections to deinstitutionalization, which we support where it is in the best interests of the retarded person; rather, they are discussed as considerations directly affecting the retarded individual.

We believe that placement should be in the least restrictive environment, and that, as a matter of preference (based on the needs of many institutionalized retarded persons, the development of community acceptance of the retarded, the savings to the public fisc, and the development of a retarded person's maximum capacities), community placement is more desirable than institutional placement. We believe, however, that retarded persons should have the right to choose where they live, whether in the community or in an institution, if they are informed of the consequences of the choice and legally and developmentally capable of making it. We also believe that legal procedures, generally conceptualized under the principles of procedured due process, should be brought into play whenever a decision to deinstitutionalize a person is to be considered, to the end that the person will have an opportunity to express his choice and test the proposed action of the mental retardation professionals, i.e., their

124

decision to deinstitutionalize him. Finally, we believe that a decision on the merits of community or institutional placement should weigh not only the interests of the institution, the community, and the public, but also and more importantly the interests and preferences of the affected retarded person, to the end that society take into account (as it has not often done when a person is institutionalized) the retarded person's own interests and preferences, not merely society's.

It is anomalous to speak of the law and deinstitutionalization without at the same time speaking about the law and institutionalization, for what is at stake in either is a decision as to the person's appropriate life style, a decision as to what is the best placement of that person, whether in an institution or within the community in some smaller institution. Accordingly, many of the legal issues that are discussed in this chapter have relevance to both deinstitutionalization and institutionalization.

DUE PROCESS

As a general rule, a "voluntary" admission of a mentally retarded person lawfully can be made by the parents or guardian of the mentally retarded person, subject only to the approval or withholding of approval by the institution's administrators. At the same time, the decision to deinstitutionalize the person frequently is also lawfully made only by the administrators of the deinstitutionalizing facility, the person's parents or guardian, and the administrators of the community facility to which the person is being transferred. Rarely in these decisions does the retarded person have a right, or even an opportunity, to make a decision for himself, to affect a decision being made for him by others, or to even participate in the decision-making process—when the decision vitally affects his life style, his "best" placement, where he will be, and who will take care of him in what situations and surroundings.

Recently in an institution for the mentally retarded, a thirty-year-old resident, who is severely physically handicapped, commented, "I am not trying to brag but I am not mentally retarded. Do you think I should be in this institution?" Upon investigation, it was discovered that he has an IQ of 77 and, arguably, he should not be in an institution for the retarded. Although the placement decision was made on his behalf and seemingly in his best interests by his parents, he was excluded from the decision-making as to his most suitable living arrangement. This particular individual has written letters to legislators and state agency officials and informed them that he has been inappropriately institutionalized. He does not understand the legal details related to due process; however, he clearly understands the basic premise that he should have a right to participate in the decision concerning his life style.

Considerations of extending due process to retarded residents in regard to discharge can also work in the other direction. When a young adult residing in a residential institution was approached as to the possibility of leaving the institution and living in a community group home, he was outraged and insulted. He was happy with his institutional life and clearly wanted to remain in the institution. The decision was made by professionals that a community placement would be more "normalizing"; however, he did not want to live in a community environment and was satisfied with his present degree of "normalization."

Many mental retardation professionals would argue that the retarded person's decision was uninformed and made without adequate community exposure and that proper exposure would result in his desire to leave the institution. However, this argument imposes the professionals' values on the retarded person. Does the retarded person have the right to refuse exposure to the community if he is satisfied with his institutional placement? In a somewhat similar situation, a retarded person was discharged to a community-based group home—a fact, and a place, he found repugnant. Although the group home parents and other community people attempted to act in his best interest and to provide a supportive and stimulating environment, he nevertheless was unhappy and begged to be returned to the institution. When his wishes were not honored, he acted out his frustration until he was allowed to return to the institution. Extending due process (in his and other cases) requires carefully considering the interests of the retarded person and not blindly adopting normalization principles and applying them in a way that might be irrelevant or detrimental to a particular individual. Who defined normalization principles? Was due process extended to retarded persons in specifying the principles through which they felt normalization could be achieved? Are we listening mainly to the opinions of mental retardation professionals?

The law has denied a right of opportunity to participate because the retarded person has traditionally been considered unable to participate in those decisions, and because the law has assumed that the person's parents and the administrators of the institution in which the person is placed will act in his best interests. Yet it is perfectly clear that the best interests of the retarded person are not always the same as and, indeed, frequently conflict with the best interests of the parents or the administrators.

If there is a conflict of interests, then it is highly inappropriate for the law to sanction any process which excludes the mentally retarded person or his independent advocate from the decision-making process. When a person is on trial for a criminal offense and pleads temporary insanity at the time of the offense or the inability to stand trial for the offense because of mental incapacity at the time of trial, he is not required to do so through his own effort but is entitled to a lawyer to assist him. It seems a bit far fetched to argue the criminal analogy with respect to the placement of a retarded person, but the considerations are the same. A decision is made to place a person (in one case in a prison or in an institution for the mentally ill, in the other case in a mental retardation facility); the person is not capable—or is not fully capable—of participating in and arguing his interests during the decision-making process; and the public's interests are represented (at the criminal trial by the prosecuting officials and in the placement process by the parents and by the administrators of the facilities). The crucial difference is that in the criminal proceeding the mentally ill person has a right to have somebody appointed by the court or selected by him to argue his interests, whereas in the placement of a mentally retarded person that person has no right to have a person appointed by anyone or selected by him to argue his interests. The decision to place the mentally retarded person in an institution or a community-based facility is analogous to, and the same considerations in those placements are involved in, placement in the parental home, a foster home, a group home, or with friends of the retarded person or his family.

The law is inadequate in other procedural matters. What process is followed in a decision to institutionalize or deinstitutionalize? Is it a quasi-judicial process in which the various and conflicting interests and claims can be advanced and impartially resolved? Who has a right to be or in fact is involved in that process? Is a judgment made on the basis of all the facts involving not only the retarded person but also his family, the institutions, and their suitability for him? Are the facts presented to and reviewed by an independent, objective person? Must his decision be made solely on the basis of the facts presented to him? What are the operative facts? Finally, does an appeal lie from that person's decision? If so, to whom—an impartial review agency? Almost without exception the answers to these questions are negative.

In practically all but one instance in which the public, through government, takes action with respect to the liberty or property of an individual, the law has insisted on "due process"—a right to confront the public or its representatives and be heard by an impartial arbiter before the public takes action with respect to the individual. The exception has been the decision to place a person in an institution for the mentally retarded or to deinstitutionalize him. The wholly inadequate state of the law now is that, as a general rule, due process is granted only with respect to the placement of a retarded person in special education programs, but not the far more confining, liberty-depriving placement in institutional or community-based facilities or in parental or surrogate parental homes.

The many persons involved in a placement decision—parents, social workers, institutional administrators, psychologists, physicans, teachers, and sometimes, in rare instances, judges—have enjoyed substantial immunity in the placement process, with the exception of the judges whose decisions are at least usually appellable to higher courts. Their decisions, both individually and collectively, have frequently been accepted by the persons affected; more often, their decisions have simply been implemented without the affected person's being involved or having a chance to approve the decision, participate in it, or object to it. This immunity, however, may soon become obsolete, for litigation is under way challenging the placement decisions, with parents and legal advocates for retarded persons suing the decision-making professionals on the grounds, among others, that due process has not been adhered to in making the decision.

PROFESSIONAL LIABILITY

A second kind of litigation challenging the professionals' immunity from legal procedures and exculpability from the effects of their decisions will be forthcoming—the lawsuit by the affected person or by his legal representatives (parents, guardians, or next of kin) based on the torts committed by the professionals—malpractice, negligence, or tortious interference with the person. Consider, for example, the case of a trainable mongoloid child who, for each of the twelve years of her life, has been in an institution and knows no life except an institutional life. The decison to place the child in the institution was made by her parents on the advice of a pediatrician who admits to having no training with respect to mental retardation and who made the decision based on his general knowledge of retardation, and particularly of mongolism—"these children simply can't learn anything, they can't be trained, they will die soon, and they ought to be out of the home." Advice such as this may be grounds for a lawsuit for professional malpractice. Malpractice litigation now bedevils the physicians. If that kind of advice had been given by a psychologist instead of a physician, it is not likely that it would have been actionable by malpractice litigation. But surely the standards of professionalism that the law applies to one profession should be applied to others, especially where the medical professionals frequently participate jointly with other mental retardation professionals in placement decisions. It is safe to predict that malpractice litigation will soon be brought against social workers, institutional administrators, psychologists, and educators whose professional advice is sought and followed in placement decisons. If they give unprofessional advice, they should be held accountable for their failure to give advice measuring up to and consistent with standards of professionalism in their respective fields.

The following passage is quoted from a report of a psychological evaluation conducted by a licensed clinical psychologist: "This young girls with an IQ of 52 will never be able to do so much as write her own name or cross the street by herself. Institutionalization should be carefully considered before the parents become further emotionally involved." Obviously, this psychologist did not realize the capabilities of a person with a 52 IQ. Luckily, the parents of this child failed to take this advice, and the child is presently achieving at the third level in a public school special education class. Where would the child be now if the advice of the psychologist had been followed? Would there have been grounds for a malpractice suit?

Determining exactly what constitutes professional malpractice by a psychologist, an administrator, or a teacher may be difficult, but the glaring cases of malpractice are not difficult to identify, and they will initially set the standards for professional competency for money damages. An additional remedy must be granted. It should consist of a review of the decision that was grounds for malpractice and an effort to correct the wrong decision, remedy the improper placement, and secure appropriate placement. If the law will hold the decision-makers accountable for their placement decisions, then no longer will it be possible for an administrator who seeks to reduce the population of his institution to single out a retarded resident and require that person to leave the institution without first making a decision that is professionally supportable and based on all the relevant evidence, not necessarily in the best interests of the administrator, the institution, or the parents of the affected person.

THE DUTY OF PREPARATION

A third emerging legal problem is that of defining the roles an institution and the community play in preparing parents, a resident, the receiving facility, and the community in general for deinstitutionalization. It should not be legally sufficient that a decision to deinstitutionalize is made if the decision is not able to be properly administered in the best interests of the retarded person.

Take, for example, the parents of the previously mentioned twelve-year-old mongoloid girl who was institutionalized at birth. They have rarely visited their child, their teenage children do not know they have a retarded younger sibling, and the family is totally unprepared emotionally and physically to have the twelve-year-old retarded child at home. The child has learned the relevant skills essential for home and community living, and the institution is ready to discharge her. Does the institution have the right to discharge a child to a family who clearly cannot handle the situation? What are the institution's duties in family preparation? If a child returns to his family and the family later discovers that it cannot effectively cope with home placement, what recourse does the family have?

The duty of preparation also applies to training the retarded person. What happens to the retarded adult who is discharged to the community with no prior training in sex education? If he commits a sex offense without being provided previous sexuality training by the institution, should the institution be held legally accountable? As an example of the need to prepare the community, consider the eighteen-year-old who, having returned to the community, bought several bottles of beer at a local tavern and was arrested for public intoxication. The officer testified that he looked "funny," slurred his words, and walked awkwardly. The court, on this evidence alone and without benefit of a breathalyzer or blood test, convicted him. But there is a hitch: the young man always looked "funny" (he was mongoloid), he always slurred his words (he had a speech impediment), and he always walked awkwardly (he had gross motor difficulty). He was not drunk, simply retarded. However, the law enforcement officials in this particular community were unaware of characteristics associated with mental retardation. When an advocate contacted the arresting officer to speak in defense of the retarded person, the advocate's explanation was discounted as "hollow excuses."

Counseling with parents, making preparations in the community, working with the receiving facility, and training the retarded person himself for community placement are not yet recognized as legal responsibilities of a deinstitutionalizing facility. Nor will these become legal responsibilities until legislative or administrative regulations are adopted requiring preparation for deinstitutionalization or until the courts hold that the professionals at the deinstitutionalizing facility and community-based facilities are professionally responsible to carry out those duties and may be held accountable in a malpractice action for their failure to perform them or may be restrained from deinstitutionalizing a person if they have not complied with the duty of preparation.

THE OBLIGATION OF EQUIVALENCY

A related concern deals with the availability or unavailability of services in the community. Again it should not be legally sufficient that a retarded person is discharged to the community if there is not available in the community the same kind and quality of services available to him at the discharging institution.

Many people falsely assume that any community is well suited to provide a continuum of services to the retarded person and that the community is unequivocally the most appropriate placement. What about the community that provides no educational programs to moderately, severely, and profoundly retarded individuals? In some cases of deinstitutionalization, the retarded person has left an educational program or a sheltered workshop in the institution and has been discharged to a community environment in which programs are unavailable. Has his life style improved or has he lost opportunities for development?

Undeniably, services at institutions and in the community are not what they should or can be. But community services should at least be the quantitative and qualitative equivalents of services at the discharging institution. If they are not, the retarded person arguably has been adversely affected by a governmental decision by being denied the same quantitative and qualititive services in the community as he had in the institution, and therefore has been injured and has a right to be recompensed for his injury. Some court decisions in right-to-treatment litigation hold that a person who is institutionalized on account of his retardation has a constitutional right to treatment as a quid pro quo of his being institutionalized. It requires only a small extension of this right to hold that person discharged into the community retains the right, although he is no longer institutionalized, as long as he can demonstrate a need for treatment. It would be not only unfortunate but also constitutionally doubtful if the state could avoid its duty of treatment by deinstitutionalizing a person.

If this extension of the right to treatment can be made, the effect will be to insure that an administrative discharge of a patient can be judicially reviewed. Even if procedural due process standards are complied with, the right-to-treatment argument will allow a patient to argue and prove that he still has a need for treatment. If the community into which he is discharged has community or home-based facilities, then perhaps his need for treatment can be met in that form.

The tough case, however, occurs when the two choices are total maximum institutionalization or complete discharge from treatment and control. In that situation the retarded person, if he can prove he is harmed (deprived of treatment) by the discharge, should be allowed to return to or remain in the institution.

If this sort of lawsuit is allowed, administrators of mental retardation facilities might defend their actions as being consistent with the "least restrictive alternative" rationale. This argument was first used by commentators who have recently been writing persuasively that a person whose liberty is infringed upon by the state should have the right to the least restrictive form of commitment; in the case of mental retardation, they argue for the least restrictive form of treatment and placement. The idea has been successfully argued in some mental retardation litigation, and the basic argument is often used by administrators to discharge patients from the facility. The argument is probably legitimate when there are adquate alternative (i.e., community) treatment facilities available to a retarded person. But when there are no alternative facilities, the least restrictive placement justification for dismissal is clearly invalid and should be no defense to a right-to-treatment suit brought with the purpose of preventing deinstitutionalization or returning a patient to an institution. The only time it should be a defense is when there are community facilities available and the patient can benefit at least as much, if not more, from the community facilities than from the institution.

If a person is going to be injured or damaged by the community placement, he should be entitled to money damages, but, as most likely will be the case, if money damages will not compensate him adequately, he should be entitled to a court order that he not be deinstitutionalized until quantitatively and qualitatively equivalent services are available in his new placement setting.

THE TRANSFER OF RIGHTS

It is not at all clear the rights possessed by a resident of an institution survive his deinstitutionalization and carry over to the community. In North Carolina, for example, legislation affords residents of mental retardation centers certain rights, but no legislation provides that they shall have the same rights when they are deinstitutionalized to a group home, a foster home, their parents, or some community facility. Do they still have the right to privacy and to ownership or personal belongings? Should they have an individual evaluation and habilitation plan as was required when they resided in the institution? Who in the community is to be held responsible for informing the person of his rights and advocating on his behalf? The same legal recourse arguably available to a person deprived of equivalent services upon his deinstitutionalization should be available if in-institution statutory rights are lost upon deinstitutionalization.

THE DUTY OF STATE SUBSIDY

A legitimate public and private concern is the cost of deinstitutionalization. How do the costs for community-based care compare with the costs of institutional care ("costs" include not only fiscal costs, which may be originally higher for community care than for institutional care but which over the long term may be lower, but also "costs" saved in terms of human gains)? If they are less, and if the retarded person is being returned to his parental home or even to some nonpublic home such as a foster home or group home operated by an association of retarded citizens, the state is saved the greater costs of institutionalization, but the cost is transferred from the public sector to the private sector. Should not the government—the public sector—provide some recompense or subsidy of the costs of retaining the retarded person in the community at a private facility? What about the case of a deinstitutionalized child who goes back to a community where he is excluded from public school programs or is possibly too young for public school? One recourse of his working parents might be to place him in a private day care center at the approximate rate of $150 to $200 per month. While he was previously living in the institution, the state subsidized the cost of his training program. However, upon discharge to the community, his parents were required to assume the financial burden from the state. One father of a severely retarded boy living at home recently commented that he is often tempted to teach his son to commit a criminal act. If the boy were a criminal, he could receive rehabilitation at state expense. However, since he is not a criminal and he is retarded, the boy is excluded from many public programs and the family must purchase private care, usually at heavy financial cost and other burden to the family. There is no clear duty now of public recompense (and the duty will come only from legislative action), but the savings to the public sector are obvious if deinstitutionalization is made to a private facility. The state should not so easily escape the costs of its responsibility of care for the retarded person. Recompense could take the form of direct transfers of money, living cost subsidies, social security benefits, and tax credits, among others.

THE DUTY TO MONITOR

A major problem is that of monitoring the quality of the care in the community. For purposes of argument, assume that the quality of care in the institutions is monitored and that standards are set and met to adequately safeguard the retarded person while he is in an institution. (To assume this is to ignore the evidence that there is insufficient monitoring or no monitoring at all and that the standards of care are far below what is legally tolerable.) The law has not yet begun to address issues of monitoring the care and setting standards for the care of retarded persons in the community, except insofar as it requires compliance by community facilities with building codes, fire codes, and related standards for the physical facilities in which the retarded will be living. The law is just now beginning to define and provide for the types of community services that make deinstitutionalization possible. The law has yet to address whether the now emerging standards for care and treatment in the institutions will be applied to deinstitutionalized persons, and if so, whether they will be applied to both governmental and private facilities and professionals. What happens when the management and operation of group homes is detrimental to the welfare of the retarded individuals living in them? Who monitors the quality of services delivered? For example, consider the case of a retarded adult in a nursing home who is afforded no opportunities for self-development or self-expression. This does happen far too often, since few monitoring systems have been developed.

The retarded person might successfully contend that he would be endangered or injured if he were deinstitutionalized to a facility or persons not required to live up to the standards set for his care in the institution. Accordingly, he might be entitled to money damages or an order restraining his deinstitutionalization.

THE RIGHT OF VOLUNTARY DISCHARGE

Another issue concerns the right of a resident to leave an institution if he has been "voluntarily" admitted or has "voluntarily" admitted himself. If voluntary admissions are in fact not made by the retarded person himself but rather by various persons affected by that decision, and if the retarded person decides that he wants to leave the institution (voluntary discharge and deinstitutionalization), should he have that right? In North Carolina, legislation provides that a person voluntarily admitted (admitted other than on court or other governmental agency order) to an institution for the mentally retarded may, upon several days' notice given to the administrators in writing, receive an automatic discharge. While one's innate senses of civil liberties and rights might be warmed by this legislation, one's senses might also recoil at it if the automatic discharge of a "voluntary" admittee results in his return to the community in which he is not prepared to live or a return to a community that is not prepared to accept him. As an example of the former, consider the following.

At one mental retardation center, a "voluntarily" admitted adult patient requested his discharge and received it within several hours after his request. He thumbed a ride down to a nearby interstate highway and then, while he was thumbing a ride along the interstate highway and not knowing the rules of the road, was struck and killed by a car the driver of which was driving lawfully but who could not avoid hitting the retarded person when he jumped in front of the car, apparently thinking that the car would be able to stop within the available distance. One wonders whether legislators should not take another look at the wisdom of providing a blanket, automatic right of discharge to any voluntary resident. A review seems required if only because administrators of the institutions have failed to prepare their residents for community living. One also wonders whether an administrator of a discharging institution should be liable to the retarded person, or his estate, if the discharge results in injury that would not have come if the resident had been properly prepared for discharge.

THE LEGAL ASSUMPTION IN FAVOR OF PARENTAL CUSTODY

Another difficult issue surrounds the legal presumption in favor of custody of a child by the parents, a presumption that assumes that the parents are the best persons to care for their child. This assumption, while it may have general validity and while it appeals to our sense of familial obligation, is not necessarily true. The parents, after all, may have been the persons who initially institutionalized their child. They also may be financially, psychologically, and physically not as well equipped to deal with and provide for the retarded child as a group-home facility, a foster home, or adoptive parents. Should parents be encouraged to deinstitutionalize their child when it is obvious they do not have the coping skills to make successful adjustments? When a retarded child is returned to a highly unfavorable home environment where supportive services have failed to bring about change, should parental custody be denied?

When the assumptions in favor of parental custody are or might be in error, the legal presumption should not exist, and an independent determination into suitability of the parents should be made.

THE PARENTAL VETO

A related issue is the almost absolute right of parents to object to or veto the placement of their retarded child in a community facility other than their own home or in a foster or adoptive home. If the institution wishes to deinstitutionalize a retarded person and if the parents do not want to have the retarded person returned to them, the only alternative for deinstitutionalization is placement in the community with some persons other than the parents. This placement sometimes will be objected to by the parents for a variety of reasons: the unsuitability of the alternative placement; the implicit rebuttal by the alternative placement of the parents' judgment that institutionalization was best for the child in the first place;

the sense of guilt that parents feel when confronted with the possibility that other persons are capable of taking care of a retarded child in the community although the parents themselves were not, as evidenced by their placement of the child; and the parents' sense that they are or will be socially stigmatized if they have a retarded child at home. A pending case at one institution involves a ten-year-old child who has developed the necessary skills for home and community living; however, her parents refused to take her home and have vetoed alternatives such as a foster home or a group home placement. In a recent parent interview the father commented: "This institution is the ultimate place to be, and it gives me such mental comfort to know my daughter is here." Should this child be required to spend the rest of her life in the institution because her parents have refused to have her at home and have denied permission for an alternative placement? Where do the parents' rights end and the child's rights begin?

The legal presumption in favor of parental placement needs to be reconsidered and the parents' ability to object to or veto other deinstitutionalizing placement should be carefully examined when deinstitutionalization is in their child's best interests but not in their own.

THE DUTY OF TRUTH IN PLACEMENT

There has been very little "truth in placement" in institutionalizing or deinstitutionalizing people. While federal and state legislation regulates truth in lending and sale of consumer products, no legislation requires "truth in placement." No legislation requires an institution or a community facility to disclose to the persons making the placement its financial strengths or weaknesses, its staff-to-residents ratio, the programs that will be made available or are not available, the types of diet provided, the fact of compliance or noncompliance with local building, zoning, or fire codes or with accreditation standards, the professional qualifications or on-the-job experience of its staff, or other matters relating to the suitability of the facility and its staff for the retarded person. Thus, the parents of a retarded person or his guardians might have to place him in an institution without having the benefit of detailed information concerning the facility itself. If, as has happened, the facility has to close for whatever reasons, the entire agonizing, expensive, and time-consuming process of replacement must be embarked upon again. A further refinement of "truth in placement" legislation would be legislation obligating a private facility to post a financial responsibility bond, or obligating a public facility to provide financial recourse, for parents or guardians who are put to any expense because of the closing of the facility. Obviously, when such an important issue as placement is at stake, some form of disclosure should be required so that the placement decision can be founded on all available facts, and some form of recompense in the form of a financial responsibility bond of assurance should be made if placement cannot be fulfilled.

REFINING GUARDIANSHIP

Finally, the entire law of guardianship needs to be explored and refined. Traditionally, a court-appointed guardian is available to a person who is incompetent to manage his own affairs; accordingly, a guardian can be appointed for most retarded persons. Traditionally also, the guardian is wholly and entirely responsible for the management of the affairs of his ward; accordingly, the guardian of a retarded person has absolute authority over the property and even sometimes over the person of his ward. This concept of total guardianship is inconsistent with the emerging models of retardation which teach that retarded persons are capable of performing some functions and making some decisions for themselves. If a retarded person is capable of managing his property and money and deciding the amount or type of social freedom he wants, the laws of guardianship should be revised to provide for a limited guardianship in which the guardian has only partial control over certain aspects of the property or person of his ward. If the emerging models of retardation correctly teach that there are degrees of retardation and capabilities among retarded persons, there should thus be degrees of guardianship tailored to the particular individual and his capability, rather than a single type of complete guardianship tailored to outdated and invalid assumptions.

CONCLUDING STATEMENT

Much of the law of mental retardation is just now being developed, and its implications are being initially explored in light of our new understanding of retardation and our new sense that retarded persons are entitled not only to human rights but also to legal rights. The warehouse-type institution is not the least restrictive setting for the care, habilitation, training, and development of retarded persons. In some institutions, the most shocking infringement of rights has been found. Living conditions are so deplorable that they raise questions of whether the Eighth Amendment, prohibiting cruel and unusual punishment, has been violated. Some types of "treatment" employed in them raise questions of unconstitutional intrusions into the life and liberty of the residents. Rights to education and treatment, although tenuous in the community, are most likely to be denied in institutions. And rights of the retarded person and his family are most likely to be surrendered under a theory of *in loco parentis*, the belief that institutions will act as parents would in the best interest of the retarded residents. It is largely because of the failure of our institutions that we have adopted the belief that deinstitutionalization by less restrictive forms of placement is the constitutionally required placement.

And yet a word of caution is in order: deinstitutionalization, without necessary legal safeguards, will not be a satisfactory answer to the problems of institutionalization, but will merely be an unwitting way for replacing the infringements on legal and person rights that retarded persons have suffered in institutions by similar infringments to be suffered elsewhere. In short we must apply the fullest legal protections that the person in the institutions are now belatedly and partially receiving to the persons who are being deinstitutionalized.

9

Legislation

PAULA BREEN HAMMER, JENNIFER HOWSE

ELINOR, who is mentally retarded and has cerebral palsy, has lived in an institution for seventeen of her twenty-one years. Her environment for these seventeen years consisted of a bed with an iron headboard, a white metal bedstand with three drawers, and a white metal free-standing wardrobe. It was her good fortune to be selected as a promising candidate for the facility's deinstitutionalization program "Homeward Bound."

The first step of the program was an intensive daily training program in a simulated "apartment" set up on one of the wards. On the morning Elinor was scheduled to begin learning how to live on the outside, she took special care to select from her closet her best clothes, and placing a pencil and small notebook in her purse, wheeled herself over to the "Homeward Bound" apartment. Upon entering the room, Elinor opened the refrigerator, placed her purse on one of the shelves, and closed the door. Most white metal free-standing wardrobes look the same.

It is a long and winding road home, but Elinor and hundreds like her are on their way as part of a national movement called deinstitutionalization. Fulfillment of this goal will bring about the return of developmentally disabled individuals from large institutions to their respective communities. Fulfillment of this goal will also require the mobilization of community programs to eliminate the need for placing such individuals in state institutions.

Generally speaking, deinstitutionalization had its genesis during the 1960s, in the discontent surrounding the increasingly publicized conditions in large institutions (Kugel and Wolfensberger 1969). National mobilization toward this goal was given strong initial momentum following President Richard Nixon's now-historic pledge during his November 16, 1971,

140

meeting with members of the President's Committee on Mental Retardation:

> Today I pledge continuing expansion of such support, and I invite all Americans to join me in commitment to two major national goals:
> 1) To reduce by half the occurence of mental retardation in the United States before the end of this century.
> 2) To enable one-third of the more than 200,000 retarded persons in public institutions to return to useful lives in the community. (p. 1112)

The stated goal of deinstitutionalization was in turn articulated in 1972 as one of the keystones in the Department of Health, Education and Welfare's "Social and Rehabilitation Service (SRS) Five Year Plan FY 74-78" (August 1972). As stated in this document, the department was to base its planning and strategy development around the two goals of non-dependency and institutional reform.

At the time this planning document was published, the Social and Rehabilitation Service had purview over virtually unlimited federal resources, available through different titles of the Social Security Act, which could be brought to bear on implementing the goal of deinstitutionalization. These included social services and assistance payments under Titles I, X, XIV, and XVI, medical assistance through Title XIX, Aid to Families with Dependent Children (AFDC) under Title IV, and the Vocational Rehabilitation Act totaling $13.5 billion for fiscal year 1974 alone.

To be sure, in 1970 the programs authorized by the Social Security Act for social services, medical services, and cash assistance to individuals constituted together a vast potential for funding community programs for the developmentally disabled. The multi-billion dollar social services program alone is one of the largest federal investments in human services at the community level. Administered in HEW by the Social and Rehabilitation Service Community Service Administration (now the Public Services Administration), the program transfers three federal dollars to the state for every one state or local dollar spent on social services.

Conditions seemed ripe for the emergence of a well-orchestrated federal/state partnership which would effectively channel funds toward training institutionalized developmentally disabled individuals for life in the community and which would provide them with services and appropriate living situations once they got there. Mott (1976) describes the pivotal role of the social services program in SRS policy in the early seventies:

The essential problem came to be defined in terms of the confusion of proliferating social service programs, many of them emanating out of categorical federal legislation. Whether sponsoring comprehensive services to different groups (the mentally retarded, American Indians, or Older Americans) or specialized services (family planning, Head Start, or vocational rehabilitation) the matrix of categories was developing into a bureaucratic jungle. The programs often had different jurisdictions, different funding rules, and different eligibility criteria. Consumer spokesmen complained that people's problems are integrated, but the services aren't. They were alternately treated as recipients, patients, clients . . . but seldom as whole persons.

Just within the SRS programs it was noted that Medicaid would pay for a patient in a nursing home, but would not pay for the rehabilitation services to get them back to their own home. Or conversely, a poor person might qualify for vocational rehabilitation but would not qualify for the public assistance necessary to sustain him or her during a training period.

SRS tried to respond by seeing itself as more than simply an umbrella agency. Early in 1970 its six bureaus agreed that their common mission was: "Enabling America's vulnerable and handicapped people—those physically and mentally disabled, the aging, the children and youth, and impoverished families—to move from dependency, alienation, and deprivation toward independence, constructive contributions to society, and realization of their potentials."

In effect, all of the agencies were to work together to achieve the goals of the Sixties: increased self-sufficiency and self-support. SCSA was viewed as a key to this mission since its social services authorization was so worded as to enable it to fill in gaps in service programs and promote the integration of services not only within SRS, but *vis-à-vis* other service programs as well.

But a treacherous chasm often exists between the policy statement or pledge of support and the realization through the concrete steps of program formulation (saying what will be done), and the program implementation (actually doing it). If deinstitutionalization seems to have fallen into the breach between promise and reality as a national commitment, then we need to take a close look at the instruments of our public policy—particularly federal legislation.

This chapter focuses on the legislative process. It is written with one group of people in mind: our colleagues in the developmental disabilities movement who adamantly contend that the legislative process is a mysterious event vaguely related to the filtering of federal dollars to local programs. Tracing the social services program 1970-76, as a case study, we hope to illustrate how legislative actions, inactions, and interactions actually influence public policy, resource allocation, and ultimately social change.

A WORD ABOUT "LEGISLATION" AND POLICY

Legislation is an instrument of public policy. Congress enacts a statute to set forth boundaries of actions which may be described generally as regulatory, structural, or allocative. Regulatory legislation, such as the Clean Air Act of 1970, polices compliance with policy. Structural legislation creates a new agency or authority to implement or facilitate policy actions. Local housing authorities established under amendments to the Housing and Urban Development Act represent structural legislative change. This chapter will be concerned chiefly with allocative legislation under the social services provisions of the Social Security Act. By distributing benefits under special conditions, allocative legislation induces or seduces compliance of others to federal policy. The social services program allocates federal funds to states to help underwrite the cost of services. Federal legislation specifies who will be eligible for what service under what conditions at the state and local level.

The broad strokes of federal legislation await administrative interpretation and leadership. The agencies of the executive branch define more precisely the eligibility rules, approved services, and budgets. For each piece of legislation passed into law, an agency representing the executive branch of government is resonsible for developing and promulgating rules and regulations (or "regs") which are designed to be both a clarification and an extension of the intent of legislation. Through rules and regulations, program guidelines, interpretive memoranda, and audits, the federal government is able to control the expenditure of funds earmarked for specific service categories. The executive branch of government uses restrictive rules and regulations to limit spending in what it determines to be undesirable areas.

The extent to which the executive branch can manipulate policy depends in large degree upon legislative controls exercised by congress.

1. *Congress controls by statute—authorizing legislation.* By writing broad, flexible laws, the congress allows greater discretion to the administering agency; on the other hand, detailed, explicit statutes prescribe executive action and proscribe executive decisions.

2. *Congress controls by the purse—appropriations.* Authorization and appropriation figures decided by Congress determine the allocation of funds available to a program or agency.

3. *Congress controls by investigation and oversight.* The General Accounting Office (GAO) and Congressional committees monitor implementation of Congressional intent, examine proposed executive actions,

and review past administrative policy.

Public policy is alternately influenced by the Congress and the administration. It is important to see legislation and the legislative process in the context of a dynamic, ongoing interchange between the Congress and the administration. Operationally, this is a complex and not entirely consistent control apparatus. Braybrooke and Lindblom's (1963) analysis of an incremental policy process might be applied to the legislative process as well: "It is decision-making through small or incremental moves on particular problems rather than a thorough and comprehensive reform program. It is also endless; it takes the form of an infinite sequence of policy moves. Moreover, it is exploratory in that the policy throws new light on what is possible and what is desirable. In this sense, it is also better described as moving away from known social ills rather than moving toward a known and relatively stable goal" (p. 71).

In the case of a national goal such as deinstitutionalization, the legislative mechanisms by which federal funds are allocated, controlled, and delivered to states has a dramatic effect on the rise and fall of programs and services designed to implement the goal. The focus of this chapter is an examination of the respective roles of both executive and legislative branches in shaping the federal policy incentives and disincentives to deinstitutionalization.

In tracing the recent history of deinstitutionalization, neither the administration nor the Congress is entirely consistent in its actions. Neither can be characterized as pro-deinstitutionalization or as anti-deinstitutionalization. This is not a story of good guys and bad guys. What unfolds is a story of the slow process of legislative and social change. The pace of the process is determined in large part by the system of checks and balances built into the federal government. The rhythm of the process is further influenced by our two-party system. In the period considered here, the Republicans controlled the executive branch; the Democrats dominated the Congress.

LEGISLATIVE ISSUES AND DEINSTITUTIONALIZATION

Has the administration proposed and supported legislation to further the goal of deinstitutionalization? Has the Congress enacted legislation consistent with the administration's stated goal of deinstitutionalization? Have administration actions remained consistent with President Nixon's stated goal? Answers to these questions have implications for the thousands of residents of public institutions who, like Elinor, could live successfully in the community as soon as basic support and rehabilitation and service programs are developed and stabilized.

It is significant to note that President Nixon did not follow up his 1971 policy statement with a legislative package or initiative to Congress addressing the goal of deinstitutionalization. White House efforts to enact human-service legislation have focused on reforming welfare programs, particularly the proposed Family Assistance Plan (FAP) under HR 1, and on replacing the categorical programs with block grant funding through special revenue sharing schemes for states and the Allied Services bill. The Nixon and Ford Administrations have not been successful in enacting these legislative objectives.

The executive branch has not addressed a key legislative issue of community-based long-term care: the fact that Medicare and Medicaid financing patterns have established long-term care services within a medical and institutional model. In fiscal year 1974, almost 36 percent of all Medicaid funds were spent on fewer than 5 percent of the total Medicaid population to pay for their care in skilled nursing facilities and intermediate care facilities:

> . . . financing for institutional long-term care—although incredibly confusing and plagued with gaps in eligibility and benefits, inequities between states and local jurisdictions, arbitrary definitions and categories of reimbursable expenses—is more readily accessible than funding for alternative care in non-institutional settings. Although this seems hard to believe, given the institutional long-term care picture, it is even more difficult for an individual to put together and finance a program of supportive services that would enable him to remain in the community. (Joe and Meltzer 1976, p. 21)

In fact administration proposals for Medicare/Medicaid changes, as well as those for National Health Insurance, assume continued funding of long-term care as a Medicare/Medicaid item which requires institutional placement. The availability of public dollars to such institutional programs, while perhaps necessary for some persons, inevitably constitutes a disincentive to deinstitutionalizing people like Elinor who have the potential for living happily in the community. What is needed is a companion financing program to support long-term care in community settings.Legislation to authorize such a program has not been presented by the executive branch.

In the absence of constructive legislative change, program advocates in SRS, including appointive officials, worked to achieve the goal of de-institutionalization by marshaling the resources authorized by existing legislation and administered by the Social and Rehabilitation Service in the Department of Health, Education and Welfare. In 1971, the new Community Service Administration Commissioner in SRS, experienced in multi-program integration, began to develop the concept of goal-oriented social services (GOSS). SRS translated the goal of non-dependency into a continuum based on the individual's dependency on income maintenance and social services. At one end of the continuum was institutional care, at the other end full self-support. Attached to each increment along the continuum was an appropriate mix of federal support including social and/or medical services and some form of assistance payments.

> GOSS was a more precise statement of social services goals than had been used before, although the goal definitions grew directly out of the legislative and professional goals of the past.
>
> There were four goals describing decreasing states of dependency from *institutionalization* through *community-based care* (halfway house, family foster care, etc.) to *self-care* (or family care in the case of children), and finally to modified (some cash assistance) or full *self-support*.
>
> SRS proposed a legislative initiative to promote further integration of all SRS programs at the community level. It was contemplated that public participation in a planning process would take place around identified target-group needs and interests and lead toward consolidation in an overall services plan.
>
> The role of the advocate, or target group agencies was thought of in terms of fostering arrangements of integrated services (e.g., Youth Service Systems or Developmental Disability Plans) to help their client group maintain or improve their position in the GOSS goal structure. The central role of the case-worker in performing the integrative function for families and individuals was to select appropriate services from those available in the community to assist the client in reaching a planned goal. It was also expected that the pressure from the caseworkers in the community would lead to the development of new services needed by their clients. (Mott 1976, pp. 16-17)

Key to this strategy was the federal social services program under SRS. It is this program that is the focus of the chapter. The social service program is part of the Social Security Act originally enacted in 1935 and amended extensively over the years. In 1970, the amendments found under *Social Security Act* Titles IVA, and I, X, XIV, and XVI authorized federal support for social services to needy families with dependent children and the needy aged, blind, and disabled individuals. The social services program has been the largest single source of federal funds for day care programs. Other approved services have included information and referral, protective services, self-support services, homemakers' services, foster care, chore services, and home-delivered meals.

The years 1970-73 were years of unprecendented growth for the social services program, with the federal budget mushrooming from $750 million in 1970 (1971) to $1.7 billion in 1972. Derthick (1975) observes the characteristics of the increased spending, including the purchase of services from state agencies serving the mentally retarded:

> Between them, New York and Illinois accounted for 70 percent of the near billion dollar increase in service grants between fiscal years 1971 and 1972. They largely account for the fact that most of the increases came from purchases. Touche Ross and Company, an accounting firm hired by CSA to find out where the money was going, reported early in 1973 that 80 percent of the increase between 1971 and 1972 was caused by an almost fourfold rise in purchased services and that over three-fourths of this was due to the jump in services purchased from other public agencies, mainly state departments of education, mental health and retardation, corrections, and narcotics and alcoholism control. Purchase from public agencies increased seventeen times over the level of fiscal year 1971. Touche Ross reported that "most of these services had been provided as state funded and operated programs prior to their 'purchase' by the welfare agency. We found little evidence to conclude that the purchased services represented new services or new programs." Clearly, federal service funds were being used by the states for fiscal relief. (p. 73)

This growth in federal social services expenditures was accompanied by upheaval and conflict about the direction of social service policy.

In the years 1970-75, the social service program was far from a stable source of funding for deinstitutionalization. The shifting sands of congressional and administrative policy about social services legislation in the early seventies seriously eroded this potential resource. The social services programs became embroiled in a series of issues much larger than services for the disabled. First, it was mired in the debate over Welfare Reform and HR 1; later, the program became a target of fiscal constraints imposed by both the administration and the Congress; and, finally, the program became a battleground for what was to be one of our nation's most serious Congressional/executive conflicts.

The Congressional/administration interchange reviewed here will focus on the extent to which prevailing federal policy facilitated or constrained deinstitutionalization by decisions regarding dollars available to states for community services, individual eligibility rules, and other conditions on state use of federal social service funds for deinstitutionalization programs.

HOW DO STATES QUALIFY TO RECEIVE SOCIAL SERVICE FUNDS? 1970-73

The Plan

The process of moving federal financial support for social services from the U.S. Treasury to people like Elinor in the community begins with a state agency responsible for administering the program, usually the Department of Welfare. The state agency submits to HEW a state plan. The plan is the state's contractual agreement to certain terms for providing service in exchange for federal funds. The state agency, in turn, regulates its local units (county welfare offices for example) and their relations with other public and private service providers in compliance with the terms of the state plan.

The Match

Until late 1972, states could earn an unlimited amount of social services dollars as long as they put up their share of matching resources and conformed with their approved state plans as called for under the relevant title of the Social Security Act. The rate of federal financial participation was 75 to 25 percent; in other words, for every dollar contributed by a state for social services, the federal government matched three dollars. Federal matching for social services prior to fiscal year 1973 was open-ended; that is, there was no limit on the amount of federal funds potentially available for social services. And practically speaking there was no limit on the amount of funds the state could ante up for match. By 1972 an increasing number of states had taken advantage of open-ended federal financial participation to build social service programs and to finance community-based services and deinstitutionalization.

The expansion resulted in the availability of needed services that had formerly been very scarce. For example, the states had moved to fill the priority need for day care and other services to assist people to be self-supporting. 29.2 percent of the funds were spent for child care, a service involving almost one-half million children. In adult services, the emphasis on deinstitutionalization was reflected in the large expansion of homemaker and chore services which accounted for 22.1 percent of the total adult services expenditures, and helped over 150,000 adults in that category. (Mott 1976, p. 26)

The 1967 amendments provided that privately donated funds could be transferred to the state for matching purposes; previously, only public funds—state and local revenues—had been used as match. Between 1970 and 1972, many private agencies for the developmentally disabled—local units of the Association for Retarded Citizens, United Cerebral Palsy, and the Epilepsy Foundation, as well as United Fund groups—donated private funds to state welfare agencies to attract federal dollars to community programs at the three-to-one rate.

By mid-1972, states were catching on to the tricks of using private matching, purchase of service contracts and interagency transfers of funds. California, Illinois, New York, and a few other states had finely tuned these techniques, and in 1972 other states, learning from the pioneers, began to project vast increases for their 1973 social services programs. The total expenditure leap projected was from $1.7 billion in 1972 to $4.7 billion in 1973. A few examples illustrate what these increases could mean for an individual state budget. Mississippi projected its growth in social services expenditures from $1.8 million in fiscal year 1972 to $269 million in fiscal year 1973. Tennessee proposed to expand from $13.8 million in 1972 to $227 million in 1973. Other states hoping to make enormous increases in 1973 social services budgets as contrasted to 1972 included: Georgia proposing to move from $32 million in 1972 to $206 million in 1973; Idaho planning to enlarge from a $1.5 million program in 1972 to $24.5 million in 1973; Maryland increasing from $20 million to $415 million; and New Jersey expecting to expand from $36 million to $415 million. Such growth would only be possible in a program with open-ended funding. Before the close of 1972, legislative and administrative actions dismantled the catapult device; the anticipated funding leaps were not accomplished.

MOVES TO LIMIT SOCIAL SERVICE
SPENDING: 1972

Authorization Ceiling

As early as spring 1970, HEW submitted to Congress as part of its revenue-sharing approach for social services a proposal to close the open end on social services funding and to authorize specific annual appropriation levels. A statutory formula would allocate social service dollars to the states (Derthick 1975, p. 38). In June 1971, the House Ways and Means Committee picked up the idea of closing the open-end funding for social services and added the provision to its version of HR 1. However, HR 1 never received Senate approval. It was not until late 1972 that Congress moved to halt what seemed to be uncontrolled federal spending by a straightforward curb on federal social-service spending. The change came as Title III of the Revenue Sharing Act (P.L. 92-512). Title III established a $2.5 billion ceiling on annual federal expenditures for the social services program. In this way, Congress dispensed the bitter medicine of funding curbs to states with the sweetner of new, no-strings federal dollars to state and local governments under General Revenue Sharing.

The $2.5 billion is not an automatic allocation; it is the upper limit on federal spending for social services nationally. Title III also prescribed a straight population formula (Sec. 1130) to determine upper limits on federal spending for social services for each state. Thus, a state with 10 percent of the national population could not receive more than 10 percent of the $2.5 billion. Again this is not an automatic formula grant to the states; it is a limit on the amount of federal funds each state may match. When a state fails to match maximum available funds, the unused or surplus funds revert to the U.S. Treasury. Unlike many federal allocation procedures, the surplus to unused funds is not available for redistribution to the other states.

Table 9.1 lists for each state the amount of the 1972 (the last preceiling year) federal allocation and the amount of the ceiling effective for 1973 and subsequent years. It is important to note that the figures for the ceiling on funds the state may receive from the federal government have remained unchanged since 1973. As long as the program is frozen at $2.5 billion nationally with no re-allocation of unused funds, only a marked change in state population will influence the ceiling established for the states in 1973.

At the state level, the impact of these restraints on federal support of

TABLE 9.1

Federal Allocations

	Ceiling on Funds Revenue Sharing Act, Section III*	Total Used in FY 1972†
TOTALS	$2,500,000,000	$1,684,626,297
Alabama	42,140,000	11,697,990
Alaska	3,901,750	4,208,286
Arizona	23,351,250	2,748,375
Arkansas	23,747,250	3,273,092
California	245,733,250	198,627,102
Colorado	28,297,500	18,908,219
Connecticut	37,001,750	9,399,607
Delaware	6,783,250	12,456,577
District of Col.	8,980,250	10,479,067
Florida	87,149,500	42,708,788
Georgia	56,667,000	32,415,041
Hawaii	9,712,500	847,787
Idaho	9,076,250	1,544,330
Illinois	135,076,500	188,381,187
Indiana	63,522,250	6,532,771
Iowa	34,612,500	9,536,046
Kansas	27,109,000	6,210,788
Kentucky	39,607,000	12,709,163
Louisiana	44,661,250	29,505,717
Maine	12,354,000	6,536,643
Maryland	48,695,250	20,946,731
Massachusetts	69,477,000	23,035,756
Michigan	109,036,000	28,039,828
Minnesota	46,774,250	26,587,809
Mississippi	27,169,000	1,833,678
Missouri	57,063,250	12,839,259
Montana	8,632,000	2,959,094
Nebraska	18,308,750	7,352,176
Nevada	6,327,000	1,616,274
New Hampshire	9,236,500	2,824,174
New Jersey	88,446,250	36,930,431

TABLE 9.1

(Continued)

Federal Allocations

	Ceiling on Funds Revenue Sharing Act, Section III*	Total Used in FY 1972†
TOTALS	$2,500,000,000	$1,684,626,297
New Mexico	12,786,000	3,680,005
New York	220,497,250	588,929,342
North Carolina	62,597,750	19,470,389
North Dakota	7,587,500	3,325,453
Ohio	129,457,750	19,517,429
Oklahoma	31,623,000	14,060,341
Oregon	26,196,500	25,297,779
Pennsylvania	143,180,230	51,293,723
Rhode Island	11,621,500	6,623,499
South Carolina	31,995,250	6,031,298
South Dakota	8,152,000	2,377,347
Tennessee	48,395,000	13,835,427
Texas	139,854,750	53,500,629
Utah	13,518,500	4,084,438
Vermont	5,546,750	2,433,568
Virginia	57,195,250	16,262,983
Washington	41,335,750	34,308,934
West Virginia	21,382,250	7,373,914
Wisconsin	54,265,750	37,937,301
Wyoming	4,142,000	590,692

*Entitlements under $2.5 billion ceiling, not actual expenditures.

†Adjusted to include Federal auditor corrections and claims from previous year; other adjustments not reflected in State data make National total $1.71 billion. "State Expenditures for Public Assistance Programs . . ." prepared by the Office of Financial Management, SRS.

Lesser of estimate or allocated share of $2.5 billion, which has been adjusted for certain States on the basis of first quarter expenditure reports in accordance with Section 403 of the Social Security Amendments of 1972.

Source: Department of Health, Education, and Welfare

social services proved to be uneven, in part because state participation in the program prior to 1973 was uneven as Derthick (1975) notes:

> With no change in federal policy, services spending doubled in the first two years of the Nixon administration, rising from $396.6 million in fiscal year 1969 to $776.2 million in 1971. In the states, growth was uneven. California continued to get a disproportionate share. In Oregon, Washington, and Pennsylvania, services spending grew at several times the national rate. (In Oregon, an extreme case, the jump was from $2.4 million to $24.6 million.) How much a state benefited could depend not only on its enterprise but also on its fortune in making connections with consultants or on the advice it got from regional officials. (p. 40)

Only four states (Alaska, Delaware, Illinois, and New York) and the District of Columbia were allocated less under the $2.5 billion ceiling than they spent in 1972. For most states, the $2.5 billion ceiling did not represent a substantial cutback, but rather a leveling off of federal support. However, the cutback did have the effect of capping the development of programs and consequently curtailing new initiatives.

The Nixon administration favored the legislative constraints on social services spending. In fact, HEW went one up on the Congress by impounding over $.8 billion of the $2.5 billion authority. In 1973 HEW provided only $1.54 billion to states in social services funds. The combination of legislated ceilings on the big-spender states and the cutbacks of HEW dropped total social service spending from $1.68 billion in 1972 to $1.54 billion in 1973. California, for instance, was limited to a 10 percent growth rate under executive actions whereas the Congressionally imposed ceiling would have allowed 20 percent growth.

ELIGIBILITY: CLOSING THE DOOR TO SERVICES

An underlying rationale for all social services is the avoidance of long-term public assistance payments to persons in need by helping those who are past, present, or future recipients of cash grants to become self-supporting. Thus, eligibility for services has always been tied in some manner to rules governing public assistance. From 1970-1975 a consistent principle of welfare programs required that a person receiving public assistance payments would be automatically eligible for social services. In 1970, recipients of public assistance included needy families (usually fatherless) with dependent children under age 18 and certain needy adults (usually age 21 or over) covered under Aid to the Aged, Blind, and Disabled. Also eligible were persons who were former recipients of public assistance and who still needed services to strengthen their self-support behaviors and prevent reversion to public assistance.

Under the 1969 and 1970 regs, these individuals were eligible for two years after they were terminated from public assistance. In a preventive fashion, 1969 and 1970 regs included a provision for persons for whom future dependence on public assistance seemed inevitable. If an individual had the potential for receiving public assistance within five years, eligibility under this criteria was established.

In addition to the automatically eligible, states could exercise considerable discretion in declaring eligible for service "former" and "potential" welfare recipients and certain "groups."

Congressional moves in 1972 to limit social services expenditures, in addition to the $2.5 billion ceiling, provided that states could spend no more than 10 percent of their federal funds on services for a category called "certain eligible people"—those who are not current recipients of public assistance but might be considered former or potential recipients of welfare payments.

ADMINISTRATION: 1973

The year 1973 seemed to mark a turning point in Congressional-HEW relations. Under a new HEW Secretary, Casper Weinberger, the administration moved early in the year to issue regulations to interpret and implement the various legislative changes in social services enacted at the end of 1972.

HEW published proposed regs in February 1973. With the opportunity to shape policy, the administration regs prohibited matching privately donated funds and eliminated many individuals previously eligible as "former" or "potential" recipients by redefining the terms: potential—expected to be on welfare within six months (from five years); former—has received welfare payment within last three months (from two years). The regs severely limited income criteria for former and potential eligibles.

Neither the "former," "potential," nor "group" eligibility rules stipulated information on eligible services. Furthermore, the guidelines discriminated against institutionalized persons in the "potential" category by allowing social services funds to be used for a maximum of only 90 days to determine their eligibility and to develop plans for community placement. The regulations abolished group eligibility determination under Title IV-A. Previous regulations had allowed the states to determine eligibility for services by residence in poverty areas. This feature had allowed greater program flexibility in the selection of clients and involved much less paperwork for program staff since each client did not have to be separately processed for eligibility determination.

The regulations went far beyond the legislation, which never mentioned income criteria. These guidelines also indicate a discrepancy between a federally stated goal of deinstitutionalization and actual program practices allowable under regulations and administration policy. Deinstitutionalization efforts for severely or multiple handicapped individuals must be intensive and fairly long term in order to be effective. For a person such as Elinor to make a successful transition from the survival mode of the institution to the more complex mode of community living requires several critical intermediary types of programming. Completing this type of program does not necessarily occur within a 90-day period of time.

THE RESPONSE AND CONGRESSIONAL REACTION

HEW received a total of 208,515 comments from 198,759 individuals and organizations, including congressmen, governors, state legislators, mayors, labor unions, and professional and religious organizations.

In the May 1, 1973, *Federal Register* HEW issued its second set of proposed regulations responding to several concerns, including the following issues noted by the department:

> Concern was also expressed by a large number of respondents over the effect of these requirements on availability of day care services for mentally retarded children who, without these services, may have to be institutionalized.
>
> The proposed eligibility requirements for potentials and the limitations on costs which could be matched, it was claimed, would make it very difficult to deinstitutionalize aged and mentally retarded recipients who, with services, could live in the community. (p. 10782)

Ironically, the May regulations included a definition of mental retardation that hardly reflects a sensitivity, much less a commitment, to the issue of deinstitutionalization. The archaic definition is reprinted here in full from the *Federal Register*, May 1, 1973:

> Mentally retarded individual means an individual, not psychotic, who according to a licensed physician's opinion is so mentally retarded from infancy or before reaching 18 years of age that he is incapable of managing himself and his affairs independently, with ordinary prudence, or of being taught to do so and who requires supervision, control and care, for his own welfare, or for the welfare of others, or for the welfare of the community. (p. 10784)

The May regulations, to have become effective July 1, 1973, continued to restrict services to very low income families. Advocates for the mentally retarded did succeed in winning some special concessions for that group. The regulations exempted the mentally retarded from the 10 percent limitation on federal match for services in the "former and potential" category.

However, Congressional action in the summer of 1973 began to supersede administration policies, and the May regs never saw the light of day. First, responding to the hew and cry of state and local officials and the general public, Senator Russell Long convened a special oversight hearing of his powerful Senate Finance Committee. The Senate called HEW Secretary Weinberger to testify and to respond to questions; public witnesses had an opportunity to present their concerns.

The result of the May oversight hearings was the enactment of a series of social security amendments attached to the Renegotiation Act (PL 93-66), placing a four-month moratorium on new social services regulations. Postponing social services until November 1, 1973, the Congress declared the May regs "out of step with the clear requirements of the statute and with Congressional intent" (Ross 1974): Senator Long warned HEW that his committee would "be going over the proposed new regulations with a fine tooth comb" to make sure they match legislative intent. Wilbur Mills, Chairman of the House Ways and Means Committee, mirrored Senate criticism of the May regs: "the stringency of the regulation will prevent effective social service programs in the field of mental retardation, mental health, family planning, child support, alcoholism, drug abuse" and aging (Gettings 1973).

The amendments also specified that aged, blind, and disabled be added to the categories of individuals exempt from the statutory restriction that no more than 10 percent of a state's allocation should provide services to "former and potential" welfare recipients.

On September 10, 1973, HEW tried once again to establish regulations for social services. This time the department required states to establish under the adult services program a plan for deinstitutionalization and prevention of institutionalization through the provision of defined services; listed fifteen defined services; broadened somewhat the financial eligibility rules for former and potential recipients; allowed additional special deductions from gross income for determining the eligibility of a mentally retarded individual for social services; ignored Renegotiation Act legislation and made no mention of the addition of aged, blind, and disabled to the groups to be excluded from the 10 percent restriction; retained what advocates for the developmentally disabled referred to as the "antediluvian and unacceptable" (Helsel 1973) definition of mental retardation; added a new-defined service—special services for the mentally retarded.

On October 31, 1973, HEW issued yet another set of proposed regulations to take effect November 1, 1973. These regulations would give states a little more flexibility in determining eligibility. Once again in December 1973, however, Congress stepped in by enacting PL 93-233, amendments to the Social Security Act which nullified all HEW regulations on social services for one year until December 31, 1974. The program would operate under the old 1970 regulations for twelve months. Congress would take hold of the policy reins to spell out social services program details.

SHOWDOWN OF 1973: IMPLICATION, IMPACT

This tug of war between the legislative and executive branches of government in 1973 must be seen in the perspective of the unique political events of the second Nixon administration. Following the impressive mandate of the 1972 landslide election, many executive agencies began flexing their muscles against a previously compliant Congress. Congressional reaction to what it saw as executive excesses in interpreting policy must be viewed in light of increasing revelations about Watergate and other scandals involving the White House.

The lack of executive leadership resulted in significant setbacks for people like Elinor in need of community services. As noted by the National Association for Retarded Citizens Legislative Newsletter in August 1973: "Much confusion still surrounds the Social Services regulations. Some states will not return to the original regulations in the fear that the new regulations will become effective November 1st. Many states have also been hesitant to set up new programs until final regulations are available. State ARC's have been hard at work to replace lost funds and to find new financial bases for new programs."

Thus many community service programs lay fallow during 1973, because states lacked clear policy guidelines for marshaling social service resources to implement deinstitutionalization.

In addition to the promulgation of regulations, the federal government also issues "Program Regulation Guides" which are intended to clarify the intent of regulation. "Program Guides," like regulations, are to be followed by state agencies administering federally sponsored programs. Ironically, at the same time social services regulations called for states to establish a plan for deinstitutionalization, the "Program Guide" issued on December 4, 1973, placed substantial restrictions on the use of social services funds in carrying out deinstitutionalization plans. The overall impact, then, was not merely a return to the 1970 regulations which were at least permissive and flexible to individual state policies on deinstitutionalization. Rather, the net effect of HEW policies was to curb and thwart efforts to increase community services that would support alternatives to institutionalization.

SUPPLEMENTAL SECURITY INCOME

Income assistance measures are an essential co-ingredient with services in any strategy for public support of long-term care in the community. Since historically recipients of cash assistance are automatically eligible to receive social services, the eligibility criteria for income assistance programs defines the basic target population for the services program. More important, however, is the role of income assistance programs as a funding resource for alternatives to institutional care. Social services funds may not be used to pay the cost of room and board. While Medicaid provides fiscal support to cover the cost of room and board for persons in institutional settings, no comparable public funding arrangement exists to subsidize the room and board costs of residents in community based group homes, supervised apartments, or semi-independent living situations. How does a needy disabled person with limited earning potential manage basic subsistence in the community? Income assistance programs (also known as transfer programs, public assistance, welfare, income maintenance) provide monthly cash payments to needy eligible individuals in the community. Recipients are expected to use assistance payments to purchase room and board.

Late in 1972, Congress enacted amendments to the Social Security Act which authorized the Supplemental Security Income (SSI) program. The statute detailed a new cash assistance program for the aged, blind, and disabled and authorized a new social services program (Title VI) for all recipients of SSI payments. The legislative history of SSI leads back to the administration's welfare reform package HR 1. Congress deleted the controversial Family Assistance Plan but approved in SSI a slightly revised version of the federalized guaranteed annual income for the aged, blind, and disabled.

Legislation authorizing the new cash assistance program, Supplemental Security Income, appeared to set policies conducive to deinstitutionalization efforts. The program set new, more liberal eligibility criteria enabling many developmentally disabled children and adults to qualify for cash assistance for the first time. SSI opened up a potential funding configuration for group homes: federal SSI payment of up to $157.50 a month to individuals to be increased automatically according to cost of living increases; state supplements to individuals (over and above SSI payment); federal/state social service funds.

Unfortunately, Congressional/administration bickering probably can be cited as a major contributing factor of HEW delays in establishing regulations for the Supplemental Security Income program. The resulting uncertainty about SSI policy and regulations has left planners in the dark as to how SSI might or might not prove to be a resource in the deinstitutionalization effort.

A major innovation of SSI is a change in the philosophy of an assistance program. One of the aims of the SSI program was to remove the stigma attached to welfare in programs for aged, blind, and disabled. Administration of the program was moved to the Social Security Administration to underscore the view that SSI is social legislation that is a legal right and entitlement of every claimant who qualifies. All people previously receiving income assistance from their state Title XVI programs were automatically enrolled for SSI payments. However, very little has been done to enroll the newly eligible population of disabled adults and children.

Two and a half years after enactment, large numbers of potential eligibles remain unenrolled. Information is a major problem. The Massachusetts SSI Advocacy Center reported on a major one-month outreach effort during testimony on SSI before the House Ways and Means Committee Subcommittee on Public Assistance in June 1975: "One of the most appalling responses concerned children. We got 300 calls in the next few weeks from parents who had severely disabled children 80% of whom, we found were eligible for SSI and who had never heard about it before in the year and a half of its existence" (p. 612).

In its report to HEW, the SSI Study Group noted in January 1976: "The original projections of potential SSI recipients and the current enrollment figures are still far apart. There is little possibility that the gap will be narrowed in the near future, if ever" (p. 87).

One policy decision has particular impact on the deinstitutionalization effort. "Inmates" of non-Medicaid funded public institutions are ineligible for SSI payments. A restrictive definition of public institution resulted in prohibiting SSI payments to individuals in group homes receiving public support. An HEW appointed SSI Study Group reported to the Secretary in January 1976 on this issue:

> As a result of this statutory provision and the regulations implementing it, SSI payments are denied to many individuals who are presently residing in homes for the aged, group homes, and residential care facilities that are established as shelter or personal care or domiciliary homes. The Study Group also heard testimony that, due to the subjective nature of these definitions and the varying characteristics of these facilities, the application of this provision may not be uniform throughout the nation. The Study Group expressed its intent that the basic Federal payment should not be influenced by a person's living arrangement. Many other SSI recipients cannot manage to live alone and need a sheltered care setting where they can have their food prepared and have assistance with personal needs. To deny these individuals SSI payments because the facility may be under the control of a governmental unit is not proper. Also, to reduce these payments because some of the services being provided are or could be provided in a Medicaid facility will do little more than force individuals into a nursing home even though in most cases this level of care is not necessary. (p. 65)

At the close of the 94th Congress, legislation is pending to address some of the shortcomings of SSI implementation. The Keys Amendment (HR 8911) would modify the public institution definition to correct the current policy disincentives to deinstitutionalization. Other legislation would authorize outreach and enrollment activities.

DECISIVE CHANGES IN SOCIAL SERVICES: 1974-75

The year 1974 brought significant changes to social services—changes in what states must do to get social service funds and in determining who would be eligible for social services in the community. These were changes on which considerable consensus exists between Congress and the administration—the enacted Social Services Amendments of 1974. In January 1975 Gerald R. Ford signed into law the Social Security Amendments of 1974, P.L. 93-647. The law consolidates the federal/state social services programs in a new Title XX of the Social Security Act. Title XX became effective October 1, 1975, and replaced social services provisions found in Titles I, IVa, VI, X, XIV, and XVI (except for Puerto Rico, the Virgin Islands, and Trust Territories). The bill was developed by Senator Walter Mondale (D-Minn.) through the cooperative efforts of Senate and House leadership, HEW, the National Governor's Conference, and a coalition of concerned consumer agencies, including representatives of the developmentally disabled.

Under Title XX, states have new latitude in defining what services will be made available, to whom, and by whom. The state will describe its own eligibility criteria, services, and fees in an annual services program plan submitted to HEW. The legislation spells out five broad goal areas for the social services program, three of which are: (1) achieving or maintaining self-sufficiency, including reduction or prevention of dependency; (2) preventing or reducing inappropriate institutional care by providing for community-based care, home-based care, or other forms of less intensive care; and (3) screening, referral, or admission for institutional care when other forms of care are not appropriate, or providing services to individuals in institutions.

For the first time, social services law articulated a commitment to a social policy of deinstitutionalization. The federal legislation outlined broad strokes and expectations about how social service funds would be used. Furthermore, the legislation put the responsibility for implementation on the individual states, not on HEW.

The Plan

Unlike the old social services plan, the new Annual Services Program Plan will require a rigorous state planning effort including citizen review and comment. This is not the familiar boiler plate or fill-in-the-blanks plan format. Each state program service plan must specify: (1) program objectives; (2) services to be provided (mandatory and optional), their definition, and relationship to objectives and goals; (3) categories of individuals to be served (including income categories); (4) geographic areas for service provision and the nature and amount of services for each area; (5) a description of Title XX planning, evaluation, and reporting activities; (6) sources of the program resources (matching funds); (7) a desscription of organizational structure, including use of public and private agencies and volunteers; (8) a description of Title XX coordination with the utilization of AFDC, CWS, SSI, Medicaid, and other related human-service programs; (9) estimated expenditures by service, categories served, geographic areas, and a comparison of estimated nonfederal expenditures for the planning year and the preceding program year; and (10) a description of steps taken to assure that needs of all residents and geographic areas of the state were considered in plan development.

The Match

A new provision [Sec. 2001(a)(1)(7)] of Title XX specifically allows private funds as well as state and local (i.e., county or city) revenues to be used in the one-for-three match.

Privately donated funds can be used for matching purposes when such donations: (1) are transferred to the state and under its administrative control; (2) are given without restrictions on use other than type of service to be supported (if donor is not the operator or sponsor of such type of service) and geographic area to be served; and (3) do not revert to a donor *other than a non-profit organization.*

Churches, fraternal and civic groups, voluntary agencies, and united fund groups are eligible for matching and receipt of federal social services funds. As before, state and local public revenues may be used for match also.

Eligibility and Services

Provisions of Title XX provide new opportunities to develop community programs for the developmentally disabled. The law significantly broadens eligibility criteria to include, at the state's option, families with income up to 115 percent of the state's median income or about $13,000 per year for a family of four. Developmentally disabled residents in community-based sheltered living arrangements including group homes, apartments, and hostels are eligible to receive a variety of Title XX funding services in the facility. Title XX can not pay the cost of room and board (so-called support and maintenance), except for halfway-type care of less than six months duration.

Title XX can pay for support staff in community residences to provide such services as protective supervision, reinforcement of self-help skills, socialization, and recreation.

Social service funds may be used for an individual in public or private institutions (including skilled nursing facilities and ICFs) as part of the plan for that individual to return to the community. So-called "in reach" services include: foster grandparent, protective and guardians by arrangement, and off-the grounds community activities. These services must be provided by an agency outside the institution and be generally available in the community.

Title XX payments may be made on behalf of an individual in a foster family to pay for a service which meets a special need of the individual. Foster parents may be providing socialization, behavior modification, and physical restoration services. Training costs and reimbursement to foster parents for the extra time and skill required to provide special services should be available under Title XX.

In October 1975, all states published Comprehensive Annual Service Programs (CASP plans) for Title XX services. HEW analysis of the plans in unpublished technical reports issued January 1976 note: "Seven states established more liberal income eligibility standards for developmentally disabled persons. All of the states (except Wyoming) describe services directed to meet the needs of developmentally disabled children and adults" (Mueller and Wolf 1976, No. 12). See Table 9.2

TABLE 9.2

CASP Data on Cut-off Point for Title XX Eligibility
Expressed as Percent of Median Income (Adjusted)

	Developmentally Disabled		Other Persons
Hawaii	79%		60%
Idaho	115%		80%
Mississippi	115%		80%
Ohio	80%		51%
Tennessee	80%		70%
Utah	115%		80%
Virginia	70%	(Includes blind and deaf)	50%

Source: Mueller and Wolff (1976)

CONCLUSION

Today we are getting the pieces together for a national deinstitutionalization effort: a policy statement by the executive branch, articulated steps of action in legislation from Congress, and administrative regs to facilitate the law. Actually doing it, actually helping Elinor move back to the community, actually moving the community to back Elinor, is up to the states. The action arena now must shift from Washington, D.C., to Annapolis, Boise, Olympia, Santa Fe, Raleigh, Boston, Albany, and the forty-three other state capitals.

National policy evolves in a slow process of Congressional and administration exchanges and assessments, a continual definition and redefinition of problems, and a constant adjustment to the flow of demands. As mentioned earlier, policy development is a series of incremental moves rather than a thorough and comprehensive reform program. And in this age of new federalism, increasingly the action will be found at the state and local levels. A national policy and national legislation for deinstitutionalization may be *necessary* to change alternatives for the developmentally disabled, but it is not *sufficient*. The machinery of national legislation can not work on behalf of Elinor and others like her without advocates at the state and local levels.

REFERENCES

Braybrook, D., and Lindblom, C. E. *Strategy of Decision: Policy Evaluation as a Social Process.* New York: Free Press of Glencoe, 1963.

Derthick, M. *Uncontrollable Spending for Social Services Grants.* Washington, D.C.: The Brookings Institution, 1975.

Duffly, F. R. Vandenberg. Hearings before Subcommittee on Public Assistance of the Committee on Ways and Means, House of Representatives, Vol. 2, Washington, D.C., June 1975, p. 612.

Gettings, R., ed. *Capitol Capsule.* Arlington, Va.: National Association of Coordinators of State Programs for the Mentally Retarded, Inc., August 17, 1973.

Helsel, E. "Action Alert." Unpublished communication from United Cerebral Palsy Association, Inc., Governmental Affairs Office, September 14, 1973.

Joe, T., and Meltzer, J. *Strategies for Long-Term Care.* Washington, D.C.: The Brookings Institution, 1976.

Kugel, R., and Wolfensberger, W. *Changing Patterns in Residential Services for the Mentally Retarded.* Washington, D.C.: President's Committee on Mental Retardation, 1969.

Mott, P. E. *Meeting Human Needs: The Social and Political History of Title XX.* Columbus: National Conference on Social Welfare, 1976.

Mueller, C., and Wolff, E. *Title XX: Comprehensive Annual Service Programs Plans—Technical Notes.* Unpublished reports, Department of Health, Education, and Welfare, January 1976.

Report to the Commissioner of Social Security and the Secretary of Health, Education, and Welfare on the Supplemental Security Income Program. DHEW Publication No. (SSA) 76-10609, U.S. Department of Health, Education, and Welfare, Social Security Administration, January 1976.

Ross, C. "Analysis: The Social Services Program." Unpublished communication from United Cerebral Palsy Association, Inc., Governmental Affairs Office, October 1974.

State Expenditures for Public Assistance Programs Approved Under Titles I, IV-A, X, XIV, XVI, and XIX of the Social Security Act for fiscal year 1972, U.S. Department of Health, Education, and Welfare, Social and Rehabilitation Service, Office of Financial Management.

"Title 45, Public Welfare," *Federal Register* (83), Part II. Washington, D.C.: U.S. Government Printing Office, May 1, 1973.

10

Approaches to Deinstitutionalization

G. RONALD NEUFELD

THERE IS GROWING SENTIMENT that large residential facilities are detrimental to the well-being of most people. Principles of normalization promote the belief that institutions should be replaced by small family-sized facilities located in communities close to the resident's natural environment. While these beliefs exist, we are confronted by the reality that approximately 200,000 persons are presently housed in large residential institutions.

In many instances these institutions are under-staffed, over-populated, and obsolete. Despite the dramatic increase in the cost of maintaining these environments, conditions for most residents continue to be dehumanizing and care is largely custodial in nature. As a result of several recent exposes of human abuse in residential institutions (e.g., Willowbrook, Partlow State Hospital) the courts have been called into the picture, and a number of these facilities have been adjudicated unconstitutional for violating the rights of residents to treatment and their right to due process.

While we are spending huge sums of money maintaining large residential facilities, it is estimated that less than 5 percent of our developmentally disabled population are served in these settings. In many instances, developmentally disabled persons remaining in the cultural mainstream are receiving no special services whatever, despite their need.

On one hand, given the outrageous conditions in many of our residential facilities, we need to find ways to depopulate these environments. At the same time, more comprehensive services are needed in the community in order to serve the large number of non-institutionalized developmentally disabled citizens.

While we are witnessing an increase in the number of community resources such as group homes, many of these resources fail to provide services for multiply handicapped and severely and profoundly retarded persons. In order to stop the flow of persons into institutions, and in order to permit the exodus of citizens from institutions, a comprehensive array of community services is needed. It is necessary that these services be predicated on a developmental model and that they be prepared to serve all developmental levels.

Unfortunately, there are forces that resist the movement from institution toward community. There are unions that strive to protect the jobs of employees in public institutions. There are parents who have children in public institutions who fear that they will lose all support service for their children if institutions are closed. There are communities whose economic base is heavily dependent upon the existence of institutions. There are comfortable residential communities which contend that developmentally disabled persons may not live in their neighborhoods, and discriminatory zoning regulations have been established to keep them out.

Although the forces listed above may be strong, it is this writer's opinion that the greatest resistance to deinstitutionalization is inertia. Deinstitutionalization can occur and is occurring where citizens have found ways to move the sluggish machinery of state bureaucracies that resist change and that presently tend to support an institutional philosophy.

A number of people and organizations have attempted to deinstitutionalize their communities since the mid-sixties. An attempt has been made here to examine several of these approaches. Deinstitutionalization is defined here as activities or programs aimed at the depopulation of institutions and institutional avoidance procedures.

The following review of approaches to deinstitutionalization is not exhaustive. The programs reviewed may not be the only ones using the approaches described, nor are they necessarily the best. Rather, an attempt has been made to distill the essence of an approach and to identify the steps that were taken or the process that was followed with the hope that other agencies, groups, or individuals may develop approaches to accomplish the goal of deinstitutionalization in their own communities.

A distinction is made in this study between a comprehensive approach to deinstitutionalization and an activity or project embracing a single idea which could not accomplish the mission of deinstitutionalization alone, but could make a substantial contribution toward a comprehensive approach when combined with other activities. The chapter is divided into six sections. The first five sections deal with comprehensive deinstitutionalization approaches according to the organization, group, or individual taking the initiative. Comprehensive approaches include state agency initiatives, regional initiatives, institutional initiatives, community initiatives, and individual initiatives. The sixth section describes several projects or activities that support deinstitutionalization activity.

There is no single source or location where one can go to find the information contained in this paper. No extensive body of literature has yet been generated in the area of deinstitutionalization. Also, in many instances, the leaders in the field are not writers but actors. The present information came largely from the following sources: (1) personal contacts, (2) telephone interviews, (3) personal experience, and (4) deinstitutionalization planning material. Persons interested in this area are urged to contact references given since activity in this field is changing very rapidly and that which is recorded today may be out-dated and irrelevant tomorrow.

COMPREHENSIVE APPROACHES TO DEINSTITUTIONALIZATION

State Agency Initiatives

Most large residential facilities are state-operated programs. Once a state bureaucracy establishes a direction, it becomes very difficult to reverse or even slightly alter that direction. In the area of deinstitutionalization, there are many state agency heads and key employees who verbally reject an institutional philosophy. They support needs assessment studies and they spend countless hours and many tax dollars developing plans but seldom reach the level of implementing the plan. The problem of non-implemented plans is increased in an era of rapid staff and administrative turnover. Each new administrative group tends to complete half of the cycle, needs assessment and planning. The important implementation and evaluation half of the cycle is often never reached and so the drawers of state agencies are filled with elaborate, out-dated plans that have never been tried.

Of course there are exceptions. In the following section of this study, deinstitutionalization activity initiated by state agencies in two different states is examined—Connecticut and North Carolina. In Connecticut, the activity is still in process and reportedly making progress. In North Carolina, the activity described was tried and failed. Attempts are made to examine some particulars of both approaches.

THE CONNECTICUT PLAN

Deinstitutionalization has been a primary thrust in Connecticut for several years. It is characterized by strong planning at the state level with the state mental retardation agency assuming a major leadership role. Judging from the Connecticut plan, it appears as if the regional mental retardation institutions are partners in planning with the state agency. Together, they have mobilized citizen support and developed community alternatives that are moving them toward their deinstitutionalization goals.

The first step in the Connecticut design was to remove the mildly and moderately retarded residents from their institutions and place them in group homes in the social mainstream. Prior to community placement, great care was exercised to help residents develop adaptive social skills that would render them compatible in community settings. Even after the residents were placed in the community, careful attention was focused upon the maintenance of these adaptive skills. Along with group-home development, attempts were made to encourage surrounding community agencies to provide support services for group-home residents. The private sector was approached to develop a citizen advocacy program. Citizen advocates were trained to help assure protection for clients and guarantee their human rights.

The second phase of the Connecticut plan focused upon prevention, or institutional avoidance through public education. As a preventive measure, persons on waiting lists for institutional placement were considered. Intensive efforts were directed toward preventing institutional enrollment by providing group or foster home placements. Prevention through public education was designed to help the public understand the role that developmentally disabled persons can perform in the social mainstream, and to describe services available to them.

The results to date of the Connecticut plan are as follows. First, a network of group homes has been developed. During the first five years of the plan, 720 residents from the Mansfield Training Center alone have been placed in the community. Institutional enrollment has dropped by approximately 40 percent and the source of candidates for institutional placement is gradually drying up due to the development of community services. At this point, residents in the institutions in Connecticut are primarily severely and profoundly retarded persons.

The next phase of the Connecticut deinstitutionalization program is to begin providing community alternatives for their severely and profoundly retarded residents. Initially, the Mansfield Training School proposes to find community placements for fifty severely and profoundly retarded persons. These candidates will be placed in their natural homes, foster homes, or group homes. In order to accomplish this phase of their deinstitutionalization plan, a transdisciplinary team of four professionals will be established. The team will include an occupational therapist, a physical therapist, a registered nurse, and a parent educator. First, the team will select persons to be deinstitutionalized, identify their individual needs, and establish necessary treatment programs. Next the team will train paraprofessionals to implement the treatment programs for the clients. Wherever possible, the involvement of parents will be sought so parents may work with the team and their own children.

In Connecticut, the state mental retardation agency has taken the initiative to move toward deinstitutionalization. There is obviously a strong alliance between the state agency and regional institutions. On one hand, residents have been carefully selected and prepared for community placement. At the same time, the support of community agencies was solicited to support residents in group homes. Along with institutional depopulation, attempts were made to reduce the flow of persons into institutions. Training was provided for parents and also for interested persons from the private sector to function as citizen advocates. Simultaneously, a public awareness effort was launched in order to gain public support for community services.

For the mildly and moderately retarded, the process is slow but appears to be occurring with minimal resistance. It is likely that resistance is limited because great care has been exercised to involve all interest groups in the process and because the Connecticut plan has included a strong public education program. It is too early to predict the success of the process for severely and profoundly retarded persons.

NORTH CAROLINA

In 1971, the Child Advocacy Center in Durham, North Carolina, was sponsored by the State Department of Mental Health. The primary goals of the Child Advocacy Center were (1) to help residential institutions develop institutional renewal procedures, (2) to develop procedures to depopulate institutions, and (3) to develop procedures to prevent the flow of persons into institutions.

For administrative and service-delivery convenience, the State Department of Mental Health divided the state into four regions. Serving each region was an Alcoholic Rehabilitation Center, a Psychiatric Hospital, and a Mental Retardation Center. Each region was divided into ten or eleven areas, each with a population base of approximately 100,000 persons. Each area is served by a Community Mental Health Center. At that time, four regional commissioners were located in the state's capital with responsibility for coordinating mental health activities within each region.

Since the provision of services to mentally retarded citizens was then and still is performed primarily through the state's Regional Mental Retardation institutions, North Carolina is characterized as embracing an institutional philosophy. It was through these Regional Mental Retardation Centers that the Child Advocacy Center planned to implement its goals through staff training and program development procedures.

The Child Advocacy Center consisted of a director, three senior staff, and a small support staff. Its annual budget was approximately $125,000. Designs to accomplish the deinstitutionalization goals were developed in collaboration with staff at each regional mental retardation facility. Although specific approaches differed in each location, the basic design provided for the training of staff to prepare residents for community placement and to develop exemplary programs or projects to accomplish the deinstitutionalization goals.

In addition to the Child Advocacy Center's training and program development activities in the regional centers, a variety of individual case advocacy situations were undertaken. Several of the case advocacy ventures were very controversial and made the position of the Child Advocacy Center highly visible.

Another controversial statewide project designed and sponsored by the advocacy program was a human rights study. The goals of the human rights study were (1) to examine existing laws and policies protecting the human rights of residents in institutions, (2) to propose new legislation to protect the rights of residents in institutions, (3) to collect information concerning the violation of resident rights in North Carolina institutions, and (4) to develop training material concerning the human rights of persons in institutions.

The total results of the Child Advocacy Center are very difficult to analyze. The advocacy program was not successful in establishing any durable structures that supported the goals of institutional avoidance or institutional depopulation in either the Regional Mental Retardation Centers or in their surrounding areas. Two of the three institutions totally rejected all of the training and program development activities as surely as the human body rejects an unfamiliar heart. Only a handful of institution residents were returned to the social mainstream as a result of the activities of the advocacy program, and the state still embraces an institutional philosophy.

Within three years, the counter-forces to the center and its goals were so great that staff at the center were unable to attend to their deinstitutionalization mission, and the majority of staff time was spent in justifying the program's existence. At that point, staff members who were committed to the goals of deinstitutionalization resigned and allowed the program to die rather than see its mission distorted.

However, not all of the activities of the Child Advocacy Center failed. For example, (1) new and improved patient rights legislation exists in the state today due to the Patient Rights Study; (2) one institution, the Western Carolina Center in Morganton, North Carolina, supports an exemplary internal advocacy program aimed at institutional renewal and protection of resident rights; (3) an outgrowth of this activity is an advocacy training program for students in the Division of Special Education at the University of North Carolina at Chapel Hill.

Insofar as the primary goal of the Child Advocacy Center was aimed at helping alter the state's institutional philosophy, the program failed. Why? First, the program was forced to look for support to internal, that is, state and local, administrators who did not respect the center's basic mission. Without support from within, the program should have looked for external support or support from the private sector. Second, the center had neither the staff nor the resources to engage in case advocacy activity. Case advocacy should have been handled by existing agencies or volunteers and the center should have rationed its resources for advocacy training, program building, and leadership development. Three, although the state maintains an institutional philosophy, communities generally are unwilling to accept leadership from the Regional Mental Retardation Centers. This is complicated by the fact that most of the community mental health centers refused to fully accept responsibility for mentally retarded citizens in their catchment area.

In two of the three target institutions, staff from the Child Advocacy Center were viewed as outsiders. In the communities they were viewed as institutionally based personnel. Finally, while the state was divided into geographic regions, power was centralized in the capital. In the capital, verbal support for the goals of the Child Advocacy Center was expressed, but the support was fickle. When deinstitutionalization and advocacy activity threatened the regional centers, no program support at the state level could be mustered. With no internal or external base of support and with a controversial mission, failure was inevitable.

Regional Initiatives

The real and stated priorities of a state are not always the same. One way of identifying a state's real priorities is to find out where the money is being spent. Most states adhere to an institutional philosophy; that is, their primary resources for serving mentally retarded citizens are large regional residential facilities.

It has already been mentioned that less than 5 percent of the total population of developmentally disabled citizens is served in these settings. Furthermore, when institutional programs have been weighed in the balance, they are found wanting. One conclusion that can be drawn from this information is that state agencies should not be involved in direct service provision. In keeping with this belief, some states have moved toward a philosophy of decentralization. Administratively, programs are regionalized, and responsibility for service delivery is contracted to private organizations, or state money is distributed to regional mechanisms to develop and provide services. Several regional approaches to deinstitutionalization are described below. They stand in contrast to state-initiated approaches since authority for service delivery is delegated to a regional mechanism and the regional mechanisms take leadership initiatives. Among the states that have developed strong regional structures are Washington, Minnesota, Wisconsin, and Oregon. Many more states have developed regional organizations but they are not necessarily related to their deinstitutionalization plans.

WASHINGTON STATE

Deinstitutionalization in Washington state is evolving through a series of piecemeal activities, programs, and legislative bills. First, given a commitment to deinstitutionalization, a network of privately owned group homes were developed under contracts for service. The group-home movement in Washington state is based on the belief that all developmentally disabled persons have a right to live in least restrictive environments. Plans have been developed to provide sufficient group homes to prevent the flow of persons into institutions, thereby stabilizing the population in institutions. The development of community-based alternatives has been supported by the passage of mandatory education legislation.

Concerning institutions, plans are under way to phase out and consolidate several institutions. According to their present plans, the institutional population for the entire state will stabilize at 2,360 in 1980.

Meanwhile, legislation has been passed establishing a network of community boards composed of local service providers and consumers. These boards are authorized by legislation to receive and spend money to operate programs and develop services in their catchment areas. They are also authorized to hire staff to conduct their work.

In addition to the decentralization impulse that established community boards, the state has been divided into six case-service districts. Positions in the case-service system should absorb the surplus of employees that results from the depopulation of the institutions. Staff in district offices are state employees and accountable to the central office in Olympia. District staff are responsible for the management of new group homes, nursing homes, and intermediate care facilities. Additional responsibility includes case management, counseling, follow-along services, and information and referral. They will constitute a single portal of entry into the total human-service delivery system.

The principle of decentralization is most clearly demonstrated in local boards. They are unique in that they have legislative authority to receive and spend money in service delivery. This authority, coupled with a strong local commitment to bringing their own citizens home from the regional institutions and to preventing the flow of persons into institutions by developing comprehensive community services, could result in an effective program of deinstitutionalization. This could be brought about by strong individual leadership or the collective leadership of a parent group. Washington state's local mechanisms deserve to be followed to see if they adopt a deinstitutionalization mission.

One unfortunate dynamic is that coordination is poor between the local boards and the case-service districts. This may be due to the fact that the Washington design did not occur through early systematic planning but rather through piecemeal legislation. Now they are faced with coordinating mechanisms that have overlapping responsibility. The case-service districts, while they are regional, are not fully decentralized insofar as they are accountable to a central administration. From this writer's viewpoint it is difficult to understand why regional staff were not organized as staff to the community boards.

Finally, Washington's long-range plan indicates a stabilized institutional population of 2,360 in 1980. Apparently the state's early deinstitutionalization efforts resulted in a high number of discharges. At this point, the exodus of residents is slow, having reached the severely and profoundly retarded residents. What is the rationale for 2,360 residents in two or three large state institutions? This provision would seem to be in conflict with the state's commitment to decentralization, community services, least restrictive environment, and normalization. Is a large regional institution the best alternative for the projected 2,360 residents?

SASKATCHEWAN

The process of deinstitutionalization began in 1962 when the Royal Commission on Health Services in Canada examined the purpose and function of large psychiatric hospitals. They concluded that large, isolated, segregated, undifferentiated mental asylums could not provide adequate treatment for mentally ill patients. In the wake of this observation, a new hospital administration was appointed consisting of Dr. F. Grunberg, Dr. H. Lafave, and Dr. A. Stewart. The position taken by the new administration was that if they could create conditions to prevent communities from extruding their citizens, then institutional depopulation would follow.

From 1921 to 1962, service provision for persons needing psychiatric care was centralized in the city of Weyburn. In 1963, a decentralization principle was adopted. The province was divided into a network of health districts locating strong central direction in each region. It was intended that each region should provide total service within its own boundaries. To this end, a system of community and regional services was mobilized. Community services included nursing homes, extended care facilities, geriatric centers, and general hospitals. The majority of these resources were in place from the outset; it was simply a matter of making their services accessible through coordination. Local services were supplemented by the development of four regional centers.

In keeping with the goal that each region should provide total service, the institution at Weyburn changed its admission policies. First, the hospital was only used an an overflow facility when all regional clinics were at full capacity. Second, long-term wards were abolished. If there were no community-based alternatives, patients were taken for short periods of time and returned to their natural community. Hospital staff were reorganized to serve specified geographic regions. Thus, no one could be admitted for custodial care; no one could be admitted to the hospital if that person could be treated in the community; no one could remain in the hospital if treatment outside was possible.

Having reduced admissions, the process of institutional depopulation was launched. First, staff in the hospital were assigned to teams who served specific geographic regions. They were responsible for in-patient, outpatient, and follow-up care in their territory. Next, residents in the long-term wards were discharged as rapidly as possible. As the long-term population decreased, there was a greater staff-to-patient ratio for dealing with the more difficult residents who remained.

At this point in the process, it became clear that deinstitutionalization could indeed be accomplished and resistance to the deinstitutionalization movement began to erupt. First, hospital employees began to fear that they would become unemployed. Second, the hospital in Weyburn was a major industry for the city, and it was felt that the loss of the hospital would result in an economic upheaval. Third, physicians in small communities would not be able to cope with the added burden of patients who were returning to their communities. Fourth, concern was expressed that residents were being dumped into inferior community programs such as nursing homes that were not responsive to their needs and could not provide adequate care.

Persons interested in the deinstitutionalization process did not ignore these negative forces. First, follow-up studies were organized to obtain information concerning the welfare of discharged residents. In the first study, data were collected on sixty-seven former residents. Of these, 18 percent were readmitted to the institution for more than one month during the first year following discharge. Fifty-four percent of the former patients obtained jobs and worked for six months or more after discharge. Most persons seemed more content in the community than they had been in the hospital, and they expressed their satisfaction with community arrangements. Even the chronically ill were often successfully integrated into the community. Later follow-up studies including a larger sample confirmed this information.

Regarding the concern about overburdened community service structures, it was discovered that existing local services along with the regional clinics were able to cope successfully with the former residents. In fact, it was discovered that the residents utilized fewer services and on fewer occasions than was at first anticipated. In the final analysis, the cost for care in communities was less than half the cost for residents in the institution. One should hasten to point out, however, that deinstitutionalization should not be adopted for economic reasons since many more persons are in need of service than institutions can serve, and adequate alternatives require many programs.

It is significant that, when provincial administrators were assured that former residents were adequately cared for in communities, deinstitutionalization was supported as being in the best interest of the patients. At that point, provincial officials cooperated with the hospital and the community in providing solutions for the employment and economic problems that were being created.

In the final analysis, no former hospital employees remained unemployed. In many instances, hospital staff were quickly hired in community services and regional centers due to their experience in the mental health area. Other persons were offered provincial assistance to obtain additional training in health-related areas and later received better jobs. One unused portion of the hospital was converted into a provincially sponsored vocational school. Another part of the hospital became one of the regional clinics and an extended health care facility. At the same time, some new industry came into the town with the result that the economy of the community was stabilized.

Several features stand out in the foregoing design. First, it is unlikely that deinstitutionalization would have occurred without the strong leadership and commitment of the hospital administration at Weyburn. Second, it was conjectured that if community services were sufficiently developed to prevent admissions to the hospital, then depopulation could be achieved. In this connection, strong regional leadership was developed with the stipulation that they would provide total service for citizens in their catchment area. Third, admission procedures to the hospital were made very difficult. Finally, there was strong support for the activity from provincial leaders.

NEW YORK STATE CAPITAL DISTRICT

In 1969, the New York State Department of Mental Hygiene planned to begin construction on the O. D. Heck Center, a $25-million residential facility with a mandate to serve the capital district of upstate New York, a seven-county region with a population of 500,000. Due to concern over the poor track record of institutions, construction plans were abandoned and the funds set aside to support the Eleanor Roosevelt Developmental Services.

Instead of building a regional institution, the state agency made a decision to: (1) move itself away from direct service provision, (2) support the development of a regional structure and allow the region to develop its own services, (3) emphasize prevention, and (4) support service provision in local communities rather than in large regional facilities. While the state took the initiative and provided resources for this approach, it became regional in the sense that responsibility for the development of services was turned over to a mechanism within the region.

With the money that the state had planned for bricks and mortar, it was possible to hire staff on the ratio of 1:1,000 on a regional basis. Establishing ratios based upon total population represents another departure from traditional institutional logic in which staff ratios are based upon numbers of handicapped persons in the institutions. Thus, more than 700 persons were hired and assigned to seven multidisciplinary teams. Each team was then designated to communities with populations ranging from 25,000 to 165,000. In addition to the community-based team, a logistics team was established for coordination, planning, and evaluation functions. The overall plan was to mobilize a partnership that yoked together the state, counties, private agencies, and consumers.

One assumption made by the teams was that no single agency could presume to provide comprehensive services for any single client or group of clients. Therefore, services were identified and the teams began collaborating with local agencies and service providers.

Another belief embraced by personnel of the Eleanor Roosevelt Developmental Services is that service provision would be based upon a client's level of functioning, a developmental model, rather than on a label, the diagnostic prescriptive model. In keeping with this belief, three program modules were developed: day, evening, and overnight. Services provided in this modular structure would be based upon individualization and normalization concepts. During the day, education, prevocational, and vocational activities were sponsored. During the evening and on weekends, attention was focused upon socialization and recreation, including activities such as respite care and drop-in centers. The overnight module provided a place where persons could come to sleep and relax—a place to call home. It was anticipated that the overnight program would not be over-burdened if the day and evening modules functioned effectively. All community services were identified according to their capability for service provision in the various modules indicated above.

In addition to staff hired by the Eleanor Roosevelt Developmental Services and the integrated network of existing community-based service providers, a large volunteer task force was organized. It was believed that all persons identifying problems should be recruited to become part of the solution. Hence, volunteer participation ranges from service provision to information dissemination. At this point, there are more than 1,400 volunteers participating in the Eleanor Roosevelt Developmental Services network.

Another belief shared by the staff is that information concerning human services should be shared with the public. First, values and beliefs should be communicated. Second, the public should be made aware of needs and services. Attempts were made to disseminate public information through television, radio, and the press. In addition to the use of mass media, presentations were made. Whenever possible, volunteers were used as speakers and presenters.

Finally, the regional approach employed by the Eleanor Roosevelt Developmental Services is one of responsiveness to the political process. At the same time, there was no centralized authority. Leadership was diversified; no single group was viewed as having excessive power; and responsibility was shared. There are some obvious advantages to this approach. First, forces that are antagonistic to the deinstitutionalization activity find it difficult to attack a movement with a large, diffuse leadership base. Second, an organization can waste a great deal of time and energy defending itself or attacking its enemies. In the human service sector, this is time that needs to be spent serving clients. At the outset, there was strong political support for this activity. The apparent agreement concerning goals and values among staff, state officials, and the community is an important aspect of this design.

Obviously, the litmus test of any deinstitutionalization approach is the result. In this seven-county region serving more than 500,000 people, more than 3,000 persons are being served; there are 150 collaborating programs; no persons are being sent out of the region for services or placed in institutions. Whereas several years ago the region had 1,400 persons placed in a regional facility, there are now fewer than 600, and it is planned to have all residents back home in less than two years. The record is impressive. Curiously, the Director of the Eleanor Roosevelt Developmental Services is Huge Lafave, one of the leaders in the deinstitutionalization activity which resulted in the closing of the Psychiatric Hospital in Weyburn, Saskatchewan.

EASTERN NEBRASKA COMMUNITY OFFICE OF RETARDATION

The deinstitutionalization movement took root in Nebraska in the late 1960s due to the activities of the Nebraska Association for Retarded Children. First, the parent organization was successful in obtaining the passage of several pieces of legislation, including mandatory education legislation and anti-sterilization laws. Second, through a series of town meetings conducted across the state, the sensibility of citizens was aroused in behalf of retarded citizens. Third, at the request of the Nebraska Association, the governor appointed the Nebraska Citizens' Study Committee to investigate conditions at the Beatrice State Home, Nebraska's only state-supported residential institution. Due to this investigation a new plan was developed in Nebraska to deliver services to retarded citizens in the state. The plan that was developed was predicated upon human rights issues, the normalization principle, and the developmental model and proposed to implement a comprehensive array of community-based services.

In order to implement the plan additional legislation was passed which established six regions in the state of Nebraska. Each region was given responsibility for developing services and programs that were responsive to the needs of mentally retarded persons throughout their lives. At the state level, the legislation provided for an office of mental retardation with the following responsibilities to establish and operate community-based services, to provide consultation for mentally retarded persons and their families, to evaluate existing facilities, and to assess future needs.

The Eastern Nebraska Community Office of Retardation (ENCOR) is one of the Regional offices that was established by the above legislation. It serves a five-county area with a population of 521,000 in both urban and rural settings. The regional staff is largely independent of the state office. At the regional level, the staff is accountable to a board of governors that consists of five voting members, one from each county. In addition to the five voting representatives from each county, the board includes five non-voting advisors. The regional office is the fixed point of responsibility for all service provision, and the governing board maintains authority for all ENCOR transactions. In addition to the governing board ENCOR has access to an advisory committee that has membership from all vested interest groups.

ENCOR was created in order to fill the gaps within the existing service structure. At present, they are serving approximately 1,400 persons of all ages and at all levels of functioning. Eighty-four different residential sites have been developed, including thirteen group homes. One interesting observation that ENCOR staff have made is that their group homes are not as successful as smaller residential arrangements serving no more than three to four persons. Regardless of where a person is served, an individual plan is developed for every client, and continuity of service between agencies is assured. In this way, mentally retarded persons are dispersed in the community and the system is inundated with supportive service.

No one has been extruded from the ENCOR catchment area in the past two years. However, there are still 300 adults and fifty children in the Beatrice Home. Current plans call for the return of these 350 persons to the ENCOR region by 1977.

The Nebraska design is an excellent illustration of a regional model since it is decentralized in a way that locates substantial authority in the region and established the regional body as the service delivery mechanism. One must remember, however, that the prime mover for this design was a parent organization. Behind the scene at all times, rendering both ENCOR and county governments accountable for providing resources and services for the retarded person, is the Nebraska Association for Retarded Children. This represents a healthy balance of power between the public and private sector. This alliance is strengthened since members from both sectors share the values embodied in the principle of normalization.

Community or Local Initiatives

In contrast to deinstitutional initiatives that have been undertaken by state agencies or regional (multi-county) mechanisms are examples of initiatives that have been taken by communities. The following section of this chapter describes deinstitutionalization activity that came about through local initiatives.

JEFFERSON COUNTY ASSOCIATION FOR RETARDED CHILDREN

Jefferson County is a rural county in northern New York which includes the city of Watertown and a total population of 100,000 persons. The population is relatively static and the citizens tend to ignore large-scale social problems to focus rather upon problems at the microscopic or local level. In the mid-sixties the Jefferson County Association for Retarded Children (ARC) had one public school sponsored class for retarded citizens. The only choice available for most families with disabled children was to keep them at home with no supportive services or training, or to send them away to a state institution. Dissatisfied with these poor and limited options, the parents determined to establish their own alternative system of education for trainable children. They had three goals in mind: (1) to provide educational opportunities for their children, (2) to prove to public schools that their children could benefit from classroom exposure, and (3) to nudge public schools to assure responsibility for providing education and training for their children.

At this point, the ARC sponsored classes are still functioning and there are four classes in the public school. Education and training resources are now available in Jefferson County along with services, including diagnostic medical evaluations, full-time infant care, sheltered employment, hostels, and supervised independent living. More than 340 persons are served each day, and admissions to state institutions have been reduced to zero.

In order to have a truly comprehensive network of community services, and in order to provide a larger number of community alternatives for handicapped persons, additional services are needed. It is proposed that the school system take over the education classes that the local Association for Retarded Citizens is now sponsoring in order that the ARC's money be directed toward the development of additional alternatives.

Meanwhile, the attention of concerned citizens has turned toward approximately 130 persons from Jefferson County who are still institutionalized in state schools. A small amount of federal money has been requested to help Jefferson County bring their citizens back home. The first step in the process is to mobilize a diagnostic team that will: (1) identify all Jefferson County residents in state schools, (2) evaluate the residents' disability and potential for community placement, (3) arrange for placement in appropriate community programs, (4) continue efforts to prevent admissions to state institutions, (5) evaluate the impact of community placement upon former residents of state schools and, (6) develop a procedure that may serve as a model to other rural communities. The diagnostic team consists of a full-time social worker and part-time consultants from psychiatry, medicine, vocational rehabilitation, and education. During the diagnostic phase of the program, the team plans to survey the needs of each institutional resident, who are now located in three different institutions throughout the state. It is the belief of community leaders that sufficient resources exist in Jefferson County to bring their citizens home.

An attempt will first be made to place residents in their natural homes. Back-up support will be provided in the form of day programming, respite care, and nighttime recreation. For residents unable to return to their natural homes, 75 to 100 family care living arrangements have been created. The New York State Department of Mental Hygiene will provide stipends to support each resident. In addition to the services indicated above, plans are under way to create a residential facility for severely and profoundly retarded persons under the age of eighteen. All residents will be involved in day programs sponsored by public schools or the ARC.

It is anticipated that fifteen to twenty of the 130 institutional residents may require ongoing medical care. It is believed that existing health care facilities including the general hospital and nursing homes can provide the services needed by this population. Discussions are under way to arrange for the provision of this service.

In connection with this project, it is interesting to note that the local ARC views itself as the sole provider of services for the mentally retarded. They express dismay at numerous attempts to launch comprehensive plans. They have grown weary of spending fruitless labor in planning and interagency coordination. They have a clear picture of what needs to be done, and there is a strong commitment to engage the assignment rather than talk about it. Their action-studded track record speaks for itself, and one is left with the impression that the job will be done.

From this writer's viewpoint, it is unfortunate that the ARC parent group has not formed an alliance with other parent organizations with similar needs and missions. Such an alliance would increase their numbers and their lobbying power.

Comparing the community-initiative program just described with the state and regional deinstitutionalization designs, one is impressed by its relative simplicity. The parent organization claims credit for all of the deinstitutionalization activity and demonstrates a strong spirit of individualism throughout their plan. Whereas the state and regional planning groups described earlier devoted considerable attention to agency coordination, the initiating parent organization in Schenectady (Capital District) indicated a distaste for collaboration with other organizations. Coming from a background of unproductive interagency council meetings and sessions with unresponsive service providers, the parent group is quick to confront but, at the same time, willing to act. An additional feature of the community initiated deinstitutionalization plan, is that the educational system was recognized as an important ingredient in the activity.

MADISON PUBLIC SCHOOLS

Historically, public school systems have been slow in responding to the education and training needs of mentally retarded populations. In the meantime many state departments of mental health and mental retardation have developed their own education and training programs. In view of this dichotomy there tends to be a great gulf at both the state and local level between education and human-service agencies.

In a conversation with persons from Madison, Wisconsin, this writer was informed that the Special Education Department of the Madison Public School System has taken the initiative in providing extensive training and education for their mentally retarded citizens from birth to adulthood. Additionally, they have assumed a leadership role in organizing an interagency council at the local level to help coordinate service provision for retarded citizens in their school system.

The total population in the catchment area served by the Madison Public School system is 300,000; this includes 32,000 school-age children. Of these, it is estimated that there are approximately 3,000 handicapped persons.

In the late sixties the Madison Public School System was assuming responsibility for working with mentally retarded preschool populations. Subsequently, this activity has gained the support of mandatory education legislation in the area of education and training opportunities for mentally retarded children.

The services provided by the school system are directed toward all ages from birth to adulthood and extend to all levels of functioning. Due to comprehensive services provided by the school system, it is reported that no preschool or school-age persons have been committed to residential institutions since 1972. In addition to the services provided for citizens within the community, it is reported that the school system is now becoming active in the process of bringing persons back home from state institutions. Supportive services are provided by the school system to youth between the ages of fourteen and seventeen who are being placed into community-based group homes.

There are several obvious gaps in the Madison Public School deinstitutionalization design. First, no information is available concerning a systematic plan for bringing institutionalized citizens back home. second, the school system reported difficulty in coordinating their activities with the local parent organization for retarded citizens. School personnel indicated a hope that the parent association would move into the area of adult services to provide services for all clients aged twenty-one and over in areas such as sheltered workshops. From this writer's viewpoint, comprehensive deinstitutionalization planning is likely to be weak without support from and cooperation with the private sector. Finally, apart from possible interaction in the interagency council, no mention was made of services provided by the comprehensive regional community mental health centers in Wisconsin. Wisconsin was one of the first states in the country to decentralize and regionalize its mental health service network and extend their mandate to serve all developmentally disabled clients in their catchment areas. Clearly, coordination is needed between the education and developmental disabilities agencies. In this way continuity of services can be assured across age groupings and at all levels of functioning. In the meantime, the foregoing program provides us with an example of a local school system that is taking the initiative to coordinate deinstitutionalization activity for its constituents.

Institutional Initiatives

There is wide variance between institutions across the country. The deinstitutionalization movement has caused some institutions to retrench in order to protect their territory and the jobs of their staffs. Other institutions use deinstitutionalization to promote internal reform and renewal, while still others participate actively in programs to depopulate their own environments. The Macomb-Oakland Regional Center is a state-supported residential program in Michigan that is assuming a leadership role in the deinstitutionalization movement in their catchment area. The center serves a two-county area with a population of 1.6 million.

The Macomb-Oakland Center is designed to serve a maximum of 278 severely and profoundly retarded residents. While their plans include a residential facility, staff are planning an array of activities to prevent the extrusion of citizens from their counties, and persons currently in institutions elsewhere in the state are being returned home.

The first step in the regional deinstitutionalization plan was to develop a network of community-based services. Within two and a half years, 140 foster homes, ten group homes, developmental training homes, and mental retardation nursing home were established. Additionally, seventeen group homes have been incorporated as private nonprofit agencies. These programs are supported by the state agency which contracts with responsible individuals in the community. Next, procedures are established to monitor these programs.

When the Macomb-Oakland Center was started in 1972, there were a thousand persons from their two-county area in institutions elsewhere in the state. Today, with support from the community services indicated, only five hundred are left in these institutions and virtually no persons are not being sent away, in contrast to an average of 61 per year prior to 1972.

The approach that is presented above and the array of services developed appear to be very similar to the approaches described in the section on regional initiatives. The difference lies in the initiating and administrative arrangement. The Macomb-Oakland personnel are state-agency employed and accountable to the director of the center. Services are extended to the region from the center. Staff are accountable to the state, not a regional board. There are, however, two standing committees with one representative from each county. No leadership role has been taken by any parent group in the area.

In many parts of the country, local communities often resist the leadership of institution staff. What factors have contributed to the progress of this institution-initiated approach to deinstitutionalization when in other parts of the country state-operated institutions providing direct service have generally experienced miserable failure? One contributing factor may be that they are relating to a small geographic area. A second factor may be due to the fact that at this time the residential component of the Macomb-Oakland facility has not yet been completed. One wonders if they are not making a mistake by building their residential facility. The Macomb-Oakland approach stands in contrast to the approach taken in New York by the Eleanor Roosevelt Developmental Services, which abandoned their plans to build a residential complex.

Individual Initiatives

The shift from an institutional philosophy to a community philosophy is not always easily attained. It often involves changes in values, social disruption, alterations in decision-making mechanisms, and economic adjustments. The dismantling of the youth corrections system in Massachusetts by Jerome Miller is an example of a deinstitutionalization activity that has caused substantial social disruption. It stands in sharp contrast to the unobtrusive deinstitutionalization tactics reported by Hugh Lafave in Saskatchewan and New York.

A series of investigations into the Department of Youth Services in Massachusetts culminated in a crisis in 1969 and brought about the resignation of the director of youth services. The investigations exposed the use of punishment, custodial care rather than treatment, authoritarian approaches in dealings with residents, regimentation, and the manipulation of personal habits and privileges. Despite this treatment, high rates of recidivism were documented for residents exposed to this approach. In October 1969, Dr. Jerome Miller was appointed Commissioner of the Department of Youth Services. Miller took charge of the department with support from both the legislative and executive branches of state government to implement progressive policies and treatment programs for delinquent youth. Miller's first approach was to establish his central office staff and support them in exercising strong leadership toward the establishment of new treatment approaches. In this connection, he proposed the development of therapeutic communities in the institutions. This approach called for a democratic relationship between staff and youth in small units. Miller also declared that youth would be allowed to wear their hair as they chose and that they could wear street clothes. Furthermore, a general order was issued forbidding any staff member to strike or physically abuse a resident.

Within the institutions themselves, power and authority was decentralized. The new treatment programs established an open climate in which staff and residents expressed feelings and concerns to each other. Additionally, youth were expected to assume greater responsibility for participating in decisions that affected them directly. It was Miller's belief that institutional placements were generally detrimental. Therefore, he encouraged a more rapid turnover of residents.

During the first year of Miller's administration, resistance was unmasked from two sectors. First of all, staff in the corrections system that he had inherited were unable to adjust to his philosophy. Second, courts, probation, and police departments resisted his liberal parole policies. It was Miller's belief that the public would not support traditional training school practices if they were exposed. He therefore encouraged the active involvement of visitors and volunteers.

Miller soon discovered that he could not purge the system of existing staff. Staff discharges were prevented due to tenure and political sponsorship. His next attempt to adjust staff attitudes and treatment approaches was to implement a staff training program. But, change did not come. The response of threatened staff was over hostility, deliberate attempts to sabotage programs, or passive resistance. Alienated staff began to muster antagonistic forces to support them. They found some allies in other public officials. By the fall of 1971, two legislative investigations had been launched.

in spite of his vigorous twenty-four-month effort to restructure the Department of Youth Services, Miller felt that very little change had taken place. He began to favor the notion of abruptly closing the institutions and providing services in the community. As a first step in the direction of community services, the department was further decentralized into seven regions. In each region, staff were assigned to establish new court liaison and work with juvenile judges and probation staff. Additionally, a network of community services were developed ranging from residential to nonresidential placements for individuals and small groups. It was planned that centralized, institutional service would be retained for only a small number of dangerous and disturbed offenders.

Initially, two institutions were closed. Transfer of the residents from the institutions into communities was conducted quickly, since opposition was expected and Miller wanted to prevent the counterforces from having sufficient advance notice to organize against the institutional closures and prevent them. While community placements were being finalized, students from the University of Massachusetts were used as advocates for the former residents of the institutions.

Staff from the institutions that were emptied had been told months in advance of the closing date. However, they refused to believe these announcements until they witnessed a motorcade of automobiles empty the institutions in a matter of hours. Officials from the University of Massachusetts reported that the juvenile population caused no problems in the university setting. Also, an eleven-month follow-up indicated that the recidivism rate for the mass discharge group was less than the recidivism rate for graduates from a traditional program.

As a result of the move toward community, seven hundred youth were placed in residential group homes, two hundred and fifty persons in foster homes, and eight hundred clients in nonresidential programs. All of these resources were developed on very short notice.

After closing the institutions, the Department of Youth Services was left with excess staff since most services were now purchased from the private sector. New regionally assigned staff helped former residents get jobs, assisted them in obtaining placements in school programs, and provided support and guidance for them in joining youth groups. In general, youth viewed the new system as more helpful than the traditional program. Certainly, the new program provided more humane conditions for the youthful offenders.

As indicated earlier, the deinstitutionalization approach used by Jerome Miller stands in sharp contrast to the approach of Hugh Lafave. Lafave worked closely with the political and administrative machinery. Jerome Miller found himself in constant conflict with the bureaucracy. In one institution it was reported that the person Miller had appointed as superintendent was occupying a maintenance supervisor's job card. Miller's quick move to develop community services also created many problems for the sluggish state machinery. Group home operators on contract for service agreements found themselves on the verge of bankruptcy because the state was unable to find ways of making payments to them.

There are some similarities between the deinstitutionalization approach used by Jerome Miller and the deinstitutionalization activity used by the Association for Retarded Children in Jefferson County, New York. In both situations, the leadership expressed impatience with the existing administrative and political structures. Both were unwilling to wait for support from the system. Lack of responsiveness was interpreted as resistance but this did not suspend action. On the contrary, administrative resistance appeared to instill increased fervor in the movement.

Another major problem confronting Miller concerned the resistance of staff that Miller inherited. All of his attempts to alter their values were eventually frustrated. Despite this lack of support, he continued to pursue his deinstitutionalization goals.

An increasing trend on the part of state agencies concerns purchase of service agreements. In addition to using purchase of service agreements to develop community alternatives, Miller also used purchase of service for staff development and program monitoring.

Finally, Miller exploded the belief that the development of community services requires long-range, careful planning. In a matter of months, Miller's staff was able to generate an impressive array of community alternatives to absorb residents from the Youth Corrections System in Massachusetts. More information is needed to examine the exact manner in which this was accomplished. Next, it would be helpful to determine if the same results could be accomplished for residents in mental retardation facilities.

THE ROLE OF SPECIFIC PROJECTS IN THE DEINSTITUTIONALIZATION MOVEMENT

An attempt has been made in the foregoing section of this chapter to describe a variety of comprehensive approaches to deinstitutionalization. A detailed examination of each comprehensive approach would likely uncover a variety of specific projects, programs, or techniques that lend a unique contribution to the over-all deinstitutionalization activity. On the other hand none of these projects standing alone are likely to accomplish the entire deinstitutionalization mission. Several techniques are reviewed below to indicate the role of project activity in contributing to the deinstitutionalization process.

Cross-Modality Teams

Several states are currently using cross-modality teams to assist them in deinstitutionalization activity (Connecticut; Denton, Texas; Marin County, California; Ellisville, Mississippi; Portland, Oregon; Madison, Wisconsin; Columbus, Ohio). The cross-modality concept involves the inclusion of members of several disciplines who transmit their skills to each other. Individual team members in turn work directly with clients or train trainers, recognizing that backup support is available from fellow team members as it may be needed.

The numbers and disciplines represented on a team varies from project to project. The Consortium Approach of Community Alternatives & Institutional Reform (CAIR), for Persons with Cerebral Palsy is a cross-modality project in Oregon. They are utilizing a five-person team consisting of a physical therapist, occupational therapist, speech therapist, nurse, and parent or surrogate. In the Ellisville State School in Mississippi, cross-modal teams include ten persons—five professionals and five paraprofessionals. Members of professional disciplines represented on their team include psychologists, social workers, parent educators, special educators, and supervisors of residential care.

Team activities likewise differ from one project to another but generally include activities such as individual client assessments, the development of individualized treatment plans, and training for clients and/or training for direct care personnel. Teams are often required to work in the area of institutional reform, institutional avoidance, or institutional depopulation activities.

From this writer's viewpoint, while cross-modality teams might be viewed as valuable instruments in deinstitutionalization, it seems unlikely that this activity alone could accomplish the very complex task of full-scale deinstitutionalization in a state or region.

Public Awareness Programming

It is obvious that deinstitutionalization cannot occur until a network of community alternatives are developed. The development of community programs such as group homes has been thwarted in many areas because of negative public opinion about developmentally disabled citizens. These negative attitudes are often the products of myths, false information, or lack of information. Some states have responded to this problem by passing legislation that prohibits exclusionary zoning. That is, communities cannot exercise prejudice against persons with developmental disabilities by denying them the right to live in certain residential areas. While exclusionary zoning should not be allowed to discriminate against developmentally disabled citizens, such communities are likely to be difficult areas to move into with developmentally disabled persons. Thus a society or a community with limited tolerance for behavioral or academic variance supports an institutional philosophy. Apparently the tolerance boundaries for behavioral and intellectual variance differs substantially from community to community. If public intolerance stems from lack of information or false information, then public awareness programs should be provided in order to set the stage for the integration of developmentally disabled persons into the cultural mainstream. In developing a model community-based service system for developmentally disabled persons in the New York Capital District, Hugh Lafave (1974) points out that a shared sense of purpose is an important ingredient: "We have encouraged the examination of value systems, tried to reconcile them where necessary and to change them where this seems desirable." Lafave was careful to share information with private sectors through public presentations and by using all forms of mass media.

In Connecticut, a carefully designed public awareness program was developed in order, as Trohanis (1974) said: to break down those commonly held prejudices which may be preventing the developmentally disabled from playing the role in society they rightly deserve. Placing its emphasis on modifying prejudices about the nature of developmental disabilities, the Connecticut program will gear its efforts to:

1. Help find jobs for the developmentally disabled.
2. Help eliminate fears about the nature of developmental disability afflictions.
3. Create an acceptance for group and foster homes.
4. Help get assignments and contracts for shelter workshops.
5. Inform Connecticut citizens about Statewide (public and private) facilities available for treatment, training and counseling for the developmentally disabled and their families.

Approaches were developed for two audiences in Connecticut, an internal and an external audience. Internally, methods of communication were aimed at supporting supervisors, directors of regional centers, and private consumer organizations. First, a public awareness manual was developed to help the audience designated above deal with the media. A short course was then developed to train persons in the use of the manual. Finally, procedures were developed to produce a two-page bimonthly newsletter in order to share information between regional centers, agencies, projects, and parent organizations.

A much more extensive program has been developed for the external audience or the general public, both lay and professional. First, two brochures were developed. One described the role that developmentally disabled citizens can play in society. Another described available services for developmentally disabled citizens. Second, a press kit was developed for editors and writers who are working on stories related to developmental disabilities. Third, a publicity strategy was designed in order to gain access to the mass media for new releases related to developmental disabilities. Fourth, a speakers' bureau was mobilized to handle face-to-face communication. Fifth, a mailing program was organized for reaching specific groups. Sixth, a photo display was developed for placement in various public environments. Seventh, a slide tape program was produced and training seminars were organized.

The above approach to public awareness programming was developed in Connecticut for the Developmental Disabilities Council. In order to implement this program, it was suggested that a full-time public information person be hired with support from a public awareness committee of the council.

Common sense inclines this writer to believe that comprehensive public awareness programs should help deal with negative public attitudes and pave the way for activities such as deinstitutionalization. At the same time research data is needed before we can comfortably assess the impact of public awareness campaigns on public values and attitudes.

Voucher Systems

Traditionally, state agencies in the human service area have assumed a central role in direct service provision. At present there is a growing tendency as seen in Nebraska, Wisconsin, the state of Washington, and Connecticut to regionalize and at the same time decentralize both in terms of leadership and decison making and also in terms of resource distribution. We have witnessed a similar trend at the national level which has resulted in more and more resources being directed back to the states and even counties. At the national level, the revenue sharing program is an illustration of this trend. Decentralization in its most extreme form would be to place all resources back in the hands of individuals and families needing services and allow them to shop for services in a free marketplace.

Christopher Jencks proposed that our educational system should adopt such a plan. According to the Jencks proposal an attempt would be made to determine the cost of education for each child. At the beginning of each school year, every family with school-age children would receive educational vouchers that they could spend in any school of their choice. Obviously such a system would place schools into competition with each other and withdraw the present cost advantage that public schools hold over private schools. Since families would control the flow of money spent in the education system, school administrators and teachers would be forced to be more responsive to the public or they would run the risk of losing their clients.

Voucher plans have met with substantial resistance. First, voucher plans have been attacked by those who fear that it would result in a totally segregated system. In response to this concern Jencks proposed that only a certain percentage of the placements in a specific school be left open for random application. In this way racial balance could be assured. A second fear is that parents might pay additional money in order to have their child accepted. This could be prevented by simply auditing the schools financial records. Still another concern is that inferior organizations would spring up, accept the money, and then close out their programs. In order to prevent this abuse, it is obvious that rigid accrediting standards would need to be established and programs would need to be monitored. The greatest fear expressed by public school educators is that a voucher plan would destroy public schools. If this fear is based upon an awareness that public schools are unresponsive to the needs of citizens or inferior to private schools, then perhaps they should be challenged and forced to compete for clients and resources.

Within the context of this chapter, one wonders what effect a voucher system would have on the development and support for human services? Given the present high cost of institutional care, it is likely that families could purchase superior services elsewhere if they were presented vouchers for an equivalent amount of money. In order for the voucher system to successfully depopulate our institutions, families would need access to a comprehensive array of community services. Additionally, since only 5 percent of the developmentally disabled population is served in residential settings, we would need to develop an equitable system for distributing the resources.

Experiments with voucher systems have been tried in both Massachusetts and California. Information concerning the strength and weakness of these experiments is needed in order to assess the possibility of extending such an enterprise into the human service arena.

The Results of Public Exposés

Several years ago, Willowbrook, a residential institution for mentally retarded citizens, became the target of an extensive investigation aimed at exposing the outrageous conditions for its residents. The results of the investigation and the subsequent exposé has made a profound impact upon the deinstitutionalization movement in America. The conscience of many previously apathetic Americans was jolted by this event, and additional investigations and exposés have been conducted in institutions in other parts of the country. Invariably, institutional environments have been found wanting and the human rights of residents violated.

At least three major categories of reactions have developed in response to the results of investigations into institutions. First, courts have intervened; second, citizens' groups have been aroused and have organized to propose solutions; and third, a variety of individual and program monitoring procedures have been developed.

COURT INTERVENTION

The courts have become involved with institutions due to the violation of human rights. Court suits that have been filed include the areas of due process, right to treatment, right to equal education opportunities, peonage suits, and suits contesting exclusionary zoning in communities.

When the human rights of citizens are ignored, court action is certainly indicated. However, in many instances court action has only served to expose the problems, stopping short of solutions—solutions that require more money, more staff, and more program alternatives. When the courts withdraw, state agencies, institutions, and communities are often left in confusion. Communities are at a loss to respond without resources to develop community-based alternatives. Many institutions are responding with requests for more staff and more money in order to improve conditions for residents. On one hand, if citizens continue to be housed in large residential settings, then our institutions should be given the resources needed to provide adequate services for their residents. On the other hand, it is possible that large residential institutions can never provide adequate services for developmentally disabled persons. If this is true, then we are squandering our resources by directing them toward institutions. To this writer's knowledge, no institutions have been closed by the courts. Are the courts failing to accept full responsibility in their dealings with institutions?

CITIZEN AROUSAL

Another reaction to the exposés of human abuse in public institutions is the arousal of citizen groups, especially parent organizations. Parent organizations have used this information to mobilize new legislation, restructure and reorganize institutional environments, fire and replace vulnerable institutional staff, and create community-based alternatives to institutions.

One of the best illustrations of a constructive response to the investigation of an institution took place in Nebraska. In Nebraska the Association for Retarded Children requested an investigation of their state institution. The investigation resulted in the production of a new statewide plan to decentralize the administration of state programs and to develop a comprehensive network of community services.

In other areas, groups and individuals have become enamored of the process of exposing inadequacies in programs, and the exposé has become an end in and of itself. The goal of program investigations should be to improve conditions for the clients—our developmentally disabled citizens.

PROGRAM STANDARDS AND MONITORING PROCEDURES

The exposés of dehumanizing services for developmentally disabled citizens have also heightened the need for individual and program monitoring; watching techniques should provide information concerning the value of programs and services for clients. In response to this need, a variety of monitoring procedures have been developed, several of which have been designed specifically for large residential institutions.

As early as 1952 activities were under way to develop standards for institutions. At that time, the American Association on Mental Deficiency (AAMD) published a report on standards for institutions. In 1964, Standards for State Residential Institutions for the Mentally Retarded was published by AAMD's Project on Technical Planning in Mental Retardation. This instrument was designed for program evaluation and accreditation. Standards were minimal and viewed as being attainable in five to ten years.

The Joint Commission on Accreditation of Hospitals was established in 1951. Between 1951 and 1965, it focused only upon hospital accreditation. In 1965, it expanded its activities to include the development of standards to ensure quality service in long-term care facilities. The goal of the Accreditation Council was to develop and implement standards and survey procedures to ensure the delivery of adequate services. The accreditation procedure provides for continuing objective service evaluation mechanisms that are external to the organization being evaluated.

The first step in the evaluation process is that the participating facility conduct a self-survey through a survey questionnaire. At a later time, surveyors are appointed to make an on-site visit. During the on-site visit the program is assessed in terms of services provided for a sample of residents. Services are expected to maximize a resident's human qualities and meet his or her unique developmental needs.

At this point, participation in program audits such as the procedure described above are voluntary. However, federal legislation has been proposed to mandate evaluation techniques for residential facilities. If such legislation were passed, it is likely that institutions would be granted a certain period of time in which to comply with the standards. After that time, all federal funds would be withheld from substandard facilities.

No attempt has been made here to identify the numerous procedures that have been developed for individual and program monitoring. As public concern over the shortcomings of institutions has grown, the number of monitoring approaches has increased. What are the implications of this trend for the deinstitutionalization movement? First, at the very lowest level, program monitoring procedures should result in substantial institutional reform. In order to bring institutions into compliance with rigorous standards, states may find themselves spending disproportionate amounts of money, considering the number of clients served, when the same clients could be served more effectively and more efficiently in community settings. From this point of view, federal standards for institutions could function as a deterrent to deinstitutionalization. A second possibility is that rigorous standards could result in the dismantling of institutions in favor of more efficient and more effective community-based alternatives.

CONCLUSION

An attempt has been made in the present chapter to examine some of the procedures that have been used in order to depopulate our institutions and in order to provide adequate community-based alternatives for developmentally disabled citizens. If the goal of deinstitutionalization is a zero extrusion rate of citizens from the social mainstream and total depopulation of residential institutions, then it is likely that none of the approaches described above can be considered completely successful. However, some of the approaches have made substantial progress in the direction of deinstitutionalization. From this writer's viewpoint, special attention should be focused upon the following approaches: (1) the Saskatchewan plan for depopulating the hospital at Weyburn; (2) the New York Capital district; (3) ENCOR; (4) the Jefferson County Association for Retarded Children; and (5) the Department of Youth Services in Massachusetts. Each of these approaches reports unusual results, and each program has utilized certain procedures that render them worthy of close examination.

One observation that should be made is that an approach which is utilized in one setting may not work in another. Information is needed to help us predict good fit between procedures and settings. At the same time, it may not be helpful to construct state models but rather to identify the numerous techniques that are used and put them together in various combinations to fit different settings. Given the information presented above, the combinations are endless.

In keeping with the foregoing observations, no attempt will be made here to identify an ideal model. However, certain recurring themes are obvious in several of the deinstitutionalization plans. Concerning underlying philosophy or beliefs, the concepts of normalization and human rights are dominant. In this connection human values are frequently considered and provided a rationale for programs that were recommended. From an organizational viewpoint, regionalization and decentralization are popular in most of the approaches. Concerning services delivery, most approaches indicate that comprehensive community service systems need to be in place before institutional depopulation should be considered. Less visible themes, but activities that seem to reflect trends, are:

1. Contracts for service arrangements that move state agencies away from the provision of direct service.
2. Court Actions have gained ground in helping developmentally disabled persons attain such human rights as the right to education and training.
3. A sensitivity to the need for interaction with the public, especially parent organizations was made popular by the use of mass media to conduct public awareness campaigns.

4. Finally, the use of program standards and individual and program monitoring procedures rendered programs accountable.

No attempt was made here to provide an exhaustive list of deinstitutionalization programs. Nor does the author claim to have identified the most effective approaches. In the total scheme of things the deinstitutionalization movement is in its youth. Hence there is a need to constantly review activity in this area and share it with persons active in human service endeavors. In particular, more detailed information is needed concerning the process used in the various approaches to deinstitutionalization. Also a system for evaluating the process or procedures is needed. Another important variable in most of the approaches and one that has scarcely been mentioned is leadership. To what extent is deinstitutionalization dependent upon individual leadership and what kind of leadership styles are likely to be effective?

Finally, activities that are reported as successful are much less difficult to identify than unsuccessful activities. In this regard the description of the Child Advocacy Center in North Carolina is conspicuous. It is likely that as much can be learned about deinstitutionalization from an examination of unsuccessful programs. The author hopes that this material will provide guidance to persons and organizations that have a commitment to improve conditions for a disinherited segment of our social structure, the developmentally disabled.

REFERENCES

"Accelerated Services for Deinstitutionalization of the Retarded." Mansfield Depot, Ct.: Mansfield Training School.

Bennis, Warren G.; Benne, Kenneth D.; and Chin, Robert. *The Planning of Change.* 2nd edition. New York: Holt, Rinehart and Winston, 1969.

Blatt, Burton. *Exodus from Pandemonium.* Boston: Allyn and Bacon, 1970.

Censoni, Diana. "House Parents Payments for In-Home Programming In-Service Training, A Model for Supervision." Paper presented at the 98th Annual AAMD Convention. Toronto, Canada, 1974.

Censoni, Urbano. "Deinstitutionalization of 'Hard to Place' Individuals." Paper presented at the 98th Annual AAMD Convention. Toronto, Canada, 1974.

"Consortium Approach of CAIR for Persons with Cerebral Palsy." Crippled Children's Division, University of Oregon Medical School, 3181 S.W. Sam Jackson Park Road, Portland Or., 1973.

"Cross Modial Approach to Deinstitutionalization." Ellisville State School, Highway 11, South, Ellisville, Miss., 1973.

Eleanor Roosevelt Developmental Services, Oswald D. Heck Developmental Center, Balltown and Consaul Roads, Schenectady, N.Y.

"Expand Mini-Team Aid to Institution and Community Care." Office of Developmental Disabilities, Division of Mental Retardation and Developmental Disabilities, Department of Mental Health and Mental Retardation, 2238 S. Hamilton Road, Columbus, Oh., 1973.

Hansen, James. "Services for the Developmentally Disabled." Spokane, Wash.: Office of Developmental Disabilities, May, 1975.

Horejsi, Charles, ed. *Services for the Mentally Retarded: The Nebraska Approach with Attention on ENCOR*. Missoula, Mont.: Department of Social Work, University of Montana, May 1975.

Kugel, Robert B., and Wolfensberger, Wolf. *Changing Patterns in Residential Services for the Mentally Retarded* Washington, D.C.: President's Committee on Mental Retardation, 1969.

Lafave, H. G. "What is a Model Community-Based Service System?" Presentation before the Massachusetts Association for the Advancement of Human Services, Boston, December 4, 1974.

______; Bonnabeau, R.; and Woodhouse, R. "Developing New Residential Services for the Severely Retarded." Eleanor Roosevelt Developmental Services, Schenectady, New York. Unpublished, undated manuscript.

______; and Grunberg, F. "La fin de l'asile." Eleanor Roosevelt Developmental Services, Schenectady, New York. Undated manuscript.

______; Herjanic, M.; and Grunberg, F. "One-Year Follow-up of Sixty-seven Chronic Psychiatric Patients." *Canadian Psychiatric Association Journal* 2(3)(May-June 1966):205-11.

______; Stewart, A.; Grunberg, F.; and March, B. "Reducing Admissions and Increasing Discharges in Saskatchewan Hospital." *Canada's Mental Health* (January-February 1966).

______; Stewart, A. R.; Grunberg, F.; and Mackinnon, A. A. "The Weyburn Experience: Reducing Intake as a Factor in Phasing Out a Large Mental Hospital." *Comprehensive Psychiatry* 8(4)(August 1967):239-48.

______; Stewart, A.; and Brunberg, F. "Community Care of the Mentally Ill: Implication of the Saskatchewan Plan." *Community Mental Health Journal* 4(1)(February 1968):37-45.

Neufeld, G. R. The Child Advocacy Center, Human Rights Curriculum Project, Room 300 NCNB Plaza, 136 E. Rosemary Street, Chapel Hill, N.C.

Ohlin, Lloyd E.; Coates, Robert B.; and Miller, Alden D. "Radical Correctional Reform: A Case Study of the Massachusetts Youth Correctional System." Boston, Mass. Undated manuscript.

Project Zero, Jefferson County Association for Retarded Children, P.O. Box 41, Gaffney Drive, Watertown, N.Y.

Provencal, Gerald. "Subtle But Significant Factors in Community Placement." Fraser, Mich. Unpublished, undated manuscript.

__________. "The Macomb-Oakland Center: Where It Is and Where It Is Going." Fraser, Mich. Unpublished manuscript, April 7, 1975.

Rosen, David, and Callan, Laurence B. "TRENDS: Residential Services for the Mentally Retarded." Fraser Michigan, unpublished manuscript.

Saenger, G. "The Adjustment of Severely Retarded Adults in the Community." Albany, N.Y.: New York State Interdepartmental Health Resources Board, 1957.

Santiestevan, Henry. *Out of Their Beds and Into the Streets.* Washington, D.C.: American Federation of State, County and Municipal Employees, 1625 L Street, NW, February 1975.

Standards for Residential Facilities for the Mentally Retarded 1976. Chicago: Joint Commission on Accreditation of Hospitals, 875 N. Michigan Avenue.

Standards for Community Agencies, 1973. Chicago: Joint Commission on Accreditation of Hospitals, 875 N. Michigan Avenue.

Stewart, A.; Lafave, H.; and Herjanic, M. Comprehensive Rehabilitation of the Younger Long-Term Psychiatric Patient. Weyburn, Saskatchewan. Undated manuscript.

Stewart, A.; Lafave, H. G.; Grunberg, F.; and Herjanic, M. "Problems in Phasing Out a Large Public Psychiatric Hospital." *American Journal of Psychiatry* 125(1)(July 1968):120-26.

Survey Questionnaire for Use with *Standards for Residential Facilities for the Mentally Retarded.* 2nd ed. Chicago: Joint Commission on Accreditation of Hospitals, 875 N. Michigan Avenue, 1973.

"Ten Year Plan." State of Washington, Department of Social and Health Services, Office of Developmental Disabilities, Olympia, Wash. May 29, 1974.

Trohanis, P., ed. Consideration for Planning and Advisory Councils on Developmental Disabilities: A Perspective Paper. University of North Carolina at Chapel Hill, 1974.

11

Regional Human Services: Citizen Participation

DAN W. DAVIS, EDWARD HUMBERGER

THE CENTRAL ARGUMENT of this chapter is, first, that substate or multicounty regional governments are a form of institutionalization for human services programs; second, that they are unrepresentative and act to exclude certain groups of citizens from effective participation; and third that effective citizen participation can occur within a regional structure and can serve as a countervailing force moving us toward deinstitutionalization. To substantiate this argument, our first objective will be to provide an overview of the concept, rationale, structure, and functions of regionalism. We will give special attention to the Council of Governments (COGs) form of regional governance, and one of its primary problems, the effective representation and participation of citizens in its programs. Second, we will propose the application of the "nominal group procedure" as a means of increasing citizen participation in potentially conflictive environments, moving us toward the deinstitutionalization of regional institutions. This procedure permits constituency groups with competing or conflicting interests to confront each other and move toward negotiation and cooperation as a means of decision-making and resource allocation, and as a means of countering elite-controlled bureaucratic procedures or institutions which act to exclude such involvement.

All too often charges are levied against human-service bureaucracies that they are elitest, nonparticipative, and hence unresponsive to the needs of their clients. Some authors argue that the degree of nonparticipation in community action or human-service programs is a function of the values and attitudes of the bureaucratic class (Stenberg 1972). Others argue that whatever participation has been allowed is or can be a strategy to coopt the opposition or to regulate those who would confront the agencies (Selznick 1966; Piven and Cloward 1971). Still others hold that the participation of clients in human-service decisions has been unsuccessful, conflictive, or undesirable and merely impedes the effectiveness and work of professional administration. Finally, there also exists a school of thought which favors citizen participation in decision-making as a means of advancing democratic values, system legitimacy, and as a means of eliminating inequities in the distribution of political, economic, and social wealth and power.

Regardless of their positions on the value of client or citizen participation, the predominant attitude of social science analysis has been criticism. One must search rigorously to find any positive, concrete proposals for ways to achieve significant or relevant participation. Thus while we do not propose to offer a conclusive alternative to the now largely dormant debate on the merits of citizen participation, we do offer a modest proposal for a positive, effective procedure which enables communities or regions who are so committed to introduce citizen participation into their decision-making system. In sum we are saying that the institutionalizing process of bureaucratic organizations controlled by elites must be met with a countervailing force: the insistence by citizens everywhere that they have a right to direct input into and effective control over those decisions, procedures, budgets, systems, and institutions which govern their lives.

THE REGIONALISM CONCEPT

A Definitional Perspective

Regionalism is a way of looking at relationships between people within a given area, their patterns of association, and their efforts to resolve their problems and meet their common needs. Regionalism as a generic concept has been recognized in a number of fields, from linguistics and religion to geography and planning. Jensen (1965), in *Regionalism in America*, devotes considerable attention to both historic, artistic, and political applications of the concept. The Advisory Commission on Intergovernmental Relations (ACIR) has suggested a typology of regionalism which will help us understand its applicability to this chapter (ACIR 1972).

As a geographic concept, regionalism implies area and space defined by physiographic characteristics such as rivers, watersheds, mountains, rainfall, or length of growing season. As an economic concept, regions are considered dynamic and of either a functionally integrated type or an economically homogeneous type. Economic regions are usually based upon a metropolitan area and its surrounding countryside. As a social concept regions define areas of social or cultural attachment. Wirth has noted that language, costume, form of social organization, architecture, use of tools, or the practice of certain social customs are ways of defining regional boundaries (Jensen 1965).

A fourth way of defining regionalism is administrative. As a grouping of states or counties and cities, administrative regions are used as mechanisms for decentralizing government operations. We are concerned in this chapter with this last form of regionalism and with their administrative arm, the Council of Governments (COGs). These structures are a particularly important focus for our attentions since national and state governments are increasingly devolving to them responsibility for planning and implementation of physical resource and human service programs. As voluntary associations of local elected officials, COGs have been created by the national government to serve as areawide, multicounty mechanisms for planning, coordination, and implementating programs meeting the needs of a region's citizens.

The Rationale

The emergence of administrative regionalism is a manifestation of the efforts of public officials to adapt to changing conditions and needs in metropolitan and nonmetropolitan areas. It is an institutionalized response to the realization that existing forms of governance are incapable in and of themselves of meeting the service needs of an increasingly complex society. The specific rationale for COGs is that they are necessary, perhaps the only structural innovation that is capable of both achieving economics of scale, permitting areawide cooperation while maintaining local autonomy, and allowing coordination without an overcentralization of program administration.

Shelton (1972) has suggested that we are no longer citizens of the *polis*, but are "regional citizens." He notes three characteristics of this new classification of citizenship:

1. It reflects the multicounty, multicommunity existence of the individual citizen within a metropolitan region.
2. The individual citizen recognizes a dependence on many different geographic locales including those where one works, lives, worships, recreates, participates in a cultural life, and seeks medical care.
3. The recognition that certain problems are regional in nature, including air and water purity, mass transportation, public health and safety, and solid waste disposal.

Other theorists argue that a recognition of the region's significance as a unit of analysis is essential.

Public administration has also recognized the need to regionalize. Single units of general purpose government are incapable of meeting areawide needs. The proliferation of special purpose districts to meet single function needs is also an inadequate response. There has been a general recognition that the piecemeal approach to complex problems simply will no longer work (Ward 1972; Martin 1963). As one organization suggests (Institute for Rural America 1969), there are four problems governmental units must address which reinforce the regionalism movement:

1. The lack of optimum scale, or the capacity to resolve a problem at its most appropriate level.
2. The inability to treat the interrelationships of problems either because they are fractionalized in the community, or general purpose governments are comprehensive.
3. The incapacity to provide comprehensive solutions.
4. The failure to achieve the appropriate pace to respond to change.

The needs of efficiency, economics of scale, administrative control, and adaptation contribute to the process of institutionalizing regional structures as units of planning and service delivery. ACIR reflects this administrative concern by using the term "regional confederalism" as a conceptual reference point for alternative means for regional governance. They define "regional confederalism" as the association of general purpose local governments in a given area for common purposes which are not necessarily temporary. It is a voluntary, interlocal government compact to promote the common interest without subordinating any of their essential powers or autonomy to the areawide organization (ACIR, 1973). This definition is synonymous with our definition of a Council of Governments. COGs are therefore created as an institutional, adaptive reaction to the need for greater efficiency and control in the administration of the public's business.

Historical Overview

There have been two major pressures from opposite directions which have pushed public administration toward regional confederalism as an adaptive, institutional response. From local levels of government, the substantial fragmentation of units of administration and the perceptions or reality that they were incapable of meeting public service needs have provided one pressure. The proliferation of special-purpose districts as well has been a hallmark of the movement toward regionalism. Special districts increased from 12,339 in 1952 to 23,886 in 1972, including thousands of school districts. They were created by local governments and states to provide services and retain local autonomy (Graves 1964; Bollens 1957).

Pressure came from the other direction as well. The national government viewed this proliferation and inefficiency as unnecessary, although its response to the problem has been ambivalent. Some legislation promoted the very problem of proliferation, supporting more single-function districts distinct from those already existing. Local politicians favored this approach since it protected their power base. Administrators and planners, however, favored more coordinative structures. Since the early 1960s, this latter group has prevailed in their view about intergovernmental cooperation, as manifested in the rapid increase in the number of COGs from thirteen in 1960 to 352 in 1972 (ACIR 1973). They, however, were not the only reason for this growth.

The evolution of the COG movement falls into four distinct stages. Each will be briefly summarized, highlighting the pressures or forces which helped institutionalize regional structures.

1. *Initiation Stage, Pre-1945.* The major forces affecting the growth of regionalism before 1945 were the need for an efficient structure to achieve economies of scale in public service delivery, the establishment of regional planning as a legitimate public function, and the proliferation of planning efforts which created duplication of efforts. The first metropolitan planning commission was established in Cleveland in 1925, and the Public Works Administration and National Planning Board in 1933 required planning as part of their $3.3 billion program in public works. The public works requirement for metropolitan planning resulted in an increase from 85 regional planning bodies in 1934 to 506 in 1937.

2. *Experimentation and Legitimation Stage, 1945-65.* Between 1945 and 1959, regionalism evolved due to factors such as public support on all levels of government for regional planning, the development of federal dominance in stimulating regionalism through legislation and grants, the emphasis on metropolitan planning, and the introduction of Councils of Governments as regional coordinating institutions. The first voluntary regional planning unit created was Oregon's Central Lane Planning Council in 1945, followed by the two-county Atlanta Regional Metropolitan Planning Commission in 1947. Major legislation at the national level defined regional policy and resulted in the institutionalization of regionalism. The Housing Act of 1949 required some metro planning as a condition for funding. The Housing Act of 1954, Section 701, provided 50-50 matching funds for metro planning agencies, and the Housing Act of 1959 broadened Section 701 eligibility requirements to increase the degree of intergovernmental coordination required to receive funds.

Between 1960 and 1965, efforts to strengthen regional planning and implementation increased substantially. This was a legitimation period as regional efforts were initially evaluated and the regionalism issue gained prominence among professionals. In 1961 regional councils were formally recognized for the first time by national organizations like the Council of State Governments, the National Municipal League, and the National Association of Counties. Two major pieces of legislation were passed as well. The Housing Act of 1961 expanded financial assistance to metro areas for the preparation of comprehensive plans from 50 to 66 percent, and the Federal Highway Act of 1962 called for a continuous comprehensive planning process as a prerequisite for federal aid for interstate highways.

3. *Expansion Stage, 1965-73.* During this period the central role of the federal government in shaping the procedural response to local needs through legislation continued to grow. In addition, there arose local problems in generating support for regionalism as the national government pursued an ambivalent policy of supporting both single function and multifunctional planning efforts. It was an expansion period in the sense that several pieces of national legislation substantially increased the number of multicounty planning bodies across the country and regionalism became an integral and inseparable part of the activities of local and state officials requiring them to create regional planning institutions.

Section 701 of the Housing and Urban Development Act of 1965 made organizations of locally elected officials in metropolitan areas directly eligible to receive funds. Section 702 extended the principle of requiring conformance with areawide planning as a prerequisite for each grant. Section 204 of the Model Cities and Metropolitan Development of 1966 gave Councils of Governments power to review and comment on applications by local governments for a variety of federal grants for public facility construction. Rural regionalism was promoted as well through the Appalachian Regional Development Act of 1962, the Economic Development Act of 1965, The Housing and Urban Development Act of 1968, and the Intergovernmental Cooperation Act of 1968. By the 1970s, regional confederalism as a concept and institutional structure had become a means of adapting to metro and nonmetro needs for service delivery.

4. *Stabilization Stage, 1973-Present.* Since 1973, a number of issues have arisen which will affect the further development of regionalism. There has been growing concern among local and state public officials that COGs could become a fourth tier of government, a "supergovernment" which might usurp local government functions. As will be noted below, regionalism has also come to be viewed by some as inherently racist and discriminatory in its structures and functions. Similarly, concerns have been raised about the representativeness of COGs and their commitment to citizen participation. Fourth, questions are being asked about the appropriateness of giving local elected officials control over the planning and delivery of public services at the regional level. Finally, there is concern about the dilution of attention being given by these public officials to meeting the needs of minority and other client groups, in fact, whether or not they should be involved in human services at all.

In conclusion, the development of regional confederalism has been a dynamic process of interaction between forces at the local and national levels in their efforts to design institutionalized means for adapting to a growing number of public service needs. At the national level there has been an unwillingness to impose a regional structure on local governments. Similarly, local officials have resisted any but a voluntary approach to coordination, largely for selfish political reasons. Pragmatic values and reactive policy have characterized the thrust of the regionalism movement, but fifty years since the Cleveland planning council, regional institutions are now an integral part of our governmental structure.

A Structural-Functional Analysis

The structure of a typical Council of Governments is quite simple. The state legislature passes enabling legislation which permits local officials to form a COG based on a joint resolution passed by the city and/or county elected officials. COGs are creatures of local and not state or federal government, and serve primarily as a coordinating council, a forum for debate, interest articulation, and problem resolution. All elected officials in a given region comprise the full board, and an executive board represents county, city, and town interests, although the representation formula may vary from state to state. In some cases, a COG that overlaps with economic development districts must have minority representation throughout its structure, although it is usually no more than 25 percent. Membership by units of government is voluntary, and withdrawal can occur at any time after passage of a resolution by the given unit. Basic financial support comes from the member governments who are assessed a per-capita fee to pay for the COG's director and staff.

Voting may be either on a one unit-one vote basis or in proportion to the population. There are standing and ad hoc committees which are created to meet specific regional needs. The professional staff are usually hired by COGs for special functions such as Housing and Urban Development Section 701 planning, economic development, law enforcement and more recently some human service areas. Mogulof (1971) has suggested three additional structural facts worth noting:

1. They receive the bulk of their financial support from federal sources to do areawide planning.
2. They receive an aura of authority from the review and comment powers over local governmental unit grant proposals.
3. They receive their legitimacy from their member governments.

Geographic designation of COG boundaries is an area of dispute given that boundaries may be determined by the gubernatorial or legislative mandate, with or without the approval of local officials or citizens. Criteria used in determination of boundaries may include: problem intensity or a "problem shed," existing political or governmental boundaries of general purpose governments, state area or population requirements, transportation linkages, economic interdependencies, cultural or social ties, and political associations and viability. The process by which boundaries are formalized depends on the state, its legislation, and politics. It is the first issue around which local interests coalesce as this new arena of political interaction is created.

While a number of authors have attempted to define a COG's functions, we propose the following ten-point typology.

1. *Administrative.* This function includes grantsmanship, A-95 re-

view and comment, planning, and in some instances implementation of programs. The movement toward implementation being entrusted to COGs is due to the belief of some politicians and planners that plans without hope of implementation are considered a waste of time, but some states permit COGs only to plan.

2. *Identification.* Regional councils are in a strategic position to identify regional needs as expressed from any number of constituency groups. The council needs to be receptive to needs, articulation mechanisms, and to translate them into programs and seek funds from state or federal sources.

3. *Consensus and Coordination.* Obtaining the consensus of a region's constituencies is an essential function if a council is to achieve legitimacy and pursue its program design. Conflictive or coercive approaches usually result in agency division, dissolution, or the restructuring of personnel.

4. *Representation.* The degree of consensus will depend upon its representativeness of the various groups in the region. While consensus may exist within the COG itself, it may not necessarily be representative, mitigating against its perceived legitimacy by other interests in the region. A second kind of representativeness is in terms of the allocation of staff time, budget commitments, and policy statements.

5. *Advocacy.* Since COGs are not directly elected, advocacy for special client groups becomes an essential component of its legitimacy in the region. Advocacy can be performed on behalf of a specific issue, need, or program as well as groups.

6. *Interpretative-Communicative.* COGs are middle-agents, standing between the identification of needs and the sources of funds on the program side; between local, state, and national agencies on the jurisdictional dimension; and between various powers or jurisdictions within its own region. Its role is to act as a clearinghouse, to assist units in applying for funds, to interpret and communicate needs based either on homogeneous criteria, and on the basis of either the entire region or areas within the region.

7. *Redistributive.* A COG can serve as a redistributive force to insure equitable distribution of resources between urban and rural sectors, the rich and the poor, the served and the unserved. The review and comment power can be used to do this if the COG so chooses.

8. *Adjudicative.* If not involved in conflict itself, the council can serve as a neutral third party, an arbiter to monitor conflict among member units, to devise strategies to defuse or constructively redirect the conflict.

9. *Allocative.* This function involved more than funds, programs, or other resources. Planning involves allocation of needs and resources through the defining process. Different criteria can be used—a constituency basis, pressure group basis, equity basis, or program basis.

10. *Evaluative.* Most regional councils need internal as well as external evaluative capacity. Review and comment requires some evaluation, but internal evaluation of COG effectiveness is needed as well. The COG can also be called upon to evaluate third parties. It can be comprehensive or superficial, process based or program based, and can be a creative, neutral, or divisive tool.

In sum, the structural and functional components of regional councils represent a comprehensive institutionalization of the principle of regional confederalism. The degree to which the COG is effective, however, depends upon the valuative orientation of its staff, their administrative capacity, political and diplomatic skills, funding, and the general context of any given COG's environment. But one major problem confronts most COGs across the country as they assume greater institutional responsibility, one of which is human-service programs—the problem of representation and citizen participation.

REGIONALISM, REPRESENTATION, AND CITIZEN PARTICIPATION

Structures and functions are created and used to meet the objectives or needs of their creators and administrators. The valuative frame of reference of those individuals is represented not only in the structures and functions of the given institution, but in the manner in which business/ policy is conducted. The particular irony of COGs as regional institutions is that in their efforts to alleviate the problems of duplication of effort, economies of scale, and governmental ambivalence in service delivery, they have created new conflicts and problems. Only in the past few years has research begun to reveal these concerns. Underlying all these problems is the implicit assumption on the part of public officials that new institutions and structures can solve human problems which are due more to the maldistribution of wealth and power in our society than to structural inefficiency. We believe that new institutions or structures by themselves cannot solve human problems or effectively meet citizen needs when these structures are created by the same forces responsible for the problems in the first place. Thus while COGs may be new arenas of political competitition, recent research on their implementation has found that they are merely new opportunities for those aleady in power to consolidate it on a larger geographic basis. Thus we must be particularly concerned here with the valuative framework represented by COGs and their officials, and empirical evidence supporting the argument that they are an unrepresentative and nonparticipative institution.

The value framework for elected officials who comprise the decision-making body of COGs has at least four components: retain control and power over the COG, avoid conflict unless it is to your advantage, achieve economies of scale and reach cooperative agreements where it benefits your government, and meet the needs of your electoral constituency. The value framework of COGs rests on one central principle: survive by avoiding conflict, achieving consensus, and providing direct and concrete service to the board. This means finding a common denominator for cooperation, ameliorating differences among members, avoiding potentially conflicting programs or citizen inputs, and giving ownership over the COG to those political, economic, and social elites who govern the region.

These two value frames are interactive and complementary in their efforts to avoid conflict. A COG can only survive by catering to the least controversial needs of all its members, who in turn reflect indirectly the preferences of the electoral majorities. The elected officials, on the other hand, can consolidate their hold on government funds and local programs by steering the COG away from programs which injure their image or do not meet the needs of their electoral majorities.

The implications of COG and elected official efforts to avoid conflict at almost any cost are substantial. The primary result is the consolidation of power in the hands of those elites who already control the decision-making and resource allocation system. This means that COGs will tend to exclude those individuals, groups, or programs which have a high conflict potential or threaten the distribution of power. Institutionalized exclusion of citizen interests can mean that the programs they promulgate cannot necessarily be said to represent the needs or interests of their citizens. They are more likely to represent the interactive needs of COG members and staffs to survive politically. In terms of human-service programs, institutionalized exclusion means a greater probability that there will be wasted funds, since programs are unrepresentative of existing needs. There is also a greater probability they will suffer from a lack of credibility among those receiving services, and there will more likely be ineffective service delivery. In essence, the regional institution designed to be an adaptive structure will tend to be maladaptive in human services because of its unrepresentative and nonparticipative character.

For evidence supporting our argument, we turn to an evaluation of existing research on how COGs have responded to the interests and needs of three groups who are particularly vulnerable to maldistribution of power and wealth, and to the nonrepresentative nature of decision-making and resource allocation systems: central city black populations, low income populations, and recipients of public social service programs. First, we find that racism is a pervasive force at many levels of COG activities. Harris (1970) has argued that it was not mere coincidence that COGs were created at about the same point in history that blacks began to win politically in the central cities. The COG became a means for whites during the late 1960s to counter their declining political power in the central cities by expanding the jurisdictional boundaries for service delivery to include suburban areas. This we will call the dilution effect since the political power of the newly elected black city administrations is reduced by the geographic shift in power.

Data from the National Association of Regional Councils shows that 60 percent of the nation's COGs have "citizen types" on their boards, but the Department of Housing and Urban Development has found that only 30 percent have any minority members at all. Harris' study of seventy-four COGs with inner city minority populations found not only low citizen participation, but a low priority being given by COG directors to increase it: "For the most part COGs have dealt with the leaders of the various governmental units in the region. . . . much of the COG energy is diverted toward tryng to bring the eligible non-members into the organization. Consequently, the councils have not put forth a very strong effort to involve the grass-roots public in their programs."

The review and comment procedure is another area where racial discrimination can occur, since it requires black central city administrations to submit grant proposals for funding through a white-controlled review process. Further evidence of COG behavior that is racially discriminatory comes from black elected officials themselves in a survey conducted by ACIR (1973). This 1972 survey of 2,215 black elected officials found that only 28 percent of the 253 respondents were on policy boards, and only slightly more than 25 percent were on COG boards. Barriers to black representation were considered to be:

1. Blacks selected as representatives fit white conceptions of representation.
2. Black representatives have no voting strength.
3. The resolute determination of councils not to appoint a black.

4. Lack of input about black needs.
5. The regional forum is not geared to discussion giving notice to cultural and human considerations.

A second dynamic exists which acts to preclude low income citizens from representation or participation in COG affairs which we will call the nonrecognition effect. In brief, the Nonrecognition Effect says that the single most important characteristic about the relationship between COGs and the poor is its near non-existence. Not only has no major research about the impact of COGs on the poor been discovered, but there appears to be little interest in that which does exist. As Rothblatt (1971) has noted in his discussion of the Appalachian regional planning experience, "the multicounty units are frequently dominated by either local notables such as leaders in business and finance, or state interests." Or as the Institute for Rural America (1969) asserted, "Although the needs and special views of the disadvantaged need to be communicated, the interests of the disadvantaged would be poorly served if they were given an inordinately large voice in development-oriented policy decisions."

A third dynamic at work against representation and citizen participation in COGs is called the Noninvolvement Effect, which applies to social service programs. Evidence has been gathered through recent national surveys to support the argument that local elected officials simply do not wish to be involved in social service programs because they are expensive and conflictive (ACIR 1973). Marando's (1971) research on COGs discovered that human service programs categorically are considered to have a high conflict potential. Harris (1971) found that 68 percent of the COGs he investigated had no budget being devoted to social programs in 1970, and another 32 percent devoted only a small portion of their budget to them. On the other hand, Mathewson (1968), one of the founders of the COG movement, argues that COGs must concern themselves with human-service programs because they are interdependent with physical resource development. Hence we have a substantial discrepancy between what some feel COGs must do to survive programatically, and what they are actually doing to survive politically.

In conclusion, the combination of the dilution, nonrecognition, and noninvolvement effects presents COGs as regional institutions involved in human service programs with a serious dilemma. As presently structured, they are unrepresentative and discriminatory. Because they represent an expansion and consolidation of the control of local power elites through the institutionalization of regional planning and service delivery they are maladaptive for human-service programs. COGs face at least two alternatives. Either they must change the valuative orientation of their members, or change their structure to permit accurate representation of all groups and their effective participation at all levels of service-planning and delivery. Citizen participation becomes a means of deinstitutionalization by opening a closed process and forcing an exclusive and discriminatory institution to be accountable to its constituents. To maintain the hegemony of an unrepresentative and nonparticipative political elite is unacceptable in a democratic society. To maintain this hegemony in the face of overwhelming human-service needs is equally unacceptable. To design and propose new ways of increasing effective citizen participation to reduce institutionalization is our challenge.

THE NOMINAL GROUP PROCEDURE

We offer here a modest proposal for introducing into regional institutions the nominal group procedure as a means of increasing representation and citizen participation in environments where conflict potential is high or community commitment is necessary to meet the needs of its citizens. The nominal group procedure is a particularly effective means of interfacing these groups in the design and implementation of human-service programs. It is a purely rational approach that is a tool for creating greater representation of interests and participation in decision-making. The underlying theme of the procedure is that a combination of a strong rationale for the wisdom and necessity for the involvement of various constituencies and a procedure for accomplishing that goal can be an extremely persuasive argument for COGs or other regional institutions to use it.

On the first point, the nature of the program requiring the involvement of various constituencies implies that developmentally disabled citizens, for example, are the only persons qualified to give information on a number of issues affecting their lives. Not only is their input needed; other data on funding, practitioner needs, and the interests of others is also required to insure an effective program. The inclusion of the clients' interests in the process is legitimated.

On the second point, many programs seem to have encountered more difficulties in designing methods for including various constituencies than determining whether or not their inclusion was appropriate. Thus we turn to the steps a regional institution could undertake to interface the appropriate constituencies in the design and implementation of human-service programs.

First, a program must have so clear a definition of its goals and purposes that it can be understood by others—that is, clarity with supporting data. Second, the formation of a neutral group that sponsors and defends the program is essential. A neutral group is defined as a combination of persons who have established social and political ties with the various constituencies needed for program design and implementation. The group may not represent these constituencies since that would bias their perspective toward representation or lobbying. Furthermore, the members of the neutral group must have a rather comfortable affiliation with one another in order informally to work out how to make contacts with various constituencies while not further alienating groups from one another. Here their credibility and power base to support the developing program is essential. The neutral group is in a minority position to push and defend a program where constituencies alone do not enjoy or usually weather those periods of criticism and program movement.

Once a neutral group is formed, all work is either sponsored by or directly done by them. Given the nature of institutions like COGs, it is the neutral group that creates communication links between them and the other constituencies not represented on COG boards such as service providers, developmentally disabled citizens, or others. Since there are varied groups with different orientations and constituencies, it is usually wise to have the neutral group first identify the relevant groups, decide who will make contact with them, when and where, and begin formulating the sequence of how the groups can interact most effectively.

The procedure presented in more detail below suggests that initial work with the various constituencies be done separately. The rationale for this recommendation is twofold: (1) each group has particular information that only persons sharing their experience have, and (2) this information is best shared among homogeneous issue-centered groups. The latter point deserves clarification. It is more accommodating for persons with common experiences to generate their priorities than for persons with divergent experiences and perspectives to reach initial consensus on issues. In the 1960s, diverse groups coming together usually experienced discomfort and sometimes felt more distant than previously; their biases became confirmed. The model presented here suggests the initial formation of homogeneous groups around issues pertinent to them and using the information generated by them as a basis for bringing heterogeneous groups together. At that point negotiations can occur based upon a greater appreciation of the experiences and perspectives of the other constituencies.

Once information is generated from various homogeneous groups such as developmentally disabled citizens, local elected officials, providers, administrators, and agency administrators, and once they understand each other more clearly, the neutral group can encourage representatives from the various groups to work out common themes for cooperative action. They can develop procedures for working on defined tasks, then determine the resources needed to accomplish them and the means to obtain available and additional resources.

THE NOMINAL GROUP PROCEDURE FOR SETTING PRIORITIES

1. With groups of five to eight participants, hand out an 8½ x 11" sheet of paper with a clear statement of the issue pertinent to that particular group types on top of the sheet.

2. Request each person to make a list of responses to the issue typed on the sheet of paper. Request no talking. Let the participants know that their lists will be shared with each other.

3. The recorder (person conducting the procedure) lists on a flip chart each person's list of responses, one item at a time per person, round-robin, until all items from everyone's list are exhausted. Allow duplication, avoid discussion, justifications, etc. Number each item (1 . . . n).

4. The recorder reads each item for clarification and understanding. Items should not be eliminated. Duplications may be grouped (for example items 3 and 8 may be grouped and treated as one item).

5. The recorder hands out five 3 x 5" cards to each participant. Have each person select and write, by name and number, one item per card, the five (or more) most important items. Once those five are chosen, give the most important item of those five a "5" and circle that number; the next most important item receives a "4"; and so on down to the least important item receiving a "1."

6. The recorder prepares a tally sheet on the flip chart as noted on Table 11.1.

7. The recorder asks for the items (column 1) and their ranks (column 2) from each participant, round robin, one item at a time, starting with the most important item, i.e., that item receiving a rank of "5" and so on until each participant's list of five is exhausted.

8. The recorder sums the ranks (column 3), multiplies that sum by

the number of persons giving that item a rank (column 4), and the highest weighted sum is the top priority, the next highest sum the second from top, etc. (column 5). Example numbers are provided in Table 11.1.

The neutral group uses this priority-setting procedure with the various constituencies, delegating one or more members to work with each constituency based upon their affiliation and credibility. After the procedure is completed and various priorities and actions are generated, the neutral group and one or more representatives from the various constituencies meet to negotiate similarities and differences among the priorities and to design the overall program for implementation. The members identify who will be responsible for the various actions, the resources needed, how to acquire them, and the phasing of different components. A word of caution is in order. It is essential to construct carefully not only the entire set of program procedures for implementation, but to facilitate initial group successes as a means of creating movement and group cohesion for later steps.

TABLE 11.1

Priorities

Item No.	Ranks assigned to item	Sum of Ranks	Weighted Sum	Priorities
2	2, 1	3	6	3
14	3, 4, 1	8	24	2
7, 20	5, 54	14	42	1
18	2	2	2	4
	2			

CONCLUSION

Our central argument has been that regional structures such as Councils of Governments are a form of institutionalization for human-service programs in concept, structure and functions. We have also argued that effective citizen representation and participation is a countervailing force, a means of moving toward deinstitutionalization. In our review of the concept and history of COGs as regional confederalism, we found that they were created as adaptive institutional response to an increasingly complex and overwhelming series of public-service problems. In our investigation of the related problems of representation and citizen participation, however, we discovered that structures in and of themselves cannot address the source of the problems, which is the maldistribution of wealth and power. In fact we found that not only do COGs expand and consolidate the power base of local elites, but their attitudes and actions toward blacks, low income citizens, and recipients of social service programs are discriminatory, exclusive, and directed at avoidance in order to survive.

Finally, we proposed the nominal group procedure as an alternative methodology for communities who desire to administer programs in a representative and participative manner and yet who may not know how to do so in a potentially conflictive environment. The nominal group procedure's greatest merit is its ability to permit constituencies with opposing points of view and competing interests to begin the process of dialog, understanding, and negotiation which is essential if the human-service programs are to be considered legitimate and effective.

REFERENCES

Advisory Commission on Intergovernmental Relations. *Multistate Regionalism.* Washington, D.C.: U.S. Government Printing Office, 1972.

Advisory Commission on Intergovernmental Relations. *Regional Decision-Making: New Strategies for Substate Districts.* Vol. 1. Washington, D.C.: U.S. Government Printing Office, October, 1973.

Bollens, John. *Special District Governments in the United States.* Berkeley: University of California Press, 1957.

Buchanan, James, and Tullock, Gordon. *The Calculus of Consent.* Ann Arbor, Michigan: University of Michigan Press, 1962.

Dahl, Robert. *A Preface to Democratic Theory.* Chicago: University of Chicago Press, 1956.

Delbecq, Andre L., and Van de Ven, Andrew H. "A Group Process Model for Problem Identification and Program Planning." *Journal of Applied Behavioral Science* (4)(1971):466-92.

Graves, W. Brooke. *American Intergovernmental Relations.* New York: Scribner's, 1964.

Harris, Charles. *Councils of Governments and the Central City.* Detroit: Metropolitan Fund, March, 1970.

Institute for Rural America. *Multi-Jurisdictional Area Development.* Lexington, Ky.: Spindletop Research, 1969.

Jensen, Merrill, ed. *Regionalism in America.* Milwaukee, Wisc.: University of Wisconsin Press, 1965.

Marando, Vincent. "Metropolitan Research and Councils of Governments." *Midwest Review of Public Administration* February 1971).

Martin, Roscoe. *Metropolis in Transition.* Housing and Home Finance Agency, 1963.

Mathewson, Kent. "A Growing Movement." *National Civic Review* 57 June 1968): 298-302, 306.

Mogulof, Melvin. *Governing Metropolitan Areas.* Washington, D.C.: Urban Institute, 1971.

______. *Five Metropolitan Governments.* Washington, D.C.: The Urban Institute, 1972.

Piven, Frances Fox, and Cloward, Richard. "Black Control of Cities." *New Republic* 157 (September 30, 1967): 19-21; (October 7, 1967): 15-19.

______. *Regulating the Poor.* New York: Random House, 1971.

Rothblatt, Donald. *Regional Planning: The Appalachian Experience.* Lexington, Mass.: Heath Lexington Books, 1971.

Schattschneider, E. E. *The Semi-Sovereign People.* New York: Holt, Rinehart and Winston, 1960.

Selznick, Phillip. *TVA and the Grass Roots.* New York: Harper and Row, 1966.

Shelton, Donn. *Regional Citizenship.* Detroit: Metropolitan Fund, 1972.

Stenberg, Carl. "Citizens and the Administrative State." *Public Administration Review* 32 (May/June 1972): 190-98.

Ward, Keith, *Metropolitan Cooperation and Coordination Tennessee Councils of Governments.* Knoxville: University of Tennessee, 1972.

Wirth, Louis. "The Limitations of Regionalism." in *Regionalism in America,* edited by Merrill Jensen. Milwaukee, Wisc.: University of Wisconsin Press, 1965.

12

Evaluating Community Service Programs for the Handicapped

RICHARD C. SURLES

COMMUNITY-INTERVENTION PROGRAMS for handicapped children have greatly increased in number in the past few years. These programs have resulted from local initiative as well as state and federal stimulation in the development of organized responses to needed specialized services and to pressures from community and professional organizations for more alternative programs for the handicapped.

On the federal level, monies have generally been provided in the form of "start-up" grants or have been given for the purpose of establishing model demonstration projects. For example, the Bureau of Education for the Handicapped (BEH) of the Department Health, Education and Welfare (HEW) has established model projects in all fifty states which serve to demonstrate the efficacy and methodology involved in early childhood intervention. Through the creation of more than one hundred fifty federally funded projects, exemplary services have been provided to a diversified population of handicapped children and infants. Each BEH project must undertake the role of stimulating the establishment of additional services for handicapped children.

The Office of Child Development has also provided resources for the establishment of programs to serve handicapped children through efforts involving Head Start. In some states, Developmental Disabilities, State Mental Health, or Mental Retardation funds have been used to establish local model demonstration projects for handicapped children. In all, such efforts have stimulated the level interest in establishing community services.

Community service projects funded through federal, as well as state or local sources, can generally be characterized along several dimensions.

First, they serve from ten to thirty children whose disabilities may range from severe retardation to language impairment to severe emotional disorders. Some projects may serve only those children with a single type of disorder while others may serve the multihandicapped. Second, the programs are generally staffed by professional educators or specialists trained to work with handicapped children. Organizational roles usually include those of a director, two or three classroom teachers, and some clerical support. Third, most projects are administratively attached to a larger organizational unit, such as public schools, a department of health, a university, or some social services agency.

Since early childhood intervention is still an emerging concept in this country, service and program strategies are usually innovative in nature. As a result, the outcome of activities relevant to programs for the handicapped come under close scrutiny from the community and from funding sources. Moreover, the expense of these programs, as opposed to more general educational programs, increases the pressure on the staff to provide confirmation that services and programs are having the intended impact.

Thus, such community service projects have had to become accountable to their local constituency and to the funding agency. As a result many project directors, who have never before been subject to requests for evaluative data, are now asked to become accountable by "proving" their program's effectiveness.

Since very few funding agencies have yet to develop a standard accountability model for projects, project directors have had to resort to a variety of strategies to meet evaluation demands. Some have employed a professional evaluator, frequently a person with educational or psychological training in child assessment or screening. Others have sought a programmatically uninvolved third party group of professionals and peers to assess what results are being produced by the project.

Frequently the professional evaluators or the third party group use a research design in which they attempt to determine a cause and effect relationship which will enable them to report to interested parties on the effect that program strategies are having on individuals. This approach of seeking cause and effect has been increasingly criticized by some evaluation specialist as to its appropriateness and manageability in a field setting (Morehouse 1972).

Evaluators feel that not only is the cause-effect design unrealistic, but focusing just on programmatic effect is too limiting when dealing with accountability demands. Gene Glass (1972), for example, offers an extensive educational accountability model. To undertake what he calls "weak accountability," Glass would have project directors engage in the following evaluation activities. First, the evaluation must indicate the strategy to be followed and the methods used to set instructional objectives. Second, it would be necessary to maintain data on the cognitive and social growth of pupils as well as their physical health. Cognitive and social growth would include information on progress toward and attainment of objectives set by the project. Third, data would exist on the procedures for selection, advancement, and dismissal of staff. Fourth, periodic audits would be made of the internal financial accounts of the project; and fifth, legal accountability would be publicized through the disclosure of the legal policies of the organization.

If a project is to have "strong accountability," it would be necessary to engage in the five activities listed above plus the following three: First, it would be necessary to maintain two or more alternative educational programs which could be conducted at the same time and evaluated. Second, random assignment would be made of both pupil and instructional staff to two or more programs. Third, assessment would be conducted by evaluators knowledgeable of program intent. Evaluators such as Glass would have educational projects provide extensive data about how well project objectives were being met and identify the type of personnel used to arrive at desirable outcomes.

While "strong accountability" may be desirable, its utility for the service projects described here is doubtful. It seems unlikely that projects attempting to serve handicapped children and infants can be accountable if requested to utilize alternative program models in each project, randomize assignments of children and staff, and, possibly, employ a full-time evaluator.

Weak accountability, though, does seem possible and there are some additional steps which could strengthen project evaluation. For example, a project could use professional or citizen review of objectives and strategies prior to their implementation. Since most childhood intervention programs for the handicapped are unique, the pre-implementation review allows the base line for an accountability situation to be established, after which the project will attempt to place into operation the objective and strategy sanctioned by both professionals and citizens. Moreover, professional and citizen review can be used during program operation.

Thus, while service projects may not be able to meet Glass's ideal, they certainly can achieve an accountability stage which will provide them with information for internal decision-making and information for external decision-makers. It seems, too, that by utilizing professional and citizen review at various stages of the program a position somewhat between "weak" and "strong" accountability can be achieved.

As for how a project establishes an accountability program, much data probably already exist which would be useful for evaluation. Usually without great difficulty, projects can characterize (1) the curriculum strategy being used, (2) the degree of disability of individual students, (3) the process of acquiring and replacing staff, and (4) the expenditure of funds. Legal accountability may require the advice of the funding agency or some professional help.

The difficulty for most service projects is to produce evidence that they are having an impact on their target population and that the impact is intended and relevant to goals and objectives of the project.

The remainder of this paper provides one example of a planning and evaluation procedure [some ideas are modifications made by Stedman and Surles (1973)] developed by Gallagher, Surles, and Hayes (1972) which could be used by service projects when responding to data demands for program impact. The procedure provides a systematic model for evaluating programs by requiring that program intentions be clearly specified for both administrative activities and treatment activities and that information be systematically collected so that description of intentions are made. Once baseline information is determined, data can be gathered which will provide an indication of the effectiveness of the strategies and their resulting impact.

Thus, the activities necessary to utilize the accountability system require both planning and evaluation. Planning is setting clear goals and objectives for action. Evaluation is assessing whether those goals and objectives are met.

Utilizing the model, it is possible to begin to answer three questions highly relevant to the planning and evaluation process: What is it that we want to do? How well are we doing it? How well did we do it? The first is a question that requires planning, while the last two require evaluative judgments.

Some procedures for answering the questions follow. One crucial factor to recognize in the accountability system is that planning and evaluation are closely related. Planning tends to provide an indication of what is intended, while evaluation attempts to provide information on results. Properly utilized, the system to be presented should provide useful data for the purpose of accountability.

WHAT DO WE WANT TO DO?

Whenever one begins the process of planning, it is useful to have a procedure which will systematically allow the explanation of intentions. A useful procedure is that of a goal-achievement planning model (see Figure 12.1), an adaptation of a model developed by James Gallagher. It consists of outlining plans in trms of specified *needs, goals* to be achieved, *objectives* related to each goal, *alternative strategy* for meeting each objective, the specification of the chosen *strategy*, the description of the *implementation methodology, evaluation procedures,* and the informational *feedback* provided by evaluation once completed. *Resources* and *constraints* are considered for all the planning elements but especially for objectives. Moreover, feedback resulting from evaluation will effect goals, objectives, and other elements of the planning model.

This planning structure represents a model that should have universal application to the many varied problems that occur during the planning of programs for the handicapped. It would be used when planning the weekly activities of children, or when planning a long-range program for a differing target population, or for actually planning an evaluation system. The following example depicts the model used in planning the establishment of such a system.

Need: An evaluative plan must be developed and carried out.

Goal: The plan must meet state requirements and must provide information to the public about the effectiveness of the program.

Objectives: 1.   To complete the evaluation plan by September 1.
                 2.   To begin collecting data by September 15.
                 3.   To complete data collected by April 30.
                 4.   To complete the data analyses and to file a final report by June 1.
                 5.   To prepare a brief report for public dissemination that will outline the successes of the project.

Constraints: 1. $2,000 is budgeted for evaluation.
                 2.   Teachers are reluctant to participate in an evaluation.
                 3.   No one on the staff is familiar with data analysis (i.e., statistics).

Resources: 1. $2,000 is budgeted for evaluation.
2.   A firm can provide consultative assistance in evaluation.
3.   A college in town has graduate students who could help with the data analysis.
4.   An evaluation consultant will help develop the plan.

Alternative
Strategies: 1.   Director hires a consulting firm to develop and carry out evaluation plan.
2.   Director seeks an additional staff person who would devote one-fourth time to evaluation.
3.   Director attends workshops on evaluation and develops plan.
4.   Director uses the staff in conjunction with the consultant.

Selection
Criteria: 1.   The consulting firm want $1,700 to create and do data analysis.
2.   Director wants to allocate at least $500 for printing and dissemination of data but could get by with $300.
3.   The consultant says that he will set up the plan (objectives and evaluation methods) and provide graduate students for purpose of data analysis for $1,000.

4.   Teachers know and trust the consultant.
5.   Graduate students will be qualified testers and will not interfere with classroom activities.
6.   With the extra $1,000 Director can hire a consultant to help decide how best to design format of and distribute data.

Choice: Director hires the consultant and graduate students for $1,000 and closely supervises their activities.

Evaluation: 1.   Director checks to see if the following events occur as planned:
     a.   evaluation plan by September 1
     b.   collecting data by September 15
     c.   data collected by April 30

          d.   report by June 30
          e.   two-page data sheets ready for dissemination by June 30

2. Director seeks information about the quality of the report.
3. Director plans to hire an independent consultant from next year's budget to study the impact of public dissemination of data.

Feedback:

1. A budget of $2,000 for evaluation is probably too small.
2. Director needs to find out how other project directors are handling this problem.
3. Director needs to hire a person for next year who could serve as an administrative assistant and as the Director of Evaluation for the project.

GOAL	OBJECTIVES	STRATEGIES	EVALUATION PROCEDURES
The model project through its parent program information exchange will increase parent's knowledge about and acceptance of their child.	1.1 By the end of the year of the parent program, parents enrolled in the program will increase knowl- of child growth and development by 30%.	1.1 Group meetings between staff and parents in which the continuous growth and development of the child is explained by the staff.	1.1 Increase in knowledge of growth and development is measured by a criteria-referenced test administered in a pre- and post-fashion.
	2.1 By the end of the second year of the project, parents' long-range expectations for their handicapped children will shift in a more positive direction.	2.1 Periodic meetings are planned and led by parent members in which they discuss their children, present and future.	2.1 Long-range expectations are assessed by pre- and post- written expectations by parents and judged independently by two project staff members having daily interaction with the children.

TABLE 12. 1. Overview of Goals, Objectives, Strategy, and Evaluation.

While all elements of the model would have utility for the planning and evaluation procedure, certain elements are essential. These include the clear specification of goals, of measurable objectives, of selected strategies, and of an evaluation methodology. Table 12.1 makes the distinction between these various elements more clear.

Goals show the general intentions and directions that a project is going to take. Related to each goal are a series of objectives which depict more specific intentions with measurable indices and time limits.

Goals reflect long-range intention. For example, a goal might be "to improve the language development in three-year-old language-impaired children so that the children are able to enter normal preschool programs by age five." Obviously, this goal does not lend itself to immediate

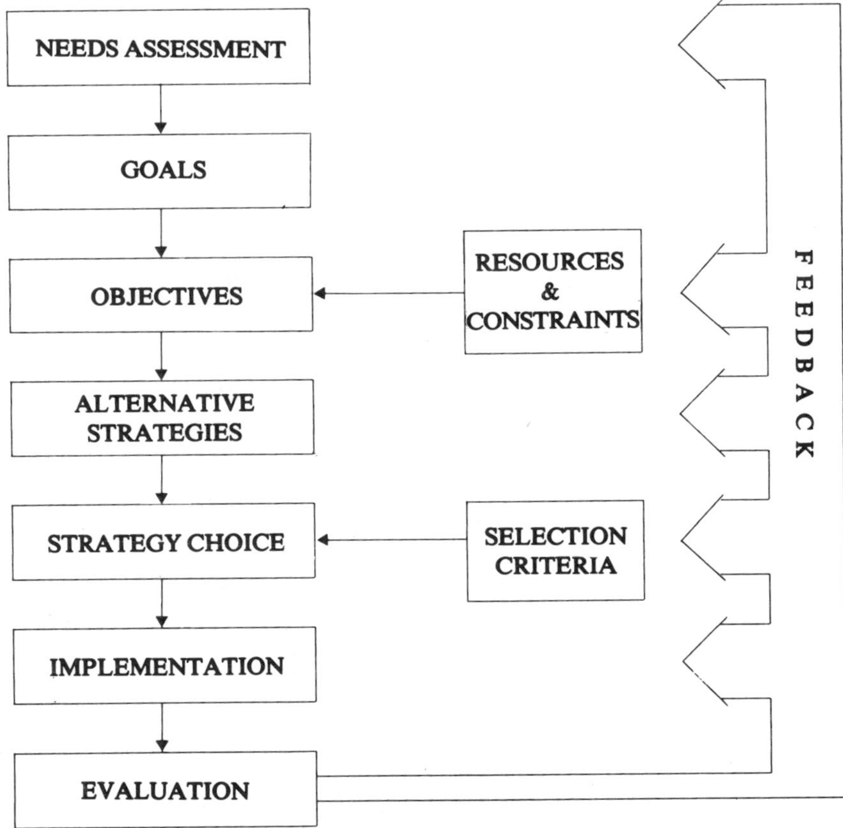

FIGURE 12.1. Goal achievement evaluation system.

evaluation or accountability. To achieve accountability, a series of objectives are specified which are relevant to the particular goal. For example, an objective for the above goal might be "to improve beyond normal expectation the receptive vocabulary and complexity of expression in the children in our center by June 1, 1976." This statement combined with other similar ones represents a description of expected project benefit.

Each objective also requires the specification, whether formally or informally stated, of a programmatic strategy. If the objective is "to increase parent personal non-hostile interaction with their children," then a procedure for meeting that objective should be established. The strategy, for example, might be that "the project will establish parent counseling groups that will meet once a week during 1976."

It is then that the planning procedures, which facilitate evaluation, require the specification of a goal with related objectives, objectives with strategies and objectives, and strategies with related evaluation procedure which will indicate if strategies are working and objectives being met. Table 12.2 provides an example of the accountability system and resulting data.

In the development of objectives and strategies, it is useful to distinguish between two types of objectives. One type is an administrative objective which indicates the management activities which must occur in order for program treatment to be undertaken. These objectives might indicate the number and type of staff to be hired, the need for the acquisition of space, the need for the development of certain types of curriculum materials, and the need for certain classroom techniques to be observed. If one has to be accountable to a funding agency on a monthly or quarterly basis these objectives are frequently very useful, for they indicate what activities a project is currently undertaking and what progress the project has had while engaging in these activities.

Another type is an outcome objective which reveals the desired result from treatment-related activities. This objective indicates the programmatic intentions of a project and what impact the project hopes to have once treatment is complete. In general, the behavioral changes which might be specified in an outcome objective do not take place easily or quickly. As a result, a project might only wish to report data on those objectives at six-month to one-year intervals.

Thus, when the planning model is used for evaluation purposes, it requires the specification of the major goal, the administrative objectives needed for reaching that goal, the outcome objective which will reveal the intended treatment results, and the strategies and evaluation meth-

TABLE 12.2

Planning Procedures

GOAL	OBJECTIVE	STRATEGY	EVALUATION PROCEDURE	SAMPLE DATA
Children develop necessary self-help skills	To increase each child's self-help skills so that by June 1 they feed selves without the aid of others	Use food as a primary reinforcer	1. Pre-post observation of criterion behavior 2. Anecdotal record	On November 1, only 10% of the children could do the eating activities unaided (N = 25). By June 1, 96% of the children were eating without the aid of others.

odology relevant to each objective. This is depicted in Figure 12.2 on the planning approach.

By utilizing the goal-achievement planning model, it becomes possible for a project to describe its plans and strategies to other parties.

HOW WELL ARE WE DOING?

The answer to this question requires frequent observations on a daily or weekly basis—observations which are related to the clear and precise objectives which have been established. Such observations may require log-

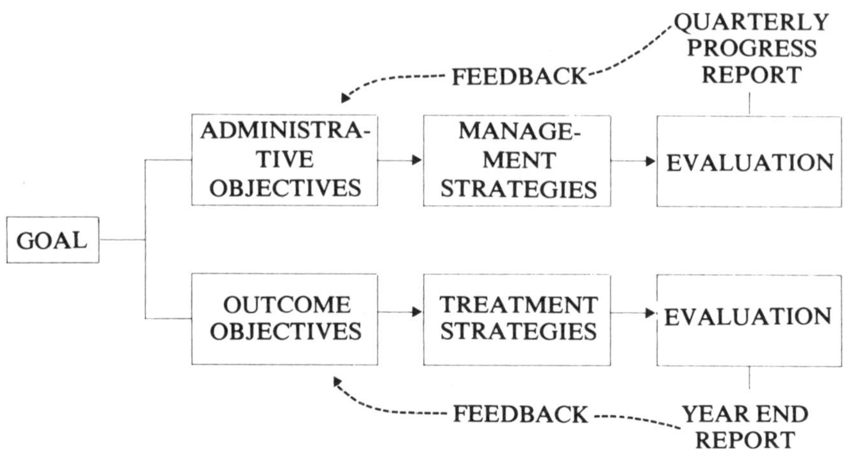

FIGURE 12.2. Evaluating differing objectives.

ging, record-keeping, check lists, or some type of behavioral rating scales. The technique is a rather "simple-headed" one but it does require good information management. For example, if an objective such as "to increase each child's self-help skills so that by June 1 he can feed himself without the aid of others" were selected and a food reinforcement were utilized, then during meals an instructor might work with the child on the task and keep an anecdotal record on success and problems. Sample data from such activities might simply describe the activities as follows: Oct. 1 —child can feed self finger food; Oct. 4—child interested in holding a spoon but not able; Oct. 10—child holds spoon poorly and often drops. Such a procedure would not only have utility for the purposes of evaluation but would also allow a careful recording of what curriculum and programmatic strategies were used and how effective they appeared to be. It would also permit the systematic review of program strategy. Such data might demonstrate, for example, that the strategy of using food reinforcement with the severely handicapped is impractical, given the skills of the current staff, and therefore the project may need to seek alternatives.

TABLE 12.3

Techniques for Evaluation

MEASURES

STANDARDIZED	- standardized tests - standardized informant-interview scales - established observation and behavior analysis schemes	
NON STANDARDIZED	- attendance at program - number sent on to regular programs - report-checklist, rating scales, letters - teacher report, check-list, rating progress report scales - acecdotal records - case studies by clinician	- recording number of: - requests to center for consultation - referrals of children by other agencies - observations and visits to school - brochure circulation - speaking engagements by staff - reports in newspaper articles, T.V., stories, magazine pieces, articles in journals
NON STANDARDIZED	- records of criterion behavior met - informant interview scales - observation and behavior analysis schemes, applied to behavior observed on video tape - letters or testimonials	- follow-ups of workshops and demonstration activities or feelings about presentation of part of it - contacts with agencies - records of new facilities modeled after yours - presentations to groups - noting changes in budgeting that allow funds to the handicapped - straw polls of agencies and city about know-ledge of project

HOW WELL DID WE DO?

Information gathered to answer the question of "how well are we doing" can be summarized and utilized to answer the question, how well did we do? For example, it is possible to use the summative data from many children with similar charactertistics that were being assisted in the same manner. The evaluation data for such activities might be the summation of anecdotal records of the individual child into one comprehensive report. These records would also be reported with some pre-post observations of certain criterion procedures which might reveal data similar to the following example. "On Nov. 1, only 10% of the children could do the eating activities unaided. By June 1, 96% of all children were eating without the aid of others." Such data certainly begin to provide validation for programmatic activities. While the utilization of information collected in a record-keeping, anecdotal method has great utility, it probably is still necessary to develop other measurement techniques. Table 12.3 provides examples of alternative procedures.

Since the behavior of individuals is very difficult to monitor and evaluate utilizing standard tests or even observational methods, it is recommended that for each major objective several evaluation techniques be utilized to ascertain the effects of any one objective. The thinking is that by collecting a variety of different kinds of information related to a single objective, one can start to build a case of circumstantial evidence to support programmatic effectiveness.

What should result from these procedures is data which, one hopes, will enable one to satisfy the accountability demands from outside agencies. The data should clearly indicate *who* the target population was for the activities, *what* the intended results were, and *what* data was collected related to each objective. An example of how data might be reported is shown on Table 12.4.

In conclusion, the evaluation strategy presented in this chapter represents a structure for planning and evaluation which could be applied in community service projects. No attempt has been made to depict a research methodology for data collection and analysis. At best the material represents a systematic way one might undertake the meeting of accountability demands.

Theoretically, well-stated plans should be an asset to a project's staff. Knowing the purpose and direction of an organization should reduce anxiety and facilitate decision-making which is congruent with the goals of the project. Well-stated plans can also be used to communicate to

13

Public Awareness Planning

PASCAL L. TROHANIS

EFFECTIVE DEINSTITUTIONALIZATION requires the development of an array of qualitative services spanning both community alternatives as well as institutional reform. According to a 1974 resolution clarifying the term deinstitutionalization, the National Advisory Council on Developmental Disabilities determined:

> Community alternatives has sometimes been construed to mean only community-based residential programs. This is incomplete. Community alternatives must be responsive to the full range of needs of families to prevent crisis, and to deal with crisis. Examples include public education, education of professionals who advise placement, a variety of kinds of respite care, family training in habilitation skills, and effective counseling.
>
> Institutional reform involves a modification or improvement in attitudes, philosophies, policies, effective utilization of all available resources, and increased financing to provide adequate programs to motivate and assist individuals to reach their maximum level of functioning in the least restrictive environment possible. Institutional reform will occur only through an increased effort on the part of all professionals, nonprofessional, and lay persons concerned with the developmentally disabled.

Basic to the planning and execution of activities in both community alternatives and institutional reform is involvement in the art and process of communication. Public and private human-service agency personnel, consumers, and university persons are constantly practicing and engaging in communication. For example, they transfer and express ideas, understandings, and information to different audiences about deinstitutionalization. Additionally, they motivate or energize decision-makers to action in the spheres of public policy or human services. Beyond state government and private agency personnel, they reach out to larger publics in order to combat the apathy, avoidance, and negative images of handicapped citizens. Finally, they communicate to many persons about maximizing the opportunities for handicapped citizens to live, learn, work, play, and pray in the mainstream of modern American life.

By virtue of their communicative nature, a growing number of human-service persons are devoting energy and resources to the development and implementation of public-awareness plans for reaching out to influence different audiences. Thus, this chapter introduces the reader to some general concepts about public-awareness planning and implementation. Also included is a short listing of a few exciting films on deinstitutionalization which might be helpful in implementing one's own awareness program.

PLANNING AND PROGRAM DEVELOPMENT FRAMEWORK

Public-awareness planning and development strategizing are crucial to public and private human-service agencies. It is hoped that the following framework will assist the reader to conceptualize an awareness program which carefully examines alternatives for communicating what, to whom, for which purposes, when, how, and with what effect.

Planning Program Purposes

Because service agencies want to nurture public awareness, information, or relations on issues related to deinstitutionalization, they must be able to clearly outline their program purposes or goals. To help the reader think about this planning activity is a list of seven purpose statements for consideration:

1. Promote acceptance and understanding for handicapped citizens and the deinstitutionalization concept.

2. Stimulate the development of new laws (e.g., fire, zoning), policies, services, and/or appropriations dictated by the needs of citizens who are handicapped.

3. Facilitate the development of a citizen's self-concept, skills, and knowledge.

4. Provide reliable, accurate, and current information on community alternatives and institutional reform.

5. Keep handicapped citizens or advocates informed about available community services and rights so that they may participate and gain full benefits from them.

6. Cultivate new publics who may act on behalf of the deinstitutionalization movement.

7. Minimize citizen resistance to the siting and operation of community-based programs.

These seven information, persuasion, and motivation purpose statements are intended as examples. They should be viewed as jumping-off points for human service communicators to delineate their own purposes. It is essential to know what is to be accomplished and what needs are to be satisfied by the audience.

Having accomplished this planning step, the communicator can move on to the next phase.

Researching

This planning phase calls for intensive and extensive data probing. All relevant opinions, observations, attitudes, and reactions of persons to be associated with an agency's public-awareness program should be consulted. Furthermore, program needs should be clarified and verified prior to additional planning. As a consequence, it is hoped that parts of a program are to be better seen in relation to the whole. Therefore, background information is vital to the next step in planning which involves the matching of specific messages and delivery channels with specific audiences.

Planning for Audiences

Audiences, like purposes, must be identified, analyzed, and agreed upon. Simply put, who is to be reached with a designated message? Most often, the audiences which will receive the messages can be subdivided along different dimensions. For example, size can be divided into meaningful categories such as a single person, small group (up to 100), and/or mass (100 or more). Occupation, sex, and education are other dimensions. Finally, assumptions about an audience's knowledge base, values, feelings, and needs should be explored by agency communicators.

Many of the typical publics (target audiences) for a deinstitutionalization-oriented program include legislators, educators, real estate brokers, doctors, lawyers, city officials, social service professionals, consumer groups, and parents. To many public-information professionals, this type of audience grouping represents around 15 percent of the total population. However, if the goal of a public awareness program is to promote greater public acceptance and understanding, the program should direct a large portion of its efforts to the 85 percent—the so-called general public.

Apathy and avoidance among neighbors can be changed. New laws and services can be stimulated. Improved training in habilitation and respite care can be promoted. However, to accomplish these and other worthwhile ends, a close examination and understanding of the intended audiences is mandatory.

Message Planning

Having delineated purposes and audiences, human service communicators must cope with the complex issue of message determination and design. What will the determined publics watch, read, or hear? Precisely what content—facts, opinions, interpretations—should be prepared? Is the message difficult or simple to understand? Does it ask for a response or offer rewards? What approach, slant, or style is most advantageous?

In general, there are two broad messages. The first deals with the deinstitutionalization concept of community alternatives and institutional reform. The second broad message (and probably the more important) concerns the rights of those citizens who are handicapped. The following general statements and questions (Nelson 1973; Waldman 1973; Paul 1974) provide a basis for both kinds of messages. They are offered in order to stimulate initial discussion on the issue of designing and clarifying messages:

1. The client, the handicapped person, has constitutional rights as a citizen. Denial of any of those rights compounds the disability. Those rights must be secured, including, or especially in, those instances where the disabled person is not able to rise to his own defense.

2. There is a need to attract and identify qualified foster parents or attendants.

3. The advantages, successes, and cost of institutional reform and alternative community methods must be explained.

4. The person has a right to live in his or her own community. If rejected by his or her own family, the person has a right to resources for a decent life without compromising his or her own personal integrity.

5. What special services need to be provided for people who are handicapped, or what is this community doing to provide special services?

6. The person has educational, psychological, and medical needs which must be met appropriately, sufficiently, and on time. He or she has a right to appropriate educational and treatment resources. No subhuman or even substandard environment—physically, socially, or morally—can be rationalized as acceptable.

7. What is the potential for a handicapped person in his community?

8. How is an institutional program reformed? Where was it before and why the change?

9. Explain how a community offers maximum opportunities for normalization of handicapped people.

10. Citizen advocacy: what it is, why it is needed, and who will implement it.

11. The person has a right to pursue a life beyond stigma. This requires an educated citizenry, an accommodating physical environment, alternative resources which are not characterized by demeaning labels or exclusive incompetency criteria for participating, and an advocate to monitor his or her well-being and assist in increasing productive and adaptive interaction between the person and the environment.

12. What are the opportunities for employing the handicapped or helping them to set up and operate small businesses?

13. There is a need to dispel myths about handicapped persons who would be living in the community.

14. How can the local citizenry best be linked to the deinstitutionalization process and give their support?

Planning for Delivery Channels

There is a need for shaping a deinstitutionalization-oriented program to meet local requirements, community by community. While this variance will naturally exist, some delivery channel requirements appear to remain the same. Raices (1974) believes that a good program should have "basic materials with relatively long lives, such as fact sheets, films, brochures, photographs, slide presentations, posters, and manuals. For the short run, news releases, reprints of recent press mentions, material for local editors and columnists, speeches, tapes for radio news editors are typical." Other delivery channels include TV (commercial, public, cable), piggy-back mailings, postage meter display, outdoor advertising, speakers bureaus, press kits, documentaries, displays, press conferences, hearings, special events, and one-to-one "jawboning." Perhaps one of the most important and often-overlooked channels is the fostering of honest and continuous personal contact between handicapped citizens and others in the community.

To assist the reader in matching and selecting channels with messages and audiences, the following planning framework is offered. While Read (1972) admits that his format is not based on a scientific formula, his intuitive guidelines may be helpful for public awareness planning and decision-making.

Mass-media channels. We should achieve maximum communication efficiency by using mass-media channels under the following conditions:
1. The audience for the message is large. The mass media, in fact, offer the only practical channels for reaching large, general audiences.
2. The message is simple. This does not mean that the message lacks importance, but the conept should be easy to grasp and understand.
3. The message is timely. There is need to reach audiences quickly.
4. The audience is exposed to the mass-media channels. A large share of the intended audience subscribes to and reads newspapers, or listens to radio, or watches television.
5. Time and money are limited.

Group channels. The following conditions suggest the use of group channels (meetings, conferences, field days, and direct-mail services):
1. The audience is relatively small, specialized, easily identified, and highly motivated.
2. The message is either complex, highly specialized, or both.
3. Communication effectiveness depends in part upon immediate audience response and feedback. The audience does more than receive the message.
4. Message content is more important than timeliness.
5. Time and other resources are available.

Person-to-person channels. The conditions that suggest the use of person-to-person channels are almost self-evident and include the following:

1. The audience is small, and motivation may be slight.
2. The message, simple or complex, must be fitted to the individual needs of the receiver.
3. The timing of the message is not critical.
4. Time and other resources are available.

The exceptions. There are exceptions to all guidelines, of course, and we find many exceptions for those above.

The packaging of credible, consistent, accurate, clear, and repetitious messages into any of these channels requires a good deal of preplanning, preparation, and execution. However, a developer is cautioned that as he or she moves from the simpler channels (fact sheet, news releases) to complex ones (16mm, color, sound sync film), to more complex ones (person-to-person contact), much more time is consumed in planning than in actual preparation.

Planning for Evaluation

No public-awareness plan would be complete without some consideration for evaluation. For just like other sponsored activities, the human-service agency must collect information in order to gauge the effectiveness of them, as well as provide data for continual decision-making purposes.

Since communicators use many different planning and evaluation systems for gathering data about program impact, effectiveness, and objectives attainment, an overall methodology for public awareness will not be suggested. Furthermore, the state of the evaluation art for this area is not that scientific or sophisticated. Of course, there are elaborate techniques and forecasting procedures which are being experimented with and implemented by large corporations. These are very expensive, however, and usually too obtrusive for agency purposes.

Therefore, what are some methods which can be designed and used to evaluate different dimensions of a plan? The following procedures could be employed to collect data for program assessment:

1. Clipping service—to keep track of how many newspapers are running releases and other stories.
2. Estimated numbers of persons reached as a result of televising a TV program or broadcasting a radio documentary.
3. Numbers of persons writing in for information about deinstitutionalization activities.

4. Names and addresses of persons responding (via a WATTS telephone number) to a radio campaign sponsored by an agency or university.
5. Evaluation forms containing satisfaction and impact questions that can be collected and analyzed following a public-awareness seminar or workshop on topics such as habilitation skills, human and civil rights, and responsive residential environs.
6. The frequency of messages transmitted via radio and TV.
7. Appearance of a new governmental ruling, community services, or appropriation attributable to the deinstitutionalization concept.
8. Data from a speakers' bureau.
9. Number of times a bank, library, or department store asks for displays or booths.
10. A third-party panel to assess, using predetermined criteria, the impact of face-to-face activities.
11. Circulation figures and feedback (formally solicited or informally provided) from readers of an agency newsletter.
12. Postcard feedback data on a film or slidetape that is circulated.

Regardless of the methods developed and used, communicators should make sure that their evaluation procedures are tied closely to their program goals. Furthermore, they should document as completely as possible their successes and failures. In this way, decisions about the overall plan can be more closely scrutinized, changed, and improved over a period of time.

Coordinating the Program

Ultimately, a decision must be reached regarding what needs to be said, what materials developed, for which audiences, and for what purposes. An agency may be fortunate to have the services of a full- or part-time staff member to coordinate its public-awareness planning; or a talented task force or subcommittee on public information, made up of advisory board members or interested local citizens; or ongoing consultative assistance provided by an advertising or public relations company or individual communications professional.

If none of these is the case, one might make use of other agencies and resources which can facilitate the development and production of messages for a given channel and audience. For example, University Affiliated Facilities (UAF), educational media centers in public schools or universities, prison print shops, Health, Education and Welfare regional communication programs, and state government media or public information offices should be contacted. Another facilitator might be consumer groups such as the Association for Retarded Children and the United Cerebral Palsy Association. Of Course, the final determination as to who will coordinate the program will depend largely on such factors as availability of local talent, regulations, purposes, and resources. It is a good idea to have made media contacts prior to execution. This means that the coordinator should contact such persons as newspaper editors, TV and radio public service directors, and photographic studio personnel.

Executing the Plan

Even with someone responsible for coordinating the development and execution of the public awareness efforts, an agency must continue to explore programmtic alternatives, keeping money and time in mind. Additionally, it should strive for program consistency, clarity, credibility, and openness. Furthermore, it should seek long-term exposures, wide input, and a good mix of delivery channels. Finally, the effort should be positive and optimistic in tone.

After a plan has been conceptualized, it is ready to implement. Read (1972) offers some execution suggestions.

Step 1. Budget time and money for each of the communication activities called for in the plan, and work up a calendar of deadlines for those activities. When will the first news story be written, the first radio program be aired, the first television program be presented? What are the dates for the scheduled meetings, and when must the first planning session be held for each meeting or the series of meetings? When and how will the meetings be publicized?

Step 2. Plan schedules to meet the deadlines. With a realistic time budget, we should be able to estimate the number of hours needed each week to carry out the plan. If the number of required hours is unavailable, we must adjust the plan to fit the hours.

Step 3. Evaluate the plan after each step and make adjustments called for by the evaluation. Our first meeting may have been so successful that subsequent meetings are not needed. Cancel them. We learn that the television station has changed its program schedule, and the show we counted on is unavailable. We must shift resources to other channels. Audience feedback indicates more misunderstanding of the problem than we anticipated. We may need an additional series of news stories.

Step 4. Make a final evaluation and prepare a report on successes and failures for future reference. We can improve our efforts tomorrow only by applying the knowledge gained today.

In essence, public-awareness planning and program development deals with the continuous communication of views about deinstitutionalization. Also, it involves building positive support for these views and the citizens most closely touched by this movement.

A PARTIAL LISTING OF 16mm FILM RESOURCES

1. *Like Other People* (43 minutes, color, 1972)
     Available: Perennial Educators   United Cerebral Palsy Inc.
               P. O. Box 236   Youth Activities Dept.
               1825 Willow Road   66 East 34th St.
               Northfield, Ill. 60093   New York, N. Y. 10016
     Also Available: United Cerebral Palsy of Denver
                     2727 Columbine Street
                     Denver, Colorado 80205
   A sensitive and powerful film on the subject of normalization. A british-made documentary of a young cerebral palsied couple who are in love and demand the right to social, emotional, and sexual fulfillment.
2. *Normalization—The Right of Respect* (14 1/2 minutes, color, 1973)
     Available: Atlanta Association for Retarded Children
                First National Bank Building—Suite 369
                315 West Ponce de Leon Avenue
                Decatur, Georgia 30030
   The film discusses the principles on normalization, especially residential facilities and focuses on developmentally disabled citizens in real-life situations.
3. *Look Beyond the Disability* (30 minutes, color, 1972)
     Available: Media Support Services
                Parsons State Hospital and Training Center
                2601 Gabriel
                Parsons, Kansas 67357
   The film was produced for TV for the Kansas DD Council to help locate developmentally disabled citizens in need of services and to alert citizens to their key role as a "pressure group" to encourage communities to provide services locally, especially education.
4. *Something Shared* (15 minutes, color, 1974)
     Available: National Association for Retarded Citizens
                2709 Avenue E. East
                P. O. Box 6109
                Arlington, Texas 76011
   A film on citizen advocacy which introduces the concept and the nature of the advocate-protégé relationship.

5. *That's What it's All About* (28 minutes, color, 1974)
   A film produced at Denver University on normalization and the Colorado Hostel Program. For information on its availability contact: Division of DD, 306 State Services Building, 1525 Sherman, Denver, Colorado 80203.
6. *People First* (34 minutes, color, 1976)
   Available: Stanfield House
            P.O. Box 3208
            900 Euclid Street
            Santa Monica, California 90403
   This film documents the lives, political, and community activities of People First, the first self-advocacy group of DD citizens.

REFERENCES

Audette, Bob. Presentation on public education, Developmental Disabilities Technical Assistance (DDTA) Chairman's Conference. Quails Roost, N.C. November 1973.

National Advisory Council on Developmental Disabilities (DD). Memorandum on clarifying term "deinstitutionalization." June 11, 1974.

Nelson, Roberta. Presentation on public education, DDTA Chairman's Conference. Quails Roost, N.C. August 1973.

Paul, James L. Working paper on Advocacy Potential of DD Councils, DDTA. Chapel Hill, N.C. April 1974.

Public Relations: How to Use It. A pamphlet by the Scholarship, Education, and Defense Fund for Racial Equality. New York, 1973.

Raices, Emanuel. "Notes on the foundations of a public information program." In *Public Awareness Considerations,* edited by P. Trohanis. Chapel Hill: Developmental Disabilities Technical Assistance System, 1974.

Read, Hadley. *Communication: Methods for All Media.* Urbana: University of Illinois Press, 1972.

Telling the United Cerebral Palsy Story. A pamphlet by the Public Relations Department, United Cerebral Palsy Association, New York.

Templeton, Ian. *Communicating with the Public.* Arlington, Va.: National School Public Relations Association, 1972.

Waldman, Leslie. Presentation on public information, DDTA Chairman's Conference. Quails Roost, N.C. October, 1973.

14

State Agency Planning

JACQUELINE FARAH

THE CONCEPT OF DEINSTITUTIONALIZATION is multifaceted and far-reaching. The philosophy itself is noble, popular, and timely—timely in that it follows closely other movements whose efforts have been directed toward bringing deviant populations into the mainstream of society. Twentieth century events which highlight this trend include the attention of the federal government to the rehabilitation of handicapped people during the 1920s, the assertion of civil rights for blacks during the fifties, the actions of Chicanos and Native Americans during the sixties, and the repeated thrusts for women's rights throughout the century. The goal of each movement has been individual dignity for every human being and opportunity for each man and woman to participate in the socioeconomic life of our communities. These are our goals now as we work to procure rights and opportunities for developmentally disabled people.

FACING THE CONFLICTS

The "rightness" of the deinstitutionalization and normalization movement should not obscure the complexity of the issue. Essentially we are asking ourselves and the other members of the dominant culture to give up old coping skills. For many years and for a variety of reasons, we have separated non-normal folk from our communities. We have used our state institutions to give them special places in which to live, to work, and to learn. This has been the thrust of our planning over the last sev-

246

eral decades. At times the separation of handicapped individuals from our communities seems to have been designed for the benefit of the handicapped person. It seems, however, that more often than not the root of it has been in our own reluctance, perhaps fear, to interact on a day-to-day basis with people who are different from and somehow threatening to us. The act of bringing heretofore hidden groups of people into the daily activities of the community cannot help but present personal and public confrontations for the members of the dominant "normal" social subculture as well as the new citizens from whom we sought to isolate ourselves over the last five decades.

While we may want to see the deinstitutionalization/normalization movement as an easy, smooth-flowing process, played out in such a way as to minimize if not avoid sudden and major changes, it will be accomplished only if we are willing to anticipate and in fact embrace the conflicts inherent in such an effort. The elimination of social barriers will challenge longstanding attitudes and values. Recognizing the prevailing character of our social-service system relative to handicapped people as virtually isolating, one can see that deinstitutionalization requires important, radical changes in the system. People from whom the "normal" population receives services—grocery clerks, doctors, taxi drivers, counselors, people behind the desks in various public offices—have had, for the most part, no contact with individuals with significant handicapping developmental disabilities. Consequently, these service providers have had no need to acquire skills for interacting with people who are not "normal." This fact has effectively prohibited the utilization of community services for seriously impaired people. Before we can implement deinstitutionalization in the strict sense of the word (phasing out our institutions) we must give careful thought to the character of our communities and to the needs of the population for which alternatives must be provided.

UNDERSTANDING THE CHALLENGE

Deinstitutionalization has three basic thrusts, the success of the first two resting on the accomplishment of the third. Deinstitutionalization means (1) moving people who are now living in institutions into the community, (2) preventing the institutionalization of people who are now in the community, and (3) the third force on which the first two depend, the development of community-based alternatives to institutionalization. It must be understood that the services which have been provided to severely handicapped people within institution walls now have to be made available to them in our communities. The viability of the alternatives depends on deliberate and thorough consideration of what the target population will need if those people are to experience a satisfying life in the community.

Since disabled people and non-disabled people are more alike than different, our needs are basically the same: to live, work, play, and learn in an environment that helps us to maintain our own health and welfare. The elements of the community that we use and take for granted—our homes, schools, doctors, modes of transportation, areas of recreation— are the same elements that must also be available to developmentally disabled people. Most of us can readily utilize the components of our social system so that our basic needs are satisfied. For those who are handicapped in any of a variety of ways it becomes more difficult to acquire what is needed from the existing system. The more deviant the handicap, the more difficult it is to find and use the essential resources of the community. The generic services and systems that "normal" people can gain access to for their use are not now accessible to significantly impaired people. One hopes that fact will change. Until it does, it is in keeping with the spirit of the nation's social consciousness to have the needs met initially through the efforts of state and federal social-service agencies.

The deinstitutionalization movement lays a serious and long-range responsibility on public social-service agencies. Decision-makers must work for programs which respond to immediate needs and at the same time keep sight of long-range goals and consequences. There are some programs which seem to provide immediate solutions to problems faced by handicapped people, but the consequences of the programs over time may be detrimental to the population being served. For example, a bill recently presented to the legislature in Oregon attacked the problem of transportation for handicapped people with two proposals. First the authors of the bill suggested that the state should require all mass transit vehicles to be accessible for handicapped people. In the same bill they wanted to legislate free transportation for the handicapped population. The first part of the bill deserves full support and implementation, but the second proposal essentially devalues the population it is trying to serve. To quote the director of the Oregon Association for Retarded Citizens, "Yes, we want to be able to get on the bus. But once we get on, we want to drop in our fare just like everyone else." The development of community programs is at first a response to immediate need. All the programs, however, must be kept in the context of increasing the perceived value of people who have been systematically devalued for many decades. This is a long-range goal.

Developing the accessibility of generic services is another long-range responsibility of public social-service agencies. For the most part, when and where people receive services should be determined by what they need, not by unrelated personal characteristics. The obvious abuse in service provision occurs when differentiation of provision is made according to race or sex. A woman rides a bus because she needs to get from one place to another. She should not be "served" by the back of the bus if she is black and the front of the bus if she is white. Similarly, we should avoid establishing back-of-the-bus services for handicapped people. It will be very easy for public service agencies to fall into a pattern of supporting a parallel and separate service delivery system for developmentally disabled people in the wake of deinstitutionalization. In order to respond to immediate and pressing needs, special services will be set up. However, the same resources that are used to set up new special services might be better used for easing access to existing services. This is happening now in the area of education. In many states TMR classrooms are part of the public school system. As more and more severely handicapped children return to or stay in the community, they will find the generic educational system, the public school, ready to provide services to them. In light of long-range goals, this is by far preferable to the establishment of separate education facilities for mentally retarded children. It has fiscal and philosophical advantages. State agencies should make maximum use of the generic service system as they plan to develop community-based services for handicapped people.

ATTACKING THE PROBLEM

The organization of agencies varies a great deal from state to state. Some states have umbrella agencies which are responsible for the administration of social services. In some states this agency has restricted planning responsibility, while in other states the umbrella agency retains the power of budget review and approval. Many states do not have a superordinate coordinating agency of this type and instead provide social services through several disconnected agencies which may have overlapping jurisdictions and target populations.

Whatever the organization of the state bureaucracy, each agency providing social services must engage in planning. Plans are developed as part of the budgeting process to anticipate costs and justify expenditures. Nearly all federal monies are conditional on the submission of plans for their use. Many states now require similar documentation of proposed service programs. The state plans of social services agencies will determine where and how resources will be used to respond to service needs.

The plans of state agencies are very important to the pattern of service delivery. The processes used to develop the plans and the principles reflected in the plans are determinants of quality. The previous section presented some principles that should be considered when planning for services to people who are developmentally disabled. There are also processes which are important in that they facilitate the implementation as well as the generation of state agency plans.

It would not be useful to offer here a recipe for planning—there is too much variation from state to state in how roles and responsibilities are delineated. Instead, the following material suggests some constructs which facilitate the development and implementation of deinstitutionalization plans. Specifically, some aspects of particular steps in the planning process are outlined and a taxonomy of services is suggested which can be useful in a variety of ways for planners in the area of services for developmentally disabled people.

Long-range and comprehensive planning begins with an analysis of the human services systems which now exist for the population as a whole. We need to ask, how are the responsibilities of human service agencies now defined? What characterizes the population being served by each agency? Is eligibility for services determined by age, economic status, health conditions, vocational potential? For the most part, state and federal agencies have been set up to respond generically to a type of need across age and economic grouping (although these factors are frequently used to establish broad parameters for eligibility). More recently, in the interest of providing comprehensive services, "specialty" agencies have been established to serve many needs of a population demographically defined (e.g., children's services, services for the aging, developmental disabilities services). While there may be immediate advantages to assigning responsibility to a comprehensive agency to assure the provision of services to a specific type of population (mentally retarded, racial minority, elderly), this format tends to prolong the isolation of a particular population. The usefulness of a specialty agency is limited to coordinating and influencing the planning of generic agencies to assure that the needs of the special population are being met. The actual provision of the services should come from the generic agencies themselves. Ideally, a "specialty" agency will work itself out of business as it works to assure the inclusion of its target population in the generic service system.

After studying the current patterns of service delivery—how, where, and to whom services are provided—the next step is to determine what will be needed. There are two ways to approach the issue of needs assessment. One technique is to conceptualize the array of services that may be needed by an individual over a lifetime. Ideally this array of services should be available within reasonable proximity of one's home. One can compare this ideal to what currently exists and see a picture of the gaps. It is then important to determine which gaps will be filled first.

The Rehabilitation Research and Training Center at the University of Oregon has developed a classification of services as part of their work in describing planning and evaluation strategies for Developmental Disabilities Councils (Halpern, Farah, and Nagle 1974). The list contains fifty-four services which are clustered into nine sets of direct services and one set of indirect services. Direct services are those which are delivered in such a way as to bring the service provider into direct contact with the disabled client or the family of the client. Indirect services are essential to the development of adequate high quality services but do not involve direct interaction with the client. The services are listed below:

1. GENERAL SUPPORTIVE SERVICES

  1.1 Casefinding
  1.2 Information and Referral
  1.3 Coordination of Services
  1.4 Follow Along
  1.5 Protective Services
  1.6 Personal Advocacy
  1.7 Guardianship Services

2. IDENTIFICATION AND ASSESSMENT

  2.1 Screening
  2.2 Diagnosis
  2.3 Evaluation

3. TREATMENT

  3.1 Medical Services
  3.2 Dental Services
  3.3 Speech Therapy
  3.4 Physical Therapy
  3.5 Occupational Therapy
  3.6 Psychotherapy

4. EDUCATIONAL SERVICES

4.1 Preschool Services
4.2 School Services for the Mildly Handicapped
4.3 School Services for the Moderately, Severely, and Profoundly Handicapped
4.4 Adult Basic Education
4.5 Special School Services

5. FAMILY SUPPORT SERVICES

5.1 Family Education
5.2 Family Training
5.3 In-home Sitter Services
5.4 Out-of-home Sitter Services
5.5 Out-of-home Respite Care
5.6 Homemaking
5.7 General Counseling
5.8 Crisis Intervention
5.9 Family Planning
5.10 Genetic Counseling

6. LIVING ARRANGEMENTS

6.1 Board and Room Living
6.2 Group Home Care
6.3 Foster Care
6.4 Sheltered Care
6.5 Nursing Home Care
6.6 Institutional Care

7. VOCATIONAL SERVICES

7.1 Evaluation
7.2 Training
7.3 Placement/Counseling
7.4 Sheltered Employment
7.5 Activity Center Programs
7.6 Other Employment Services

8. RECREATIONAL SERVICES

8.1 Therapeutic Recreation
8.2 Leisure Time Recreation

9. TRANSPORTATION

10. INDIRECT SERVICES

10.1 Planning Coordination
10.2 Public Education

10.3 Primary Prevention
10.4 Basic Research
10.5 Manpower Development
10.6 Data Management
10.7 Funding
10.8 Elimination of Architectural Barriers

These terms, which have been defined elsewhere for utilization, provide a conceptual framework for assessing resources and needs. They may also have applicability to data management for the purposes of monitoring client progress and conducting the cyclical process of evaluation and planning.

The second approach to needs assessment is one of monitoring the pressure points. Where are demands being made? Where are there obvious overloads or waiting lists? Using only this approach to determine where resources will be utilized becomes a brush-fire routine. However, this type of analysis can be combined with a conceptual approach when one undertakes the task of deciding which gaps to fill first.

As an aid to carrying out the needs assessment part of the planning process, the taxonomy of services shown above has been utilized in two ways by state Developmental Disabilities Councils. The council in the state of Oregon used this conceptual framework to develop a grid which shows on one dimension the state social service agencies and on the other dimension the services that may be needed by a developmentally disabled individual during his or her lifetime. Each social service agency in the state provided information about the services that it is able to provide or purchase, and with that information the Developmental Disabilities planner was able to indicate in the grid the services that are currently available within the state. This graphic description of services proves to be very useful to those who are trying to coordinate the planning for and provision of services in two ways. It facilitates the understanding of agency responsibilities, and it allows one to begin identifying gaps and duplications in the service system.

The Developmental Disabilities Council in the state of Utah used a small group process similar to nominal groups to assess the needs of developmentally disabled people as perceived by practitioners and consumer representatives at the local level. The taxonomy of services shown above provided the initial framework which allowed participants in all regions of the state to describe their local service patterns in common terms. The commonality of the frame of reference permitted the State Council to integrate local concerns in the state planning effort.

The discussion of how states are to plan for deinstitutionalization moves along rather smoothly if we keep talking as though one agency were solely responsible. One decision-maker, one monitor, one developer with everything easily controlled. However, services are provided by a variety of agencies and should continue to be provided in that way. A specialty agency, if it exists, will not have control over the entire system. It is more likely to have advisory, monitoring, and coordinating responsibilities. The assessment of resources and assessment of needs will probably be done by each generic agency relative to its particular service. Each agency will also establish priorities for the utilization of its resources. With as many as five or more agencies planning for the development of community services, the results could be haphazard and counterproductive. It is essential for each state to have a forum where agencies come together. The agencies can be supportive of each other, build complementary programs, identify ancillary services which will augment the primary service each delivers. It is not easy to establish a cooperative constellation of state agencies, but the development of community services will suffer significantly without such an effort.

The coordinating forum at the state level may take the form of a superordinate agency, the umbrella-type agency discussed earlier, which pulls together the plans and budgets of the social service agencies to facilitate non-duplicative, full-range service delivery. A Human Resources Division or Division of Health and Welfare functioning in this way is not itself a deliverer of services but rather an administrative unit which has responsibility for assuring coordinated and cooperative planning and resource utilization.

Another vehicle for coordinating state agencies' efforts is the Developmental Disabilities Council. The Developmental Disabilities Act, PL 91-517, authorizes federal grants for planning, administration, provision of services, and construction of facilities for persons with developmental disabilities. One of the prime concerns of the act is the development of comprehensive services through the combination and integration of specialized and generic services. The act intends to draw together the efforts of diverse state agencies such as health, welfare, education, and rehabilitation. Consequently the major thrust of the program is comprehensive planning. The council itself provides a structure in each state whereby agencies responsible for specific social services can cooperatively review programs, establish policies, and communicate across agency lines.

The development of good community alternatives to institutions depends as much on community support as it does on interagency cooperation. Unfortunately community support is usually difficult to generate and channel. As they develop plans for community services, the planning agencies should identify local consumer groups which can be used as advisors throughout the planning process. Two purposes are served in tapping local involvement. First, a local advisory group will often be able to provide valuable information about how things really work in its community. Local politics, attitudes and patterns of service usage are sometimes known only to those who live with them. Secondly, involving local citizens in the planning process will help establish a base of support for the changes that will be taking place. Individuals from the community who have participated in decision making, whether it is in an advisory capacity or with stronger approval power, would feel as if they share "authorship" for the plans that will be affecting their neighborhoods. They can then lend a very positive local influence to the deinstitutionalization movement.

CONCLUSION

The replacement of institutional services with community-based services will be a complex and slowly growing phenomenon. Some services will need to be expanded in order to respond to a greater number of requests. Within other types of services, providers will need training in order to respond to a more heterogeneous population. Still other service areas will have to be developed almost from scratch. The last group includes living accommodations, educational opportunities, and vocational programs for severely disabled people.

Severely handicapped people can have richer and more valuable lives if they share in our communities. Resources must be directed toward this commitment. It will require redirection of state budget money—into community services rather than institutions. It will necessitate professional and public education. Most important, agencies must work in coordination and cooperation at all levels in order to assure responsible progress in the movement toward deinstitutionalization.

REFERENCE

Halpern, A.S.; Farah, J. L.; and Nagle, J. M. "A Planning and Evaluation Strategy for State Developmental Disabilities Councils." Working Paper No 79, Rehabilitation Research Training Center in Mental Retardation, University of Oregon. 2 (August 1974).

15

The Developmental Disability Council

ELSIE D. HELSEL

IN CONCEPTUALIZING THE DIMENSIONS of the deinstitutionalization issue and discussing ways of developing an improved service delivery system, Developmental Disabilities Councils can and should play a major role in getting it all together. Councils have the mandate, the expertise and knowledge, the decision-making personnel, the access to the power basis of state government, and the money to facilitate the translation of an idealistic concept into an operational reality.

In addition Developmental Disabilities Councils have something else in their favor relative to deinstitutionalization. Both the concept that brought Developmental Disabilities Councils into being and the concept underlying deinstitutionalization are ideas whose time has come. Both issues have the support of professionals and the laity involved with the handicapped. Both have public support, at least philosophically. Both are in tune with consumerism and advocacy. Let us hope that Victor Hugo was right when he said, "Greater than the tread of mighty armies is an idea whose time has come." For it will take extraordinary power to move the bureaucracy to make the system changes needed if deinstitutionalization is to remain a viable concept and one capable of providing for the developmentally disabled one of their basic rights—the right to live in the community with their peers.

UNIQUE ASSETS OF DEVELOPMENTAL DISABILITY (DD) COUNCILS

Realizing that deinstitutionalization is a complex issue requiring the committed and coordinated effort of all levels of government, all groups serving the handicapped, all citizens living in the community, what assets does a DD Council have to contribute to the solution of this problem?

THE DEVELOPMENTAL DISABILITIES ACT ITSELF

The Developmental Disabilities Act is an unusual piece of legislation and potentially a very powerful one. Not only was the act uniquely conceived by groups outside state and federal government, but the original coalition that framed the act, helped with its passage, and monitored its implementation has managed to keep itself together and continued to exert influence over the legislative and regulative bodies. The group has good communication lines to Congress and knows how to use its power judiciously. With each renewal of the act, the group has seen to it that the power of the DD Councils at the state and federal levels was strengthened.

By mandate, DD Councils are to develop a state plan which will assure quality comprehensive services for individuals who are developmentally disabled; approve, monitor, and evaluate the implementation of the state plan; establish priorities for the distribution of funds; review and comment on all federal-state plans which have an impact on persons with developmental disabilities; re-evaluate the status of implementation annually; revise the plan accordingly; and report to the governor and legislature. This mandate gives DD Councils wide latitude for addressing problems. Many have chosen to address the deinstitutionalization issue.

Specifically, the new DD Act places priorities and goals for using developmental disabilities funds for deinstitutionalization. Some of the goals written into the act are: (1) to reduce and eventually eliminate inappropriate institutional placement; (2) to improve the quality of care, habilitation, and rehabilitation of persons with developmental disabilities for whom institutional care is appropriate; (3) to provide counseling, client program coordination, follow-along services, protective services, and person-advocacy services; (4) to support the establishment of community programs as alternatives to institutionalization; (5) to protect human rights; (6) to provide for interdisciplinary intervention and training programs for the multihandicapped.

With such specific mandates, DD Councils can readily formulate strong goals and objectives for deinstitutionalization, set priorities, and target funding on this area. Such a mandate can be a powerful tool in the hands of an active, informed, and aggressive council.

COMPREHENSIVE AND FLEXIBLE MANDATE

Not only does deinstitutionalization require the commitment and coordination of all the state's human, material, and financial resources that have an impact on the DD population, but it requires the willingness and capacity of individuals and institutions within the state to change. Never before has a federal-state program been authorized to put together a state's resources in so flexible a manner. Development Disability Councils have the mandate to: operate outside the bureaucratic system with its own staff; plan non-categorically for services across departmental lines; establish priorities for implementation and funding; control the implementation of the planning through council approval; review and comment on other state-federal plans having an impact on the developmentally disabled population; advocate for and protect the rights of individuals with developmental disabilities; monitor and evaluate the implementation of the plan; co-mingle funds; and report to the governor and legislature.

This broad mandate gives councils the opportunity and the power to be effective change agents.

In addition to the comprehensive mandate, the placement of councils outside the bureaucracy with authority lines to the governor yet with administrative responsibility to a state agency gives councils the flexible posture so necessary to devise innovative solutions to the massive problems of deinstitutionalization. Since councils do not have a vested interest in preserving old patterns of care, old buildings or bureaucratic empires, or budgets, they are free to plan and to act innovatively.

Councils have a unique opportunity to devise deinstitutionalization plans which have as their central focus the needs of the developmentally disabled individual. They need not and should not become involved with planning for the bureaucratic department within which they are housed. Councils need not be locked into present delivery systems or administrative patterns. By keeping the primary focus on the developmentally disabled individual and their needs, councils can plan for a delivery service that serves disabled people rather than perpetuates old patterns which are convenient for the professional staff or utilize old buildings that have long outlived their usefulness. Councils can carefully assess the needs of individuals, the realities of costs and manpower, and the available facilities and services. They can then do what good systems planning dictates —namely, keep their focus on the individual's needs and what they are really trying to accomplish in the meeting of these needs.

Although the amounts of money allocated to councils are small in comparison with state budgets assigned to present programs for the developmentally disabled, the judicious use of these monies can be as leverage to assess, free up, and direct the much larger sums.

Such flexibility and comprehensive planning authority are absolutely necessary for attacking deinstitutionalization issues since the resources of so many state departments must be tapped and coordinated in order to provide community residential alternatives with a full complement of support services.

PEOPLE POWER

The mandated composition of DD Councils with appointments made by the governor produces a powerful coalition. The composition of one-third state agency representatives, one-third nongovernmental agency representatives, and one-third consumers or their representatives provides an excellent mix of professionals and ordinary citizens. The face-to-face opportunities for cooperation, coordination, and confrontation around problems and issues can be stimulating and productive. State agency heads learn, often for the first time, what other state agencies are doing and how programs can be interfaced and interdigitated to the benefit of developmentally disabled clients. Consumers and representatives of nongovernmental agencies learn, often for the first time, about problems that state administrators have to deal with in operating within a state bureaucracy. Representatives from the university affiliated facilities provide theoretical inputs to council planning. Consumers and representatives from voluntary agencies keep the planning and the decision-making reality oriented. As trust and mutual respect grow among council members, productivity increases and public-private coalitions from councils have already accomplished near miracles in legislative changes, budget increases, extension of services, changed policies, and changed attitudes. As councils become more knowledgeable concerning the services needed by the developmentally disabled in order to accomplish deinstitutionalization, as they become more sophisticated in their planning and more expert in advocating, testifying, and lobbying, they acquire the people power to accomplish the job that needs to be done in order to provide appropriate residential alternatives for the developmentally disabled population.

CONSTRAINTS

Statutorily, philosophically, and politically it would appear that if a DD Council got itself together, hired good staff, planned astutely, and used its power base effectively, DD Councils would be effective mechanisms for facilitating deinstitutionalization.

What is possible, however, is not always what is probable. There are many constraints which prevent councils from being the effective instruments they could be for deinstitutionalization.

In some states councils are weak. Appointments to councils have been politically motivated. Administrative agencies have usurped the power intended for councils. Council members have been well intentioned but have lacked the necessary technical assistance and support needed for effective planning. The legislative history of the DD Act itself has been one of delay and confusion. This has tended to keep councils off balance in that they were never sure of the continuing legislative mandate, continuing funding, and their continuing role or responsibility.

Probably the biggest constraint on councils, however, is the fact that bureaucracy resists change at every level. Councils are impeded in subtle —and some not so subtle—ways from exercising their mandate. Illogically, councils are usually placed with the administering agencies now operating the present institutional system. These agencies control a large portion of the budget which supports the present institutional system. They have their own ideas about deinstitutionalization. They do not look kindly on a council with a small amount of funding trying to influence the spending of much larger sums in keeping with a council plan. Furthermore, at a time when inflation is making it ever more difficult for the administrators of institutions to retain the minimal gains they have made during the past few years, they are not at all enthusiastic about a new plan for new decentralized services that would at best siphon off money from their presently underfunded, understaffed institutions and at worst replace them entirely. Administrators of the present institutional systems are understandably not always enthusiastic supporters of council plans and activities to implement community alternatives.

Another more serious constraint on effective council action in the area of deinstitutionalization is the band-aid approach being used by many councils. Despite the broad definition of *deinstitutionalization* promulgated by the Division of Developmental Disabilities, not everyone agrees on the essential elements encompassed by the concept of deinstitutionalization. There is consensus that individuals should not be inappropriately placed in institutions, that community alternatives for placement should exist, that small living arrangements are to be preferred over large living arrangements, and that appropriate programming should be available regardless of where an individual lives. Consensus breaks down when planners identify the populations for which community living arrangements are appropriate. Most, even at this late date, feel that severely and profoundly and multiply involved individuals are appropriately placed in institutions. The concept of the "least restrictive alternative" for all developmentally disabled individuals has not been incorporated into most plans.

An even more disturbing omission is the recognition of the fact that a dependent, dispersed population in a community needs careful monitoring. Most deinstitutionalization plans do not acknowledge the fact that some developmentally disabled individuals do need help in managing themselves and their affairs and do need protective services and support. Such a system should not only provide for regular re-evaluation of residential placements and day-to-day programming so that human and civil rights are protected, but they should also provide for a flexible degree of help so that individuals, regardless of the degree of disability, are permitted to make their own choices and decisions wherever possible.

Perhaps one of the most distressing and disappointing constraints to deinstitutionalization with which councils must come to grips is the attitude of the general public. As councils begin to plan and help to implement the establishment of small-group living arrangements in communities, it is indeed discouraging to find, after all the public education and public relations programs of such groups as The President's Committee on Mental Retardation, The National Association for Retarded Citizens, and United Cerebral Palsy Associations Incorporated, that ordinary citizens are still afraid to have the developmentally disabled living in their midst in the community. Such groups will engage in open harassment and court battles in order to keep handicapped individuals from living with them as neighbors. Councils must come to grips with the zoning battles which citizens are mounting in order to keep group homes from being established in their communities. Philosophically citizens accept and support developmentally disabled persons. Pragmatically they reject them. If such attitudes are not changed, the entire deinstitutionalization thrust can be blocked.

THE OHIO DD COUNCIL AND DEINSTITUTIONALIZATION

The Ohio DD Council has made a significant impact on the implementation of deinstitutionalization. What it has been able to accomplish in the last four years provides a good illustration of the successes, failures, constraints, and potentialities for the future.

Residential services were targeted by the Ohio DD Council in its first DD plan for priority attention. Already alerted to the danger of implementing a program of dispersed residential placements without first having in place a protective monitoring system, the Ohio Council used its resources to put in place, statewide, a protective advocacy system. This is a two-pronged system with a state system of protective workers authorized under law and a companion volunteer personal advocacy system operated with DD funding. At this time the 125 client-protective staffers in the Division of Mental Retardation and Developmental Disabilities are fully funded by the division and deployed across the state in twelve district offices. Approximately ten thousand clients are in this system. The personal advocacy system is still primarily funded with DD monies and has twelve advocacy offices, one in each district. DD funding is further involved in this system through the provision of training monies to a University Affiliated Facility (UAF), the Nisonger Center, for in-service training for protective workers and personal advocacy directors. The DD Council is also funding the Client Tracking System which is still in the testing phase. An additional component to the protective system, the provision of a stable of young lawyers to assist protective workers in the courts, has just been given.

At the time this protective support system was being put into place, the Ohio DD Council provided funding for residential planning. One of the first acts of the DD Council was to call and to fund a statewide residential services seminary. Governor John J. Gilligan was invited to give the closing address, at which he endorsed the recommendations of the seminar attendees to phase out within a ten-year period the present institutional system of residential care and phase in community alternatives. The seminar further recommended to the DD Council that the three primary voluntary agencies—the Epilepsy Foundation of Ohio, the Ohio Association for Retarded Children, and United Cerebral Palsy Associations of Ohio—submit a proposal to draft a State Residential Plan. The council funded the proposal and instructed the three agencies to form a new incorporated organization in order to facilitate planning. Ohio Developmental Disabilities (ODD) was incorporated, hired a Residential

Director, and set about collecting data on which to base a Residential Plan for Ohio. The governor in his closing address at the Residential Seminar had asked specifically that the plan be developed with the involvement of citizens at the grassroots level. The DD Council therefore also funded the reactivation of District Citizens Committees in each of the twelve districts. In addition to the Residential Director, the council funded a Personal Advocacy Director for ODD so that a personal advocacy system could be developed concurrently with the planning for residential care. Not only was a plan for the development of community-based alternatives prepared and presented to the governor in a statewide Report and Call Back Conference in August 1974, but many spin-off benefits accrued along the way.

The Residential Director and her staff activated Residential Committees within the District Citizens Committees. These groups not only assisted with the collection of data but served as focal points for consultant help to other community groups wanting to start group homes. Even during the planning phase it became necessary to develop resource and training materials for community groups who were asking for help. Two publications were produced: *Guidelines for the Establishment of a Community Group Home* and *Resource Guide for Persons With a Developmental Disability*. Two additional Operational Handbooks have also been prepared—one for house parents and one for administrators of group homes.

Even during the planning phase more than a dozen group homes came into existence. As they reached operational phase, new problems were brought to council. Zoning battles were joined in several cities, and a model zoning ordinance was drafted in order to facilitate starting group homes. Two new laws were written and passed by the legislature in order to permit state monies to be used for purchase of residential services from nonprofit voluntary groups and in order to provide additional construction and remodeling monies to such groups for community-based homes. The Residential Director assisted the Division of Mental Retardation and Developmental Disabilities in drafting the rules and regulations for the implementation of these laws.

Despite all that has been accomplished to date, the council is aware that only the most meager beginnings have been made. We are confronted with massive programming gaps, particularly in the area of services to adults. As more adult individuals remain in the community, the lack of comprehensive services at the community level is becoming critical. Individuals in community homes are under protective services, and the protective workers are reporting that in most parts of the state there simply are no services for adults who cannot work or who need supervised employment. Another problem that demands immediate attention of the council surfaced when protective workers, who had had clients under their purview for one year, began to look for resources for fulfilling the requirements of the protective services law for an annual review of the physical, social, educational or vocational, and emotional social status of their clients. Once again there simply were no organized resources at the community level to provide such annual evaluations for adults. The Ohio DD Council therefore has assigned monies to the Department of Health to put together a statewide network which will have the capability of providing these annual evaluations. Not only will this network fulfill the need for evaluation under the protective services law, but it will also be a mechanism for documenting program needs so that the council will know where to assign gap-filling dollars, where to be an agency advocate to see that other agencies provide mandated services, and where to assign DD Council dollars in order to develop or tie together resources.

Although the primary effort of the council has been on getting community residential alternatives developed, the council has not forgotten about those developmentally disabled who still must live in institutions. Funds have been given to the Division of Mental Retardation and Developmental Disabilities, which is responsible for the institutions, to have Ohio institutions surveyed by the Joint Commission on Accreditation of Hospitals, Accreditation Council for Facilities for the Mentally Retarded, so that we can document for the legislature and the public where Ohio fails to meet standards, and what it will cost to bring those institutions up to accreditation level.

The DD Council has also funded mini-teams in each of the institutions in order to start eliminating back wards of severely and multiply disabled individuals. The Ohio DD 1974-75 plan called for phased-in establishment of mini-teams in each of the twelve district offices of the division so that the severely and multiply handicapped can be properly cared for in community living arrangements and will not have to be institutionalized.

The enormity of the task ahead for the Ohio DD Council in the area of deinstitutionalization and the development of community alternatives is just beginning to become apparent. In addition, the Council has different priorities and different concepts from its administering agency. The council has become over-involved in the implementation of its plan and is presently reevaluating its position. However, there is no doubt that the DD Council has had a marked impact on the deinstitutionalization movement in Ohio and will continue to be a powerful and effective mechanism for change in the state.

CONCLUSION

The potential of DD Councils for facilitating deinstitutionalization and for developing the improved delivery and advocacy systems necessary for implementation is enormous. DD Councils are just beginning to learn how to use their power of public education, of lobbying, of aggressive advocacy, of collaborative action with groups with similar goals, of public-private coalitions, and of access to the political power bases.

As councils become more skillful planners, as plans become more clearly goal oriented, as councils become more sophisticated in wielding their power, as councils become more knowledgeable concerning what is possible under federal-state statutory mandates, as councils learn how to be change agents they can make the difference between deinstitution-alization's being just an impossible dream and its becoming a reality in the lives of a segment of our citizenry who have too long denied their right to live their lives with dignity in the community with their peers.

16

Child Advocacy Within State Government

The North Carolina Experience

DONALD E. TAYLOR

THERE ARE MANY RISKS as well as opportunities for the handicapped in providing services in the least restrictive setting. Deinstitutionalization is a complex concept, and, as noted in other chapters, it must be implemented carefully if the interests of the handicapped are to be best served.

Advocacy should be an important aspect of deinstitutionalization efforts. Advocacy is important in accomplishing the goals of deinstitutionalization and in protecting the individual interests of the handicapped during the difficult process of institutional change. This chapter focuses on advocacy in state government as one part of the larger efforts needed in advocacy. Other aspects of advocacy inside the system have been described by Paul, Neufeld, and Pelosi (1977).

Child advocacy in state government suffers from the same definitional problem encountered by child advocacy programs in general. The only certain element of the definition is its focus on children, and even that certainty may fade if child advocacy is successful, as the question is raised, "Why not advocacy for all?" Strict definition may hinder the procedures and programs that need developing under the advocacy banner. Loose definitions evoke twinges of territoriality among existing line or services agencies. Having no definition at all is apt to apall even the most generous member of a legislative appropriations committee.

Efforts to define advocacy within a state bureaucracy are compounded by the varying expectancies held by different levels, elements, and individuals within state government. That is, no matter what definition is established or what role is undertaken, a set of expectancies has already been established at least among those who are familiar with and sup-

portive of the concept of child advocacy. In its struggle to survive bureaucratic bullying and political pressure, advocacy within state government
runs the risk of being defined as all things for all children. To a state
legislator, child advocacy may be the long-sought coordination device
for all children's services provided by the state. To a Commissionor of
Human Services, child advocacy will ascertain the needs and set the
priorities for children's programs provided under the umbrella of human
services. To the director of a state agency, advocacy will be an objective
agent in selling the agency's budget request to the state legislature. To
organized consumer groups, child advocacy will monitor the services
provided by all state agencies. To the theoretical purist, it must not
operate programs, while the hard-nosed pragmatist does not see why
child advocacy cannot "take over" a faltering program and "run it." To
the family or child in trouble advocacy should provide direct assistance
in dealing with the problem.

In fact, each expectancy is based on problems that hinder a state's
responsiveness to the needs of children. Furthermore, each expectancy is
probably an important element of someone's operational definition of
"child advocacy." A child advocacy program within state government
must recognize and be sensitive to the expectancies held by the citizens,
policy-makers, and service providers. Conflicting expectancies can lead
to conflicting roles that confuse both staff and clients. Positive efforts to
integrate roles, on the other hand, result in evolving advocacy concepts
and broadening a constituency for advocacy support.

Analysis of North Carolina's brief history in developing a formalized
advocacy program as an internal part of state government yields a statutory definition of child advocacy that encompasses various expectancies.
The internal positioning of the child advocacy program indicates an attempt to find the place of best fit for operationalizing the statutory definition.

The North Carolina experience in formalized child advocacy began
in 1969 with the creation of the Study Commission on North Carolina's
Emotionally Disturbed Children by the North Carolina General Assembly.
Mandated to study the condition of emotionally disturbed children and
the mental health needs of all children, the study commission documented
the fragmentation, lack of coordination, and service-delivery gaps among
child-serving programs at both the state and community level.

In an effort to improve the delivery of services to children and youth,
the study commission developed its major recommendation: the establishment of a Governor's Advocacy Commission on Children and Youth
by legislative action. According to the study commission report, *Who*

Speaks For Children, "the Advocacy Commission would plan, facilitate, and coordinate services and would serve as an advocate in the interest of children, youth, and their families. It should take as its mandate the security and rights of all children and youth in North Carolina. The Commission would not be responsible for providing services directly, as this function would be incompatible with its role as advocate." Also, the study commission recommended that the advocacy commission be directly responsible to the governor and the general assembly.

In 1971, the North Carolina General Assembly ratified Chapter 935 of the 1971 Session Laws, creating a Governor's Advocacy Commission on Children and Youth to be organizationally located in the Department of Administration. The commission was composed of seventeen members consisting of four youth members (below age twenty-one), four members of the North Carolina General Assembly, a representative of the Superintendent of the North Carolina Department of Public Instruction, a representative of the Secretary of the Department of Corrections, and seven at-large members. The major powers and duties of the Commission included the following: (1) to act as an advocate for children and youth within state and local government and within private agencies serving children and youth; (2) to provide assistance in the development and coordination of child advocacy systems at the regional and local levels; (3) to conduct a continuing review of existing programs for children and youth, including evaluations of the delivery of services, and to review new programs prior to their implementation; (4) to recommend new programs and improvements in existing services; (5) to help state, local, public, and private agencies in coordinating existing services more effectively; (6) to make reports and recommendations to the governor and the general assembly concerning children's programs; (7) to provide information concerning the needs of children and youth to state, local, public, and private agencies and to the general public; and (8) to conduct studies relevant to the needs of children and youth.

The Executive Organization Act of 1973 (1973 Session Law, Chapter 476) changed the name of the commission to the Governor's Advocacy Council on Children and Youth and placed the advocacy council in the newly created Department of Human Resources. In the context of the Executive Organization Act, a *council* is defined as "a collective body which advises the head of a principal department or his designee as representative of citizen advice in specific areas of interest." In addition, the responsibility of the former commission to report directly to the governor and the general assembly was amended to provide that the council make reports to the secretary of human resources for transmittal to the governor. However, the enactment of Chapter 1293 of the 1973 Session Law re-established the responsibility and the authority for the council to make reports directly to the general assembly concerning programs and services for children.

Chapter 1293 also clarified and strengthened the Child Advocacy Council's role in several areas. Each state agency having responsibilities for providing services to children and their families may be required to submit, at the request of the council, a plan of services for children. In addition, the duty of acting as an advocate for children and youth was expanded to include assisting children and their parents or guardians in obtaining services provided by state, local, and private agencies or organizations. Finally, the advocacy council was authorized to hear appeals resulting from the denial of services to children by agencies under the jurisdiction of the Department of Human Resources.

In November of 1974, the Governor of North Carolina approved the formation of the North Carolina Office For Children within the Department of Human Resources. The Office For Children was created to provide coordination of effort in the planning for and delivery of services to children. Four primary areas of concern of the Office For Children are: (1) assistance to all children and their families in obtaining the service which are available and to which they are entitled; (2) services complementary to public school programs with emphasis on support systems for children with special needs and their families; (3) services for all preschool children who want and need services, including health services and quality child care; (4) assistance to consumer, religious, civic, and professional organizations, at both the state and local level, in promoting and developing interest and action in behalf of children and youth. Additionally, the Office For Children is mandated to provide staff and support services to the Governor's Advocacy Council on Children and Youth. This mandate is the specific responsibility of the Advocacy Section of the Office for Children.

Based on a review of statutory and policy changes, a definition of child advocacy as an internal part of the state's child serving system has emerged. The direction taken by both legislation and policy is firmly toward the integration and improvement of services and away from the delivery of services, except for direct case advocacy assistance. The array of duties and powers granted to child advocacy by North Carolina statute includes activities such as planning, program development, program evaluation, research, public awareness, and assistance to children and families.

The positioning of child advocacy within state government is a direct reflection of its legislative mandate to improve the delivery of needed services to children and youth. Since most of these services are provided through resources administered by state agencies, it seems appropriate that advocacy be an internal part of the agency structure. Achieving and maintaining the necessary autonomy for effective advocacy functioning within a state bureaucracy are difficult tasks, but not impossible.

The organizational pattern of governmental agencies is obviously bureaucratic, and the typical characteristics of a bureaucracy present broad problem areas with which an advocacy system must deal. Specialization and routinization of activities, the assignment of roles on the basis of technical qualifications, and the designation of mandated areas of jurisdiction are all features of child-serving departments and agencies. Even if these characteristics are necessary and productive in many ways, they can create problems in the delivery of services to children. Among the most flagrant faults of bureaucratic service systems are an inability to respond expediently to atypical problems and needs of children, and awkwardness in coordinating and integrating the services provided by different agencies. An advocacy system operating within the bureaucratic structure can monitor, from within, the occurrence of problems and bring pressure to bear on that structure in behalf of both individuals and client classes.

To be effective, an advocacy system in a bureaucratic setting must maintain its conceptual identity and carry out its functions in a non-bureaucratic manner. That is, advocacy should avoid being coopted and controlled by the bureaucracy it seeks to change in behalf of its clients. To do this, several strategies can be identified and implemented.

An internal advocacy system should develop close ties with a constituency outside governmental jurisdiction. Special interest groups that result from and focus on the needs of children and youth are the core of such a constituency. Stimulating and assisting citizen groups through identifying and providing information on child-related issues is a way to expose more citizens to the need for child advocacy.

At the same time, an internal advocacy system should not segregate itself from the agencies with which it must work to improve services. Often the professional staff of child-serving agencies are acutely aware of and resistive to the bureaucratic shortcomings of their agencies. Raising and supporting the advocacy consciousness of child-service workers at all levels should become one of the essential goals of advocacy within the system. It is important that those who wear the official title of "child advocate" recognize that many others have earned the same title through years of service to children. An active internal advocacy program promotes the advocacy potential of all agency employees and encourages resistance to the encroachment of bureaucratic restrictions on the service delivery system.

In its relationships with other agencies, an internal advocacy system must take great care in describing and explaining advocacy procedures and activities which may be employed in the solution of specific problems. An advocacy program within the system should be free to intervene in any child-related problem in any agency. The interventions may range from simply identifying a problem about which the agency is unaware to insisting that the agency successfully resolve a problem by a specified time. By far the most frequent activities will involve service agencies and the advocacy system cooperatively. However, child advocacy systems must reserve the right to go directly to the sources of governmental power when cooperation or negotiation have failed.

Advocacy must maintain linkages with the political system which supports services through appropriating resources and setting broad policies. Individual legislators as well as legislative commissions and committees can be active supporters of an independent internal advocacy system. In addition, state legislatures should be the recipients of objective data concerning the effectiveness and efficiency of state-supported services. An advocacy system completely divorced from the political system cannot be successful.

The North Carolina Governor's Advocacy Council on Children and Youth has developed programs and procedures for implementing its legislative mandate. These programs and procedures are also designed to cope with the constraints imposed by being located within a bureaucracy.

Four interrelated programs are currently conducted by the Child Advocacy Council. For the most part, they can be fitted into the classical continuum of case and class advocacy.

Child advocacy provides assistance to the various state departments and their agencies which have responsibilities for providing services to children and youth in improving and coordinating their services and programs. Particular attention is given to negotiating cooperative agreements and arrangements between agencies which lead to coordinated planning and progam development. Target issues or problems are derived from within a service-providing agency or from the advocacy program or from a consumer or special interest group. The role of the advocacy staff is to function as both a facilitator and a monitor. An example of this kind of activity is a negotiated agreement between the Departments of Human Resources and Public Instruction to jointly develop and operate services for preschool deaf and hearing-impaired children.

Assistance is provided to consumer and citizen's groups committed to enhancing and/or providing services to children and youth. Periodic contact with such groups identifies concerns and problems which emanate from agency policies and practices which are perceived to be detrimental to children. Advocacy staff may serve as liaison between the agency and the organization in resolving problems. In addition, the advocacy staff provides assistance to groups in developing communications systems.

The third major program is one of direct advocacy assistance to children and youth and their families. Any problem or concern related to an individual child may be referred to the child advocacy program. Referrals come from parents, relatives, professionals, and directly from children, and each case is assigned to a staff member. Most cases have resulted from the lack or inaccessability of a needed service for a child. The role of the advocacy counselor is to locate and contact appropriate services in behalf of the child and to monitor the situation until some satisfactory solution is secured. Referrals are not "re-referred" to another agency, although any appropriate agency is identified and contacted. The client's problem becomes the advocate's problem. Periodic follow-up reveals that more than 80 percent of all cases are successfully resolved. In addition, each case, successful or unsuccessful, is analyzed for its relevance to the initiation of class advocacy proceedings. Individual cases have resulted in major policy and legislative changes affecting all children and youth.

The Child Advocacy Council takes an active role in initiating and/or supporting legislation responsive to the needs of children. The staff designs and implements strategies for effecting the council's position on legislation. In accordance with the statutes described earlier, the Child Advocacy Council is free to support or work against legislation independent of the position of any agency. An example of legislation introduced by the Council is House Bill 652 of the 1975 Session which would allow minors to seek and receive medical treatment for certain conditions and problems without the consent or knowledge of their parents.

The North Carolina experience in developing a child advocacy system within the state government service delivery structure is difficult to assess. The system has survived and is growing in terms of the breadth and depth of activities and the resource capacity to carry out advocacy functions. Autonomy within the bureaucratic structure has been established and maintained through legislation and the support of state government policy-makers in positions of authority, and the support of consumer and citizen groups. As long as state governments plan and provide services for children, internal advocacy systems should be given strong consideration.

REFERENCE

Paul, J. L.; Neufeld, G. R.; and Pelosi, J. W., eds. *Child Advocacy Within the System.* Syracuse, N.Y.: Syracuse University Press, 1977.

17

A Training Design

G. RONALD NEUFELD, JAMES L. PAUL

T HIS CHAPTER describes the design and rationale for one approach to deinstitutionalization. The main thesis is that institutionalization is maintained, in part, by institutionalized staff both in the residential regional institutions and in the communities that reinforce institutionalized staff behavior. The chapter is divided into four sections. The first section, an overview of certain problems and issues involved in deinstitutionalization, provides an orienting framework for the design proposed later. The second section described a historical perspective for the institutionalization task being undertaken. The third section includes a description of the forces that resist deinstitutionalization and make the job difficult. The fourth section describes an approach to deinstitutionalizing staff.

PROBLEMS OF DEINSTITUTIONALIZATION: A POINT OF VIEW

People have a right to community and to appropriate services in their own community. When removed from their own community they have a right to a responsive human environment. Disability should not constitute the basis for discrimination such that the disabled are denied the normalizing experiences of community and habilitative or rehabilitative resources as they may require. The social good we would like, however, we have not. Large numbers of developmentally disabled citizens enjoy only limited citizenship in large institutions set far apart from any natural community life.

The circumstances which have maintained this situation are many and complex. The problems have been described frequently, but the front doors of institutions remain wider than the back doors, while the front doors of communities remain exceedingly small in contrast to community exits.

The problems have more to do with the social situation, the community's institutions, and service delivery systems than with the developmentally disabled person. The problems have more to do with the beliefs, attitudes, and behavior of the community which identifies and defines community-alien disability. The problems have more to do with organic or functional deficits of the disabled. This is not to underestimate the importance of good treatment programs to the disabled. It is, rather, to lift to consciousness the crucial importance of the ecology of disability, particularly the bureaucratic dimension of that ecology. It is also to suggest that in deinstitutionalization these issues must be accorded special attention.

The problems embedded in the systems themselves include, for example, lack of coordination of services, lack of viable mechanisms to advocate for individual rights, restricted alternative community living arrangements, deep entrenchment of the institutional and tracking network, inefficient consolidation of professional resources, territorial distractions in the service-delivery systems, bureaucratic drain on direct services, administratively impotent and demoralized direct-care staff, bureaucratic cooptation of family power and authority, and a rather nebulous legal foundation for assuring accountability to the developmentally disabled.

There has been an upsurge in litigation relative to the deinstitutionalization issue, expressed in the language of least restrictive alternatives. The moral arguments of the rights of the disabled having substantially failed to secure those rights, the litigative support of the courts is now being sought.

We run the serious risk, now, of moving from the tactics of persuasion and negotiation—such as education of and consultation to the public—to the extreme alternative of an exclusive power orientation. A mandate can be successful only if there is the potential for appropriate response. Strategies of power and persuasion must be combined to the end that a deinstitutionalization mandate can have meaning. Ways and means must be developed of deinstitutionalizing the developmentally disabled and, more importantly, the institutional settings and systems in which they become institutionalized.

Deinstitutionalization emerges in the context of social problems created by institutionalism. Institutionalization has been a social process for removing the developmentally disabled from the community, frequently in the service of narrowly conceived community interests. Inappropriate institutionalization is a bureaucratic byproduct of organizations. It is a problem of social systems which survives because of the political, economic, and human support it is given. The "human" support ranges from the bureaucratic mind, which produces personnel policies apart from client interest, to staff attitudes and behavior, which regard the client as an artifact of a job. Institutionalization, from this perspective, is organizational client-blindness.

Any substantial redirection of this course must account for both the system issues and the dehumanizing aspects of bureaucratically dehumanized staff. Change must be accomplished by: (1) specifying the structural, behavioral, and psychological aspects of bureaucratized institutional processes as a system resistant to change, and (2) programming the reduction of those resistances.

HISTORICAL PERSPECTIVE

The history of those special clinical populations, now combined to form the group designated as developmentally disabled, has been characterized by (1) increasing specificity in delineating the disabling condition, (2) increasing public understanding and support for treatment, and (3) increasing sophistication in the technologies of treatment. The handicapped were unchained and unjailed with the tacit social conviction that disability was neither criminal nor immoral. Disability came to be viewed as incompetence of person requiring compensatory interventions including protection, sanctuary, and therapeutic detention.

The treatment of the developmentally disabled is now embellished with sophisticated bodies of knowledge, a cadre of highly trained specialists, well-developed technical procedures and instrumentation, a powerful political lobby, and considerable financial support. The disabling conditions of the handicapped have received substantial attention which has resulted primarily in altered environmental situations, including institutions which are now large and complex bureaucratic structures, and technical procedures aimed at the behavioral anomalies of the disabled.

That history has now, however, reached a crest in its orientation to remove, protect, and treat the disabled. There are important tributaries emerging which have the potential for redirecting these major historical currents. These new tributaries include institutional reform, normalization, advocacy, litigation, consumerism, patient rights, redirected accountability, and deinstitutionalization. All of these tributaries, in basic terms, reflect a generic anti-institutional, pro-person commitment. While embracing widely variable tactical, strategic, and stylistic approaches, the problem they all seek to address is basically the same. They seek to acknowledge the bureaucratic pollution of the historical mainstream thrust of segregating, extruding, and demeaning the disabled. They further seek to reform the special institutional system by reducing its size, removing all who could better benefit by community programs, and preventing inappropriate admissions. Finally, they seek to improve the quality of life and services inside the institutions for those residents who need to be there.

One of the major problems of deinstitutionalization is that of engineering. How do we develop a system to reflect a basic change in social policy? What social strategy will accomplish a redirection of institutional practices?

Social change is always difficult. The engineering issue is most difficult, however, because of already existing institutional systems must be reworked. There is not just a new institutional form to be created, although that is a dangerous distraction in deinstitutionalization program development. There are old professionalized and bureaucratized practices described here that must be changed.

It has appeared considerably more efficient and effective in engineering change at individual, group, and system levels to reduce the resistances to change rather than to simply develop counter forces which outnumber and outweigh the resistance. The following section deals with some of the major forces that oppose institutional change.

RESISTANCE TO DEINSTITUTIONALIZATION

The institutional system which serves the developmentally disabled population is embedded in the cultural attitudes toward and values of deviance and disability. The institutional system cannot be understood apart from the social context which gave it life and sustains it. The deep entrenchment and resulting inertia of institutionalism can be understood as an interaction of three principal issues: (1) institutional structure, both organizational and architectural, (2) institutional behavior, and (3) institutional psychology. That is, the institutional forms, the behaviors that support those forms, and the participating members that give life to those forms interact to comprise institutionalism. We are more able to cope with the structural and behavioral issues. Certainly our record is not impressive in coping with the interaction. We have changed organizational and physical structures and we are increasingly adept at modifying behavior. The institutionalized system of care for the developmentally disabled, however, seems to have its own tidal rhythms and boundaries. Structural and behavioral changes have appeared to produce little more than rivulets, leaving the larger current unaffected. Four areas could be described which contribute substantially to the problem of change and illustrate the interaction of the structural, organizational, and psychological issues. They are: (1) the threat-recoil cycle, (2) the labeling system, (3) the Parkinson effect, and (4) bureaucratic pathology.

Threat-Recoil Cycle

Rhodes (1972) has described a social dynamic that operates in a community to stabilize the institutionalized management of deviance. The community has a threshold of tolerance for deviance which, when exceeded, serves to trigger a variety of community behaviors. Those threat-produced behaviors are relatively predictable in style and are directed at reducing community anxiety and concern. These community behaviors include (1) attaching the concern to a "condition" such as delinquency, disturbance, or retardation; (2) generating resources to do something about the condition; and (3) turning those resources over to those systems and professionals who have traditionally had responsibility for "treating that condition."

There are some negative consequences of this process. The community rarely interacts directly with the real-life decisions concerning the disabled. Economic responsibility supplants the whole range of more personal human responsibilities, depriving *both* the handicapped and the community of growth.

Labeling System

Mercer (1973) and others have described and documented the processes by which the retarded are identified and flow through rather well-defined channels which lead from the mainstream of the educational system into the sometimes stagnant cultural backwaters of remote institutions. The process seems to be lodged in the systems themselves and their bureaucratic connections rather than in the problems of the client involved. Since the classical study by Hollingshead and Redlich (1958), the lack of correspondence of treatment and problem has been demonstrated in several studies. The intervention systems have their own style and social class criteria, in contrast to the characteristics of psychopathology as criteria for clients. Rhodes (1974) has more recently characterized the different social classes and ethnic groups as "recruiting pools" from which the various intervention systems obtain support in the form of client bodies.

The system of labeling and the social and moral consequences, including stigma and extrusion, may be characterized as the wiring that completes the circuitry of the deviance and disability systems in communities. Labels connect concerns with ways of responding to those concerns. Labels are the language that interface identification and intervention systems.

Futures of Children (1975), a report to the Secretary of Health, Education and Welfare developed under the direction of Hobbs, is the most complete and current description of the labeling issues available at this time.

Parkinson Effect

This phenomenon is so well known and simple that its importance is easily underestimated. The tendency to fill existing space operates across a large range of physical and social situations. One situation is that of institutions for the developmentally disabled. If there are one thousand beds, there will tend to be one thousand residents.

The direction of change is usually to increase or enlarge. Waiting lists are as characteristic of institutions as are the resident clients themselves. Consequently, there is always the request for additional beds to accommodate "those who need it" as demonstrated by those waiting to get in. The systems that keep the beds filled also keep the waiting lists full. As long as these systems remain intact, the institutional space will remain full and expanding.

Since there are limited funds available for the handicapped, they are expended for those who "need it"—in the manner determined by those who receive the money, frequently institution-oriented professionals who continue to build systems to identify, label, and refer the handicapped to institutions. Only recently have community alternatives obtained new support to hold out some hope for reducing or reforming the existing institutional space.

Bureaucratic Pathology

One of the negative byproducts of a highly organized social system is a bureaucracy which operates apart from or sometimes counter to the goals of the system. The pathology of that overhead of human organization constitutes a very serious problem for deinstitutionalization.

There are many manifestations of bureaucratic pathology. The Peter principle is now a popular concept. It is a serious matter, however, that the bureaucratic dynamic tends to push incompetence upward. It is especially serious when it is recognized that one of the major problems in human service systems is that most important, client-relevant, decisions are made "up" from where the client is. This maintains the flow of accountability toward the system and away from the client.

Another byproduct of institutional bureaucracy is the paternalism of the institution. For the institution to protect and "take care of" the client, the client must defer to and become dependent upon that caretaking system. Such dependency, deeply rooted in the institutional style, works in opposition to the goal of a self-supporting and self-sustaining person out in the community.

This dependency dynamic is proliferated in the bureaucratic behavior of staff over time who learn and support the infantilizing energy of a paternalistic system. Staff behavior, then, is socialized or institutionalized to become bureaucratically oriented rather than client oriented. Many sins of authority are committed in the name of protecting the client.

One of the consequences of the "job" of working with and for people in a system that deducts its own premium first has to do with the personal status of the staff. The job of caring and caring for in a bureaucracy has produced an alienation which precludes the development of a sense of community. Alienated staff who work at rehabilitation can hardly be expected to provide the ego and competency foundations for the flow of the dependent institutionalized population back into the dynamic mainstream of community activity.

The consequences of bureaucratic pathology are that institutions for the most part tend to become lethargic, inert, and intractable. One important reason they do not change is that the staff become alienated, and their beliefs and perceptions come to fit the institutional situation: "The world as I know it—institutional—is as it should be." The power of bureaucratic persuasion is increased factorially by the lack of energy left over for staff to deal with the human questions of who they are and who are the people they serve.

The problem is not that we do not know enough or that we do not have enough resources or that we have been operating with poor designs— though each of these is indeed true. The problem of deinstitutionalization is that we have not got together what we do know, what we do have, and the design ability we have to deal with the institutionalizing gestalt. That gestalt includes the structures of institutions, institutionalized behaviors of staff, and the attitudes, perceptions, beliefs, and values of professionals in institutions and in the community who maintain the system directly and the public that maintains it indirectly.

The following section describes one design that follows from the position outlined here. It is based on the belief that the negative features of institutionalized human-service systems for the developmentally disabled must be reduced; this requires interventions to be concerned with the total spectrum of institutionalism. The design outlined here involves working directly with the staff of those systems that interact to maintain and nurture the institutionalizing arrangement.

A STAFF DEINSTITUTIONALIZATION DESIGN

The primary concept of this design is that staff can be deinstitutionalized and consumers involved to the end that enduring, productive, and deinstitutionalizing consumer-benefactor-staff alliances are developed.

This design seeks to demonstrate the process by which staff, the primary bureaucratic life of institutions, and the policies which govern them can be deinstitutionalized, and consumers can be involved in a productive alliance to (1) prevent unnecessary admissions to institutions, (2) remove those from institutions who can currently be better served in the community, (3) renew or reform the institutional environment for those who need an institutional placement, and (4) create alternative community services to preclude or replace institutionalization by default.

The basic program consists of the following: (1) a community-institution staff exchange strategy to develop procedures for reconstituting the existing community-institution network in which institutionalizing activities, policies, and attitudes are embedded; and (2) the development of a deinstitutionalization training curriculum for both staff and consumer-benefactors. The strategies seek to (1) weld together the systems which serve the developmentally disabled in more client-responsive patterns; (2) more efficiently integrate professional knowledge and make it available to the client-staff-benefactor units; (3) articulate deinstitutionalization procedures that are replicable and reasonably effective.

The following design is based upon the assumptions that (1) deinstitutionalization training should take place within the context of service provision; (2) procedures must be developed on the basis of a careful analysis of the forces that prevent persons from being deinstitutionalized and support the flow of persons into the institution; (3) deinstitutionalization is unlikely to occur unless staff from the institution, community agency staff, and parents work together; and (4) the forces preventing deinstitutionalization will be more fully understood if institution and community staff develop an understanding of the forces confronting each other.

An effective and complete deinstitutionalization program calls for the simultaneous activities of institutional renewal, institutional depopulation, and institutional avoidance. It is therefore necessary that this activity bring together resources from both institutions and communities. In the following design it is proposed that a county or community be identified that is within the catchment area of a regional institution. An equal number of staff from both the institution and from community agencies within this area will be invited to participate in deinstitutionalization training activity. Staff from the institution and from community agencies will then be asked to exchange roles for the full eight-week training period. Once each week participants in the training program will meet for four hours. Also, each participant will adopt one client for whom they will function as an advocate. Institution staff now assigned to a community agency will adopt a client who is on the institution's waiting list or a person who is viewed as high risk in the sense that removal from natural environment will occur apart from effective intervention and community mobilization in the client's behalf. The deinstitutionalization goal of the advocates for the high risk client is to implement an intervention program that will prevent the institutionalization of the client. Community staff now assigned to the institution will adopt an institution resident as their client. The goal of the advocate in this instance will be to move the institutionalized resident as far toward community placement as possible.

Seminar Content

The seminar participants will be broken down into teams of four, consisting of two persons from the institution and two persons from the community. Each week, participants will complete a force-field analysis on their client (see Table 17.1). The force-field analysis procedure consists simply of listing forces that support or resist the attainment of the advocate's deinstitutionalization goal. Four force-field analyses should be completed each week by each participant for each client as follows: (1) an analysis of forces within the client that support or resist deinstitutionalization; (2) an analysis of forces within the client's home that support or resist deinstitutionalization; (3) an analysis of forces within the community that support or resist deinstitutionalization; and (4) participants with clients in the institution will complete an analysis of forces within the institution that support or resist deinstitutionalization. At each weekly seminar participants will review their deinstitutionalization activities from the past week and adopt new objectives for the following week. The small team of four will assist each other in analyzing the forces and establishing new weekly objectives. After each participant has presented client data and established new objecives, the total group will convene to compare data on the forces that resist deinstitutionalization activity. As a group they will develop strategies to deal with significant counterforces that appear on more than one force-field analysis.

TABLE 17.1

Case Study Presentations Using Force Field Analysis

Three hours are allotted for case study presentations, thus allowing approximately one-half hour per program participant to present information concerning a client. Groups are divided into units including membership from both the institution and the community. Each participant shall review his client goals for the week, indicate activities leading toward those goals, identify supporting and constraining forces relative to those goals and finally entertain consultation from the rest of the group concerning goals for the following week and strategies for achieving them. A recommended format for case study presentations is an analysis of forces surrounding each client. Four variables concerning each consumer client should be analyzed (1) person centered; (2) institution centered; (3) home centered; and (4) community centered. For clients within the cultural mainstream, the institution-centered component would be omitted. It is suggested that blackboards or overhead projecters could be used for program participants to present their material to the entire group. A desirable alternative would be to have secretaries xerox copies of each analysis of forces for the total group during the general session. In this way program participants would provide each other with models to follow.

Overall Goal
(1) Move client as far toward deinstitutionalization as possible.
(2) If institutional placement is clearly warranted, assure program responsiveness in the institution.
First Week Objectives:
(1) Spend as much time as possible with consumer client to determine client needs.
(2) In lieu of client needs–is institutional placement warranted?
(3) Indicate best possible placement for client.
(4) Complete goal statements and an analysis for forces to discuss with total group.

I. *Child Centered Analysis of Forces*
    A. Goal–Place Johnny in group home in three months.
    B. Analysis of forces–

Supporting Forces	Constraining Forces
1. Enjoys Trips to Community	1. Not toilet trained
2. Willing to work at domestic tasks	2. Aggressive with peers
3. Communicates needs well	3. Hostile to adults
4. Likes to swim	4. Tendency to wander and get lost
	5. Poorly controlled epileptic seizures
	6. Wears unsightly helmet at all times

C. Strategy–
1. Attempt to eliminate 1–4 by immediately enrolling Johnny in training program.
2. Obtain more information concerning subjects strengths.
3. Strengthen subject's communication skills.

D. Resources–
1. Behavior Modification Consultant
2. Language Development Consultant

E. Weekly Objective–
1. Enroll subject in language development class.
2. Enroll subject in toilet training program.
3. Visit Burke County group home.

II. *Institution-Centered Analysis of Forces*
A. Goal–Deinstitutionalize subject.
B. Analysis of Forces–

Supporting Forces	Constraining Forces
1. Johnny enrolled in school	1. Cottage parent dislikes Johnny.
2. Teacher likes Johnny.	2. Peers dislike Johnny.
	3. Language Development Director says no room for Johnny.
	4. Apart from school (2hrs.) three times per week—no program.
	5. No one in institution thinks Johnny suitable for placement.

C. Strategies–
1. Eliminate 2–5 by negotiation.
2. Strengthen 2–2.
3. Have Johnny moved to another cottage.

D. Resources–
1. Unit Director
2. Language Lab
3. School Teacher

E. Weekly Objective–
1. Meet with Unit Director to change Johnny's placement.
2. Meet with Director of language lab.
3. Collect data on Johnny's behavior that offends peers.

III. *Home-Centered Analysis of Forces*
    A. Goal—Deinstitutionalize Johnny
    B. Analysis of Forces–

Supporting Forces	Constraining Forces
1. Parents seem to like Johnny.	1. Parents want Johnny to stay in institution.
2. Large extended family.	2. Parents are poor, cannot provide support.
	3. Parents seldom visit.
	4. Siblings do not like Johnny.

    C. Strategies–
        1. Work with parent attitudes.
        2. Identify financial aid.
        3. Transportation for family to visit and participate in decisions.
        4. Identify behavior in Johnny that angers siblings.
    D. Resources–
        1. Social Worker in institution who related well to parent.
        2. Other members of extended family who could interact with Johnny.
        3. Transportation committee-local service club.
    E. Weekly Objectives–
        1. Team up with Social Worker to visit home.

IV. *Community-Centered Analysis of Forces*
    A. Goal–Deinstitutionalize Johnny.
    B. Analysis of Forces–

Supporting Forces	Constraining Forces
1. Group home in Burke County.	1. Antagonistic Social Service Dept.
2. Group home near YMCA swim pool.	2. Lack of funds to support.
	3. Poor transportation.
	4. No school program.
	5. Far from sheltered workshop.
	6. Group home residents older than Johnny.

C. Strategies–
1. Unknown yet.
2. Check with Welfare Department.
3. Check with Welfare Department and Vocational Rehabilitation staff.
4. Conference with Special Education Director.
5. Check with Vocational Rehabilitation.
6. Conference with group home parent.
D. Resources–
1. Local child advocacy program.
2. YMCA Director.
3. Need to consult with CDATF participants for suggestions.
E. Weekly Objectives–
1. Meet with Social Service Director in institution.
2. Meet with welfare representative
3. Phone local child advocacy director.

Data from analysis of forces will be used not only in systematic planning for the clients, but also to provide data concerning forces that support or stand in the way of deinstitutionalization activity. The shifting of forces will be recorded as well as the introduction of additional forces during the program.

On Developing an Individual Curriculum

Given the manner in which participants for this seminar are to be selected, one would expect to find great variance in skills and background. It is therefore necessary to individualize instruction for each class participant. This is accomplished by organizing a training resource network consisting of persons with specific skills that may be needed by classroom participants. Trainers will be asked to participate on call and to work with individuals from the deinstitutionalization seminar. Candidates for the training pool will be recruited from the institution, from community agencies, and from local colleges or universities. For example, it is possible that a participant from the class may request assistance in developing a program for the client to reduce or eliminate aggressive behavior. An attempt would be made to identify a skilled behaviorist who could then work individually with the participant in order to develop a sound intervention program for the client. In the process of this inter-action, it is anticipated that the participant may lack skills in working with a client's family. The trainer bank should include persons from community agencies who are skilled in these areas and could work with class participants, helping them develop skills in the area of family counseling and community mobilization.

Regardless of the request from a participant, the trainer bank should be able to respond with someone to support the request and either help the participant develop a program or identify a resource to undertake the task. In many instances it is expected that there will be existing resources to do the necessary work. The advocate will be called upon to bring together the resource and the need. It should also be pointed out that the entire curriculum for the class revolves around actual experiences that class participants encounter with individual clients. Deinstitutionalization principles and procedures will flow out of this experience. The curriculum design is shown in Figure 17.1.

The Role of Parents and Politicians

While the combined involvement of institution and community staff is important, the likelihood of launching a successful deinstitutionalization design is much greater if parents, legislators, and local political representatives are involved. It is therefore proposed that the participants conduct three sessions to include parents of clients, guardians, and legislators. These sessions would be conducted at a convenient time for these persons, an evening or on a weekend. The final goal for all three sessions will be to organize and leave in that community a deinstitutionalization task force. In the first session, the community group, consisting of parents, interested citizens, and politicians, will be introduced to the goals of the program and the project design. In the second session, midway through the project, data will be presented that identifies the forces that support and resist deinstitutionalization. In the final session, the community deinstitutionalization task force will be organized and goals will be developed for the group. The goals will be the outcome of problems identified in the seminar. The deinstitutionalization task force will consist of parents, interested citizens, local politicians, institutional staff who worked with the community agencies, and community agency staff who worked in the institution. At the end of eight weeks, it is hoped that each of these participants and interest groups will be committed to the concept of deinstitu-

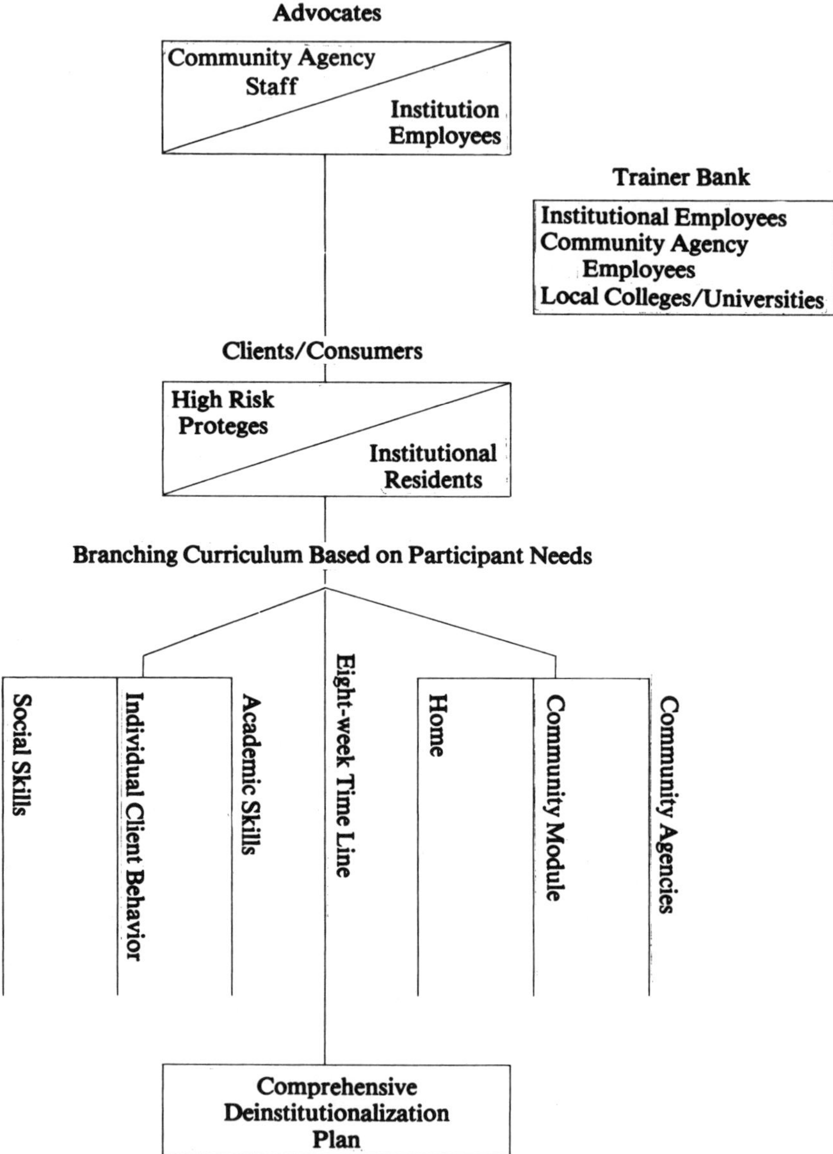

FIGURE 17.1. A Branching Curriculum.

tionalization. If they have a committment to the concept, it is assumed that they will have a comprehensive picture of the resources available to engage the mission and a comprehensive picture of the problems.

Summary and Conclusions

The foregoing design is an attempt to accomplish deinstitutionalization through training. The anticipated outcomes are (1) individual plans to deinstitutionalize a number of clients; (2) a list of forces that support and resist deinstitutionalization; (3) a deinstitutionalization task force in the community; (4) a deinstitutionalization task force in the institution; and (5) a group of institutional employees that will be prepared for jobs in the community as services are developed. The design is based upon several principles—first, that training in deinstitutionalization should be based upon direct experience; second, given the variance in experience and background, training must be individualized; third, trainers from the service-delivery network should be utilized who have had relevant experience; and fourth, learning that grows out of one experience is likely to generalize to other situations. Finally, it should be pointed out that if this design is successful, it should be replicated in every community within the institution's catchment area. With each cycle, a community deinstitutionalization task force will be left behind with linkages in the institution. Also each new cycle would include a new group of participants from the institution. Eventually all employees from the institution will have experienced case advocacy and employment with a community agency. This experience could be a major step toward preparing institution staff for community employment as comprehensive community programs evolve.

REFERENCES

Rhodes, W. C. *Behavioral Threat and Community Response: A Community Psychology Inquiry.* New York: Behavioral Publications, 1972.
Mercer, J. R. *Labelling the Mentally Retarded: Clinical and Social System Perspectives on Mental Retardation.* Berkeley: University of California Press, 1973.

Hollingshead, A. B., and Redlich, F. C. *Social Class and Mental Illness*. New
    York: Wiley, 1958.
Hobbs, N. *The Futures of Children*. San Francisco: Josey-Bass, 1975.
Rhodes, W. C., and Head, S. *A Study of Child Variance. Volume III: Service
    Delivery Systems*. Ann Arbor, Mich.: University of Michigan Press, 1974.

DEINSTITUTIONALIZATION

was composed in 10-point Compugraphic Times Roman, leaded two points,
with display type in Times Roman by Focus/Typographers;
printed on Warren 55-lb. Antique Cream,
Smyth-sewn and bound over boards in Columbia Riverside Chambray
by Vail-Ballou Press, Inc.;
and published by

SYRACUSE UNIVERSITY PRESS

SYRACUSE, NEW YORK